POLITICAL TRADITIONS IN FOREIGN POLICY

Kenneth W. Thompson, Editor

The values, traditions, and assumptions undergirding approaches to foreign policy are often crucial in determining the course of a nation's history. Yet, the interconnections between ideas and policy for landmark periods in our foreign relations remain largely unexamined. The intent of this series is to encourage a marriage between political theory and foreign policy. A secondary objective is to identify theorists with a continuing interest in political thought and international relations, both younger scholars and the small group of established thinkers. Only occasionally have scholarly centers and university presses sought to nurture studies in this area. In the 1950s and 1960s the University of Chicago Center for the Study of American Foreign Policy gave emphasis to such inquiries. Since then the subject has not been the focus of any major intellectual center. The Louisiana State University Press and the series editor, from a base at the Miller Center of Public Affairs at the University of Virginia, have organized this series to meet a need that has remained largely unfulfilled since the mid-1960s.

CHARTING A NEW DIPLOMATIC COURSE

CHARTING A NEW DIPLOMATIC COURSE

ALTERNATIVE APPROACHES TO
AMERICA'S POST-COLD WAR
FOREIGN POLICY

CECIL V. CRABB, JR.

LEILA E. SARIEDDINE

AND

GLENN J. ANTIZZO

LOUISIANA STATE UNIVERSITY PRESS))|((BATON ROUGE

10 09 08 07 06 05 04 03 02 01
5   4   3   2   1

Designer: Melanie O'Quinn Samaha
Typeface: Bembo
Typesetter: Coghill Composition Co., Inc.
Printer and binder: Thomson-Shore, Inc.

ISBN 0-8071-2704-3 (cloth)
ISBN 0-8071-2748-5 (paper)

CONTENTS

CHARTING A NEW DIPLOMATIC COURSE

INTRODUCTION

T HE END OF THE COLD WAR HAS PRESENTED AMERICANS WITH A number of problems—none perhaps more difficult and complex than attempting to redefine the nation's role in global affairs in the new era. To say that the collapse of the old "bipolar" international system has presented a traumatic and extremely difficult challenge for Americans would be to understate the matter.

After the defeat of communism as a global force posing a threat to international stability and to the security of the United States and its friends abroad, what now ought to be the role of the American nation on the global stage? What new set of diplomatic principles or strategy ought to supersede the now obsolete "containment" policy that guided America's diplomatic behavior for almost a half-century after 1947? (Indeed, in today's increasingly diverse world, is it even possible to follow a single unified and coherent diplomatic strategy comparable to the containment policy?) If Soviet communism no longer poses an ominous threat to the nation's security and diplomatic interests, what global tendencies and developments *do* threaten the well-being and future of the United States in the post–Cold War period? From a different perspective, devotees of *Realpolitik* have always insisted that the diplomatic behavior of the United States must, in the last analysis, be guided by the dictates of the "national interest." On that premise, how should the national interest (or interests) of the USA be redefined after the Cold War?

In the new era, Americans have found such questions difficult to answer unambiguously. Indeed, it is perhaps no exaggeration to say that at no time in the nation's diplomatic experience has there been such a wide diversity of opinions among well-informed students of foreign relations regarding America's proper international role. Prescriptions for the nation's behavior beyond its own borders cover an extraordinarily wide range of proposals and guidelines. For example, at one extreme, some Americans (a relatively small minority of the people) call for a return to isolationism, which characterized the era that lasted from the foundation of the Republic to World War II, when citizens and their leaders were almost exclusively preoccupied with domestic policies and problems. For this group, it seems clear enough, the nation's massive involvement in foreign problems and crises is viewed as essentially a worrisome and costly distraction from the American society's principal business: the solution of a long list of serious internal problems.

In the contemporary period, the most poignant example of the revival of classical isolationism is provided by the phenomenon known as "Buchananism," named for presidential aspirant Pat Buchanan. Urging policymakers in Washington to put "America First" (not by coincidence, the name of an active isolationist movement before World War II), Buchanan called for abandoning most of the global commitments the USA had assumed since World War II, especially its membership in, and support of, international organizations like the United Nations. (As was true of the pre-war isolationists, Buchanan was convinced that membership in such organizations inevitably entailed a loss of America's sovereignty.) Similarly, Buchanan and his followers were extremely dubious about efforts by the United States to engage in a long list of other activities overseas, such as successful "peacekeeping" operations abroad and efforts to promote democracy in foreign societies.

In the realm of national trade policy, Buchanan's isolationist inclinations were especially pronounced. In effect, he called for a return to the pre–New Deal era, when the USA erected high tariff walls against imports in an effort to "protect" American workers from foreign competition. (Nothing in Buchanan's approach revealed an awareness that such restrictive trade policies by the USA and other nations were a significant factor in precipitating and perpetuating the Great Depression. The longterm effect of this approach, of course, would be to dry up or significantly reduce international trade altogether, meaning that the jobs of the workers engaged in producing America's exports would be totally lost.) The classical isolationist approach to American foreign policy, along with recent manifestations of this mind-set, are analyzed in detail in Chapter 1.

Other citizens advocate what might be called "neo-isolationist" viewpoints regarding America's global role after the Cold War. Two reasonably distinct species of the neo-isolationist frame of mind in the contemporary period may be identified: a conservative, or right-wing, version and a liberal, or left-wing, version.

Those Americans championing neo-isolationism from a conservative perspective emphasize a number of ideas and principles that, in their view, ought to serve as a foundation for American foreign policy in the new era. Substantial unanimity exists upon the idea, for example, that no return to the period of comfortable isolationist seclusion by the USA is possible in today's world. Conservatives broadly agree that, while the Cold War is now over, the external political environment remains essentially Hobbesian, sometimes posing ominous threats to America's security and its diplomatic interests. In contrast to isolationists before World War II, neo-isolationists today are convinced that at times the United States must act decisively to protect its security and diplomatic interests. For this group, the 1941 Japanese attack on Pearl Harbor serves as a graphic reminder of the perils and hazards of an isolationist approach to foreign affairs.

At the same time, most conservative neo-isolationists also agree that other lessons from recent diplomatic experience indicate beyond any real doubt that the USA must scale down its international commitments. This was, of course, one of the transcendent "lessons of Vietnam." But it was also a lesson to be derived from unsuccessful interventionist episodes that followed in Lebanon, East and Central Africa, the Caribbean area, and the Balkans. As conservatives view it, policymakers in Washington must always keep in mind the difference between America's possessing great power and its possession of *infinite power*. Although it may be a superpower, as one recent observer commented, the USA cannot function as a diplomatic Atlas, bearing the entire world upon its shoulders.

On this premise, conservative neo-isolationists call for greater selectivity and discrimination than has often been exhibited in the past regarding the commitments assumed by the United States beyond its own borders. In the new era, these should be dictated by a clearer, and more narrowly defined, conception of the "national interest" and of the limits of American power. At the same time, substantial agreement exists among devotees of conservative neo-isolationism that, when policymakers in Washington *do* decide to commit the nation's power abroad, they will take those steps necessary to achieve the objective (or objectives). Failure to do so can result in serious undermining of the nation's diplomatic credibility and in deep-seated political divisions at home. We shall examine the conservative version of neo-isolationist thought at greater length in Chapter 2.

At the opposite end of the political spectrum, a number of liberal and left-wing observers also espouse a neo-isolationist approach to American foreign policy after the Cold War. The underlying rationale supporting their position is, of course, fundamentally different from that relied upon by conservative neo-isolationists. For many liberals, the end of the Cold War offers the USA a long-awaited opportunity to reduce its overseas commitments drastically and to concentrate on the solution of too-long neglected domestic problems. To the minds of many observers in this category, a regrettable consequence of the Vietnam War was that President Lyndon B. Johnson's "Great Society" was a primary casualty. Indeed, for many years the American society neglected increasingly critical domestic problems precisely because it was dissipating its resources, time, and energies by engaging in unjustified interventionist activities abroad. For a century or more (as in the Populist movement around 1900), it has been an article of faith among liberal and left-wing groups that a "strong" or dynamic foreign policy is inimical to achieving "the American way of life" at home. (Indeed, some liberals were convinced that the Eastern-dominated political establishment has at times *deliberately* engaged in costly foreign ventures in order to avoid devoting attention to the nation's internal problems and needs!) A neo-isolationist approach to foreign policy is also frequently advocated by those who want to achieve a "peace dividend" by slashing the national defense budget.

In calling for a neo-isolationist approach to external policy after the Cold War, many liberals also cite the lessons of recent diplomatic experience to support their position. To their minds, in the cases of Southeast Asia, Lebanon, East Africa, the Western Hemisphere, and most recently the Balkans, an objective examination of the evidence convincingly indicates that interventionist behavior has paid few discernible dividends, either for the United States or for those societies such behavior was intended to benefit. More often than not, in fact, the outcome has been the expenditure of American lives, resources, and energies in futile interventionist ventures which not only failed in the end to achieve their goals, but in the process resulted in serious and longterm negative consequences for the USA. For example, in many instances such interventionism alienated the United States from its friends and allies in the international community. In too many cases also, it undermined Washington's diplomatic credibility and America's claim to a position of diplomatic leadership. It created long-lasting resentments toward the USA by foreign societies, reinforcing anti-American sentiment abroad. And as already noted, it diverted the nation's resources from the solution of pressing domestic problems. In brief, based on the record as many liberals assessed it, interventionist diplomatic conduct by the United States has little to recommend it.

More perhaps than any other group within the American society, in their approach to foreign affairs, liberals have been obsessed with "the lessons of Vietnam." (As later chapters, especially Chapter 6, will emphasize, there are of course many, and sometimes highly divergent, "lessons of Vietnam.") To the liberal mind, paramount ones are that policymakers in Washington must demonstrate greater selectivity in their decisions to intervene in foreign societies. They must make a greater effort to ensure that interventionist moves are supported by the nation's friends and allies, and by the United Nations and regional organizations. They must also try to make certain that foreign governments with which Washington is closely identified have the support of their own people—and this, in turn, requires that such regimes respect the rights and endeavor to meet the needs of their citizens.

Above all perhaps, America's leaders must understand the limitations of military power as an instrument of national policy. While very few liberal neo-isolationists are pacifists, they do tend to believe that in recent diplomatic experience Washington has relied much too heavily upon military power in responding to problems and crises abroad. In the post–Cold War period, relatively few regional and global problems confronting the USA overseas have lent themselves to "military solutions." And attempts to solve them by the application of military force often in fact have compounded existing problems or created new ones. The liberal version of neo-isolationist thought is analyzed more fully in Chapter 3.

The opposite side of the coin of conservative neo-isolationism is an interventionist policy for the United States, as advocated by certain conservative and right-wing groups. The conservative interventionist is cognizant of the fact that, as a result of the outcome of the Cold War, the USA is left as the only superpower within the international system. Certain other countries (such as members of the European Community, Japan, and Communist China) may aspire to that position. Moreover, nations like India and Brazil are increasingly prepared to assume greater *regional* responsibilities. But for the foreseeable future, only the United States has the power and force-projection capability needed to assume and carry out *global* responsibilities.

This fact creates inescapable obligations for the American nation in its foreign relations. As many conservatives assess it, if the USA does not take the lead in efforts to preserve international peace and security, then what nations *are* in a position, and have the incentive, to do so? The alternative to a role of American diplomatic leadership is a global system that is increasingly characterized by chaos, violence, and instability. In turn, such conditions can—and in some instances, unquestionably would—directly jeopardize the security and well-being of the American society.

If liberal neo-isolationists are preoccupied with "the lessons of Vietnam," conservative interventionists believe that other lessons from diplomatic experience are no less applicable to the conduct of American diplomacy in the new era. For example, "the lessons of Pearl Harbor" provide an indelible reminder of the dangers inherent in America's failure to act to protect its security and its diplomatic interests in response to crises and challenges abroad. One applicable lesson of the pre–World War II era, in other words, is that at times the United

States must engage in what might be called "preventive diplomacy." On some occasions, it must act to avert a serious crisis abroad or to keep an emerging challenge from reaching crisis proportions, such as occurred in U.S.-Japanese relations before 1941.

Devotees of conservative interventionism are for the most part skeptical about what is sometimes called the "new realism" or the notion that after the Cold War, military force no longer is a useful component of national power. (Proponents of the "new realism" are convinced that non-military forms of power—such as America's ability to create and lead coalitions in solving regional and global problems—provide the key to diplomatic success.) Nearly all right-wing advocates of an interventionist foreign policy reject such reasoning. Far from having become obsolete, to their minds a powerful and varied military arsenal is essential if the United States is to respond successfully to a wide variety of threats and challenges arising out of the post–Cold War global environment. As they contemplate the continuing threat posed by Iraq to the peace and security of the Persian Gulf area; or the ongoing conflict that keeps the Balkans in a state of violence and turmoil; or the prospect that mainland China may once again assert its jurisdiction over Taiwan by relying on armed force—in these and other instances, conservative interventionists are convinced that military power *remains* a crucial instrument enabling the USA to achieve its foreign policy goals.

Admittedly, conservative interventionists today widely believe that policy-makers in Washington must be selective in assuming overseas commitments. Most conservatives accept the proposition that the USA cannot serve "as the policeman of the world." Or as one spokesman for this approach expressed the idea, America must avoid the temptation to function as the Mother Teresa of the international system. Americans possess neither the power, nor do they have the insight into problems existing abroad, needed to serve in this role successfully. At the same time, conservatives are convinced, to continue the analogy, the USA *is* from time to time required to serve as an international or regional "policeman" in responding to certain kinds of crises abroad. Other governments quite clearly look to Washington to take the lead in efforts to solve urgent global and regional problems—as, for example, in meeting Russia's critical financial needs and in launching the Russian society upon a democratic course, or in efforts at long last to resolve the intractable Arab-Israeli conflict. Experience leaves little doubt that, if the USA fails to act in response to such challenges, little or no progress can be expected in meeting them successfully. At times, in other words, a strong impetus for interventionist behavior by the United States comes from other nations and from foreign political movements.

Yet conservative interventionists also believe that the nation's policymakers must exhibit greater discrimination in arriving at decisions to intervene in crises and developments within the international system. For example, officials in Washington must define the "national interest" of the USA more clearly and narrowly than has sometimes been true in the past; and they must also always keep in mind the limits of American power. In other words, the nation's leader must clearly understand the difference between overall national power and, in any particular case, usable policy options. As the popular expression has it, they must avoid the temptation to "use a sledgehammer to kill a gnat," or other instances of the grossly inappropriate use of American power in responding to widely differing conditions abroad. From another perspective, policymakers must continually remember the earlier admonition of Secretary of State John Quincy Adams, that the United States does not go abroad "in search of monsters to destroy." As Secretary Adams believed early in the nineteenth century, the nation should reserve the application of its power to those instances in which its own interests *are clearly and directly at stake,* perhaps because American lives and property are in danger, or because of a threat to the nation's economic and financial well-being, or because an ally or friend of the USA confronts imminent danger.

Under such circumstances, the United States has no choice except to follow an interventionist course. And in doing so, conservatives widely believe, policymakers must take whatever steps are necessary to achieve the objective (or objectives). They must, in President Ronald Reagan's phrase, "stay the course" and accomplish the mission for which the intervention was initially undertaken. In turn, this dictates that sufficient power—military force, economic resources, and other components of American power—must be available to policymakers in order to accomplish the purpose for which interventionism was undertaken.

Included in the idea of adequate power is the necessary resolve or will exemplified by the American people and their leaders that is indispensable for achieving the goal. In effect, the motto of conservative interventionists is "No More Vietnams" to mar the nation's diplomatic record. The conservative interventionist mind-set is dealt with more fully in Chapter 4.

The counterpart to liberal neo-isolationism is an interventionist foreign policy advocated by certain liberal and left-wing groups within the American society. In fact, it is no exaggeration to say that liberal interventionism has been the dominant state of mind exemplified by the American people and their leaders in their response to external problems since World War II. Even earlier, during the First World War, President Woodrow Wilson defined a leading Allied goal as making "the world safe for democracy." Similarly, during the Second World

War President Franklin D. Roosevelt was recognized as the spokesman for the Allied cause. FDR enunciated a long list of idealistic goals of the Allies during that conflict—such as achieving the Four Freedoms, eliminating colonialism, and implanting democracy in regions like Eastern Europe.

Presidents Roosevelt and Truman were determined that after the defeat of the Axis powers, Germany and Japan would have new democratic political systems, and following a prolonged period of military occupation, these goals were achieved. Then in the late 1990s, during his historic visit to mainland China, President Bill Clinton declared that democracy was a "universal" system of government. In the course of his visit, Clinton left little doubt that a dominant goal of American diplomacy was to encourage and strengthen the emergence of a democratic political order within the world's most populous society.

Liberal interventionists are also mindful that with the end of the Cold War, the United States is the only remaining superpower within the international system. In the light of that reality, the nation's leaders have an inescapable obligation to *use* American power for goals that rank high on the liberal diplomatic agenda. As already indicated, these include promoting democracy and the cause of human rights abroad; opposing racism in other societies (especially on the African continent); taking the lead in efforts to combat poverty, improving educational opportunities, and raising levels of health and nutrition throughout the Third World; and eliminating pervasive corruption, especially in the developing societies. Expressed differently, for many liberals the period following the Cold War affords the United States a long-awaited opportunity to exercise leadership in efforts by the entire international community to attack what are often called "the indirect causes" of war and violence throughout the world.

Liberal interventionists of course have other causes to which they are devoted. These have included efforts (extending now over a period of almost fifty years) by the United States to bring about a peaceful resolution of the Arab-Israeli conflict. Time and again, officials in Israel and the Arab states have acknowledged that whatever progress has been made—or is likely to be made—in reaching that goal is crucially dependent upon American diplomatic efforts. And throughout the Middle East, voices continue to be heard calling upon Washington to renew the quest for peace between the parties to this intractable dispute.

Another high-ranking objective of liberal interventionists is achieving a long list of humanitarian goals in foreign societies. These range from efforts to relieve human suffering as a result of natural disasters (as in the Sudan, East Africa, and Bangladesh); to refugee relief (as in East and Central Africa and the Balkans); to steps necessary to respond to problems existing in what are sometimes described as "failed states," from Latin America to East Asia. (The concept of the "failed state" is a broad designation denoting the inability of an incumbent government to make its authority effective and to maintain peace and security within its borders.) The phenomenon has been endemic on the African continent and in the Caribbean region.

Liberal interventionists are also frequently outspoken in urging dynamic leadership by the USA to promote international "peacekeeping" operations. For example, they generally approve of Washington's efforts to preserve peace (or in many cases, more accurately perhaps, to bring peaceful conditions into existence) in the Balkans, Central Africa, and (if the differences between them are ever resolved) in maintaining peaceful relations between Israel and the Arab states. It seems beyond dispute that if an overall settlement of this conflict is ever reached, the USA will be required to assume major responsibilities for its implementation. Moreover, liberal interventionists believe that the USA is often justified in using its power to prevent civil wars and internecine conflicts within foreign societies.

Still another high-ranking goal espoused by liberal interventionists is revitalizing the United Nations and encouraging the emergence of strong regional organizations. Forceful diplomatic initiatives by the USA were of course crucial in the establishment of both the League of Nations (which the American nation in the end refused to join) and the United Nations, along with other multinational institutions, such as the World Bank and the International Monetary Fund (IMF). After the war, Washington's influence was a key factor in the emergence of several European unity schemes, leading in time to the creation of the European Community (EC, formerly the European Common Market) and, more recently, the European Union (EU).

Since the Vietnam War particularly, liberals have emphasized the necessity for the United States to concert its diplomatic moves with other nations. In contrast to conservative interventionists, liberal observers and groups almost always oppose a "go-it-alone" policy for the USA. This group believes that as the traumatic Vietnam War experience illustrated, America can seldom accomplish its purposes abroad by acting unilaterally. Washington needs the tangible and intangible support of its allies and friends throughout the international community if it is to accomplish worthwhile purposes.

Among the other attractions of this approach, it promotes another objective which both liberals and conservatives have widely endorsed in the post–Cold War era: "burden-sharing" by all nations whose interests are affected by the outcome of interventionist undertakings. (In recent years, the model in this regard was the Persian Gulf War, which entailed a broadly based multinational effort to preserve the security of the nations within the region.) Yet as liberals see it, Washington cannot insist upon greater "burden-sharing" on the part of its friends abroad without concurrently admitting other governments to a larger voice in decisionmaking involving interventionist conduct. The kind of interventionist diplomacy advocated by those in the liberal political tradition is examined at greater length in Chapter 5.

The last approach to the post–Cold War foreign policy of the United States to be examined here is what has been called *pragmatic interventionism*. While the diplomacy of nearly every incumbent administration since World War II has from time to time exemplified this approach, it is prominently identified with the foreign policy activities of President Bill Clinton, especially in his second term.

The pragmatic approach to problem-solving is a noteworthy characteristic of the American way of life. While antecedents of the phenomenon can be found in the intellectual traditions of other countries, pragmatism is uniquely associated with the American society's philosophical heritage. The movement's two most influential proponents—William James and John Dewey—were leading American philosophers; and their ideas took deep root in the American psyche.

Space is not available at this stage to attempt a definition of "pragmatism" as a coherent philosophical or ideological mode of thought. (The subject is analyzed in considerable detail in Chapter 6.) Suffice it to say here that the central precept of the pragmatic perspective is the belief that to be accepted as true, ideas must be *validated or confirmed by experience*. For the pragmatist, human experience—not logical reasoning or conformity with a pre-existing ideological code—serves as the only really reliable test of ideas. In the foreign policy sphere, therefore, pragmatists shun what they view as arid and usually inconclusive ideological debates and attempts to respond to challenges abroad by relying upon *a priori* and inflexible ideological codes. The pragmatic mind insists that the first requirement in successful problem-solving is to "face facts" or to examine fully and objectively all the factors and circumstances bearing upon the solution of a given problem. (This requirement in turn of course presupposes that policymakers have access to relevant information bearing upon their decisions, which further demands the existence of a skilled diplomatic corps and an intelligence network that are capable of providing accurate and objective information to decisionmakers.)

In formulating a response to problems at home and abroad, the watchwords of the pragmatist are flexibility and adaptability, creativity, realism in weighing the likely consequences of proposed actions and policies, and objectivity in judging the gains and losses for the USA to be anticipated from following a particular course of action. In the process of policy formulation, the pragmatist routinely relies upon the concept of "cost/benefit analysis," long used by economists. For possible alternative responses, the salient questions are: What are the gains and losses to be expected from each proposed response? And on that basis, what is the most beneficial course of action open to the United States under existing circumstances? In other words, in any individual case the "national interest" of the USA is determined pragmatically, following a careful examination of the circumstances of the case and an objective assessment of the policy alternatives available to policymakers in responding to them.

This means that, in a phrase widely used by pragmatists, in the foreign policy field each case should be examined and decided "on its merits," without what might be called ideological commitments or preconceptions that distort the judgments of policymakers. In a given case, the precise challenge facing the USA abroad is identified clearly; possible responses by the USA are delineated and the anticipated consequences of each response are weighed; and a course of action is finally decided upon and promulgated. After the policy has been put into effect, its consequences are evaluated; and in the light of findings made, the policy is continued largely unchanged, modified to improve its effectiveness, or abandoned as no longer in the national interest.

The epitome of this mode of diplomatic problem-solving since World War II perhaps was the decisionmaking process relied upon by the Kennedy administration during the Cuban Missile Crisis of 1962. The administration's ultimate response to Moscow's overt challenge to the security of the Western Hemisphere serves as a textbook example of policymaking according to pragmatic guidelines.

Once the threat posed by the installation of Soviet missiles in Cuba was discovered by agencies of the U.S. government, the formulation of Washington's policy basically followed the process specified above. For example, several possible policy alternatives were carefully and fully examined; President Kennedy and his advisers were realistically mindful of the nature and scope of the power available to them for responding to the Soviet threat; and they were no less aware that the policy ultimately adopted entailed serious risks, with its advantages viewed as somewhat greater than its disadvantages. (Pragmatists, in other words, are always mindful of something that often escapes the notice of those who approach foreign affairs with strong ideological preconceptions: in most instances, any course of action open to the USA is likely to involve a risk, with its positive features often only slightly outweighing its drawbacks. This is another way of saying that in the vast majority of cases, almost any policy that might be adopted entails serious liabilities.)

As it turned out, the diplomacy of the Kennedy White House throughout the course of the Cuban Missile Crisis resulted in a spectacular victory for the

United States—in some respects, the most outstanding example of diplomatic skill exhibited by American officials since World War II. Although it was not apparent at the time, Moscow's defeat in this episode was unquestionably a contributing factor to its ultimate loss of the Cold War.

The pragmatic mind-set was also poignantly illustrated over a generation later by the diplomacy of the Clinton administration, especially during the president's second term in the White House. In responding to a wide variety of developments and challenges confronting the United States abroad, the Clinton White House followed a policy of what we have called "pragmatic interventionism" or what some commentators described as "pragmatic engagement." By definition of the term *pragmatism,* this meant that the administration deliberately avoided the formulation of some kind of overall global strategy to replace the now obsolete containment policy. Critics of Clinton's diplomacy widely complained, and correctly so, that they were unable to discover any diplomatic grand strategy or consistent set of overall principles that integrated Washington's separate diplomatic moves from the Western Hemisphere to East Asia. To the mind of many critics, the diplomacy of the Clinton administration often amounted to little more than a series of unrelated and ad hoc responses to events abroad. Other governments were often mystified and surprised by the "unpredictable" moves of the Clinton White House. And, on balance, for Clinton's detractors the diplomatic behavior of his administration appeared to be erratic, devoid of predictability and consistency, lacking in moral and ethical content, and nearly always without positive results for the United States.

Needless to say, President Clinton's supporters took a totally different view of his policy of "pragmatic engagement." To their minds, the concept served as the diplomatic compass that was needed to chart America's course abroad in the post–Cold War era. For example, Clinton's approach quite clearly acknowledged that fundamental changes had occurred (and were still taking place) in the nature of the international system. The old "bipolar" structure (which as it operated *did* provide considerable stability to the global system) no longer existed. Accordingly, ideological guidelines and precepts derived from earlier periods often had little relevance for the kinds of challenges facing the United States in the contemporary period and in the future. (Throughout the world, rigidly ideological modes of thought, and political systems based upon fixed ideological principles, were being widely abandoned.) As often as not, the United States confronted novel and rapidly changing conditions and problems abroad, and these called for novel and creative responses if America's diplomatic efforts were to be constructive.

In the post–Cold War period, officials in Washington were required to take account of a wide variety of often diverse forces and influences affecting the foreign policy process. A major one, for example, was the necessity to take more fully into consideration the viewpoints and desires of America's friends and allies abroad. (And as was clearly illustrated from time to time by the viewpoints and positions of the members of the European Community, the opinions and diplomatic positions of allied governments were often far from monolithic.) On another front, if American foreign policy at times seemed unpredictable, the basic reason was easily explained: officials in Washington confronted unpredictable and rapidly unfolding developments in settings like the Russian society, the African continent, the Persian Gulf area, and a number of societies in East Asia.

As explained more fully in Chapter 6, a particularly striking example illustrating the pragmatic orientation of the Clinton administration in foreign affairs was the president's policy of "engagement" or "dialogue" with the People's Republic of China. This approach was highlighted by Clinton's visit to the Chinese mainland in July 1998. The policy of the Clinton White House reflected awareness of the reality that ongoing and fundamental changes were occurring within the Chinese political system. (Incidentally, it also represented a complete reversal of the position that Bill Clinton took in criticizing the policy of the Bush administration toward Beijing during the 1992 presidential campaign.)

If the political regime existing within the PRC by no means conformed to the standards of Western democracy, nevertheless, qualified observers agreed that considerable liberalization had occurred in recent years, and the evidence offered realistic hope that other beneficial changes could be expected in the years ahead. Economically and financially, mainland China was making impressive progress; and in some aspects of the economic system, Chinese authorities had permitted the market economy to operate more freely. By the late 1990s, China had amassed a sizable credit in its balance-of-payments account with the USA. (In other words, the PRC was selling more to the American society than it was buying.) Thus far, Beijing had not made radical changes in its administration of Hong Kong.

Moreover, it was clear that after many decades of diplomatic passivity, the Chinese government was becoming more assertive, both regionally and globally. For example, in solving a number of regional problems—such as escalating tensions between India and Pakistan, and preventing a possible nuclear threat by North Korea—the PRC had an essential role to play. As President Clinton discovered on his trip to the mainland, Beijing had in no sense abandoned its long-standing claim to jurisdiction over Taiwan. At the same time, China's leaders did not appear inclined to pursue their objective to the point of precipitating a crisis over Taiwan with the United States. (Chinese authorities posed no overt objection to Washington's "two Chinas" policy, or the maintenance of co-operative relations with both Taiwan and the PRC.)

These were the primary considerations leading the Clinton White House to seek what was sometimes called a "strategic partnership" or dialogue with the PRC and to collaborate with the Chinese government in the solution of a number of outstanding regional and global problems. As President Clinton and his advisers were amply aware, a pragmatic approach to mainland China was not without disadvantages and risks. It left a number of major issues in Sino-American relations unresolved. Authorities in Beijing, for example, still did not hesitate to suppress overt political opposition to their directives. Religious minorities from time to time suffered official discrimination. The PRC's rule over Tibet continued to evoke widespread criticism, especially in the United States. As already noted, Washington had not been successful in persuading Beijing to abandon its claim to jurisdiction over Taiwan; and Taiwan's politically active and often vocal supporters within the USA remained apprehensive about the possible eruption of a new crisis on that front.

Moreover, in the recent past, Beijing had unquestionably sold nuclear technology and equipment to other nations (such as Iran) that aspired to become nuclear powers. Little evidence existed that censure and criticism from the United States and other foreign countries had achieved any positive results in compelling Beijing to permit internal political opposition movements within the society. Today, as in the past, Chinese officials reiterated their customary position that foreign countries (traditionally viewed by the Chinese as "barbarians") could not legitimately interfere in their nation's internal political affairs.

Recognizing such drawbacks, the Clinton White House, nevertheless, was convinced that on balance, a policy of "pragmatic engagement" with the PRC paid real dividends for the United States. In the pragmatic assessment, it was better than a confrontational approach or any other alternative approach to Sino-American relations in the post–Cold War era. And based upon the results of public opinion polls, the reaction of the nation's new media, and studies of opinion on Capitol Hill, along with the overwhelming majority of the American people, believed that President Clinton's position was fundamentally correct.

Some two centuries ago, after facing deep-seated and recurrent disagreements among his advisers on diplomatic issues, President George Washington observed wearily that the United States ought to have the most successful foreign policy of any nation on the globe, since it had so many secretaries of state! According to the standard used by the Father of the Country, in the post–Cold War era the USA seems destined to have outstanding success in the foreign policy field.

CHAPTER 1

ISOLATIONISM—TRADITIONAL AND CONTEMPORARY

F|ROM THE EARLY CONSTITUTIONAL PERIOD UNTIL THE OUTBREAK of World War II, the foreign policy of the United States toward the European powers was defined by the term "isolationism."[1] (Other guiding principles and concepts served as the basis for U.S. policy toward Latin America and Asia.) In the view of a number of commentators on the nation's diplomacy, the "natural" or normal inclination of Americans in dealing with international questions is isolationist. Thus, after the United States entered its third century as an independent nation, former president Richard M. Nixon was convinced that Americans "are essentially isolationist" in their approach to global issues. In his view, the people are motivated to support an active American role in solving international problems only when two pre-conditions were present: an overt threat exists to the nation's interests abroad and the people are convinced that the nation is "engaged in a great idealistic cause" beyond its own borders. In Nixon's judgment, a pervasive belief among citizens that the solution of international problems ought to be primarily the responsibility of other nations was a major factor in President George Bush's failure to win reelection in 1992.[2]

Another commentator has said that only a bipartisan consensus after World War II, in which it was agreed that Communist expansionism posed an ominous threat to global peace and security, kept the American society's "latent isolationism at bay." With the end of the Cold War, however, isolationist propensities resurfaced and in some instances served as a serious obstacle to a role of global leadership by the USA.[3]

Still another recent observer has referred to what he calls the "willful escapism or incipient isolationism" of Americans in dealing with external policy questions. To his mind, most citizens exhibit little or no sustained interest in, or concern about, international problems. This reality was highlighted by the fact that during the presidential campaign of 1996, relatively little debate centered on the role of the United States in international affairs. This commentator lamented that during his first term in office, President Bill Clinton had done little or nothing to inform and educate the people concerning critical global problems.[4]

From the earliest days of the Republic down to World War II, a number of factors combined to make isolationism an attractive diplomatic orientation for Americans. For example, many citizens were convinced that a benign Providence had decreed such a policy for the new American democracy. To the east, what was often called "the Atlantic moat" kept potential enemies at a distance from American shores. (Somehow, it escaped the attention of most citizens that, both during the Revolution and the War of 1812, Great Britain was able to bring formidable military power to bear against the American society. And during the revolutionary struggle, France furnished invaluable assistance to the American campaign for independence.) The impenetrable polar ice cap effectively blocked any threat from the north. (Canadians usually had more to fear from possible expansionism *by the United States* than the reverse.) Distance and geographical barriers, along with the chronically unstable political conditions existing south of the border, meant that the USA confronted no real danger from Latin America.

Moreover, the settlement and colonization of North America signified a profound spiritual and ideological "break" between the New and the Old World. Throughout their history, Americans have exhibited deep skepticism about "diplomacy" and international intrigue. (The United States did not even have ambassadors to other countries until late in the nineteenth century—in part because of a belief that as the world became more democratic and hence more peacefully inclined, there would be no need for large and expensive diplomatic establishments.) Throughout their history, many Americans have viewed "diplomacy" and "democracy" as antithetical ideas. In the American view, based on the experience of the Old World, diplomats too often spent their time planning wars and engaging in intrigues leading to conflicts with other nations, from which ordinary citizens derived little or no benefit. Even today, the State Department—the agency of government that is directly charged with conducting political relations with other nations—ranks at or near the bottom in terms of its budgetary allocation.[5]

An example of this frame of mind from the post–World War II period was provided by the approach of President Lyndon B. Johnson to foreign policy problems. According to a number of commentators on the Johnson administration, LBJ had a genuine aversion to foreign affairs. He exhibited little interest in, or real understanding of, this aspect of public policy; and Johnson believed that deep involvement in international problems—especially if it entailed major military commitments by the United States—would lead to a number of negative consequences for the American society.[6] (Judged by the outcome of the Vietnam War, of course, LBJ's anxieties appeared to be fully justified. At the same time, in common with all other post–World War II chief executives, LBJ was firmly committed to the containment of expansive communism around the globe, to the preservation of the nation's alliances, to providing assistance to Third World societies, and to other ventures involving the projection of American power abroad.)

From the earliest days of colonization, Americans sought to avoid involvement in Europe's seemingly endless political quarrels and wars. For example, the need to pay the costs of the Seven Years' War (known as the "French and Indian War" in the New World) between England and France (1756–1763)—a conflict from which Americans believed they derived little benefit—was a primary reason why London felt compelled to impose new taxes on its colonies in the New World.

The American Revolution and its aftermath provided new reasons and conditions attracting Americans to an isolationist stance. Lingering antipathy and suspicion toward Great Britain; apprehensions about the emperor Napoleon's ambitions in the New World; awareness of the military weakness and vulnerability of the newly independent American republic, caused in large part by the people's aversion to "a standing army"; the determination of citizens after independence to get on with creating "the American way of life" by concentrating primarily on domestic affairs—these factors reinforced pre-existing isolationist impulses.

However, the isolationist credo never provided a totally cohesive or fully consistent set of diplomatic principles. As illustrated by the sometimes highly divergent opinions among devotees of isolationism during the 1930s, those groups and individuals favoring this course for the United States often disagreed fundamentally about the specific steps Washington ought to take in responding to the accelerating global crisis.[7]

Yet certain basic principles were also shared by proponents of traditional isolationism. There was the pervasive conviction, for example, that the United States must avoid involvement in Europe's political controversies and wars. A corollary tenet of isolationist thought was the concept of "no entangling alliances": the United States should refrain from joining European alliance systems (although *temporary* alliances were not precluded by the policy). Other isolationist axioms were the American society's attachment to the principles of "neutral rights" and "freedom of the seas." Time and again, Washington insisted upon the right to trade with all parties to European conflicts—a demand which, for example, led to increasingly tense relations between the USA and Imperial Germany during the period of the First World War.

As President Woodrow Wilson's well-known clash with the Senate over the Treaty of Paris illustrated, isolationists were outspoken, and nearly always successful, in demanding that the United States refrain from membership in international organizations and judicial bodies, like the League of Nations and the World Court. Yet experience during the pre–World War II era also indicated that—in accordance with the diplomatic doctrine of the "free hand"— America did at times co-operate independently with multinational peacekeeping efforts, with the important proviso that the nation's diplomatic actions abroad were determined by officials in Washington, not by other nations or multinational agencies. Traditionally and in the contemporary period, devotees of isolationism have always been highly protective of America's "sovereignty" and have actively resisted what they perceived to be actual or possible infringements upon it. As we shall see, this was a dominant concern of the movement known as "Buchananism" during the 1990s.

Throughout much of the era of classical isolationism, another concept was closely associated with this diplomatic orientation. This was the American society's long-standing opposition to a "standing army," or strong peacetime military establishment. Widespread popular aversion to a standing army derived from the colonial period. London's policy of stationing large troop contingents in the American colonies—and of expecting their colonial subjects to pay much of the cost of doing so—was a major cause of the Revolutionary War. With respect to naval power at least—which Americans have always differentiated from land forces—official and public attitudes began to change around 1900, when the USA began to acquire a "new navy," making the American nation in time the most potent sea power on the globe. Yet it was not until Japan's attack on Pearl Harbor in 1941 that the United States began to build the kind of military establishment needed to defend its security and vital interests. (Significantly, in accordance with the isolationist tradition, the American military machine was dismantled rapidly at the end of the war.) In other words, as late as World War II Americans still did not comprehend the relationship between national power and diplomacy.

Following Japan's attack on Pearl Harbor late in 1941, a leading isolationist spokesman—Senator Robert A. Taft (R–Ohio)—declared that "Only an idiot would be an isolationist today." Another longtime champion of the isolationist approach, Senator Arthur H. Vandenberg (R–Mich.), said that December 7, 1941, was "the day isolationism ended" for the United States.[8] In fact, by the early postwar period Vandenberg had become an outspoken and influential advocate of an "internationalist" role by the United States. After Pearl Harbor, as often as not the term "isolationist" was used as an epithet. As one of its former advocates lamented, the concept frequently became identified with "everything that was bad, terrible, un-American, and indecent"![9]

Under the diplomatic leadership of President Franklin D. Roosevelt, the United States was launched on an "internationalist" course in global affairs—an orientation that the overwhelming majority of the nation's leaders and citizens supported for almost a half-century after his death in 1945. Once the United States formally entered the Second World War, FDR quickly emerged as the acknowledged spokesman for the Allies. His initiatives were largely responsible for establishing the United Nations, along with a long list of other multinational agencies. FDR's successor, President Harry S Truman, promulgated the containment policy directed against expansive communism, and the Truman White House formulated such specific undertakings as the Greek-Turkish Aid Program, the European Recovery Program (ERP), the North Atlantic Treaty Organization (NATO), and the Point Four Program of aid to developing nations.

If the United States formally abandoned isolationism after World War II —and from the available evidence, is unlikely to revert to classical isolationist modes of conduct again in the foreseeable future—anyone wishing to be well informed about the nation's behavior abroad needs to understand this diplomatic orientation for several reasons. As a number of commentators have emphasized, even after the war isolationist impulses were never far beneath the surface of American life; at times, they break through and become conspicuously evident in popular attitudes toward foreign policy issues. A poignant illustration of this reality was provided by the results of a *New York Times*/CBS News poll of public attitudes early in 1997. Citizens were asked to identify the "most important problem" facing the American society today. Heading the list of the ten dominant concerns were such problems as the condition of the economy and the availability of jobs, the federal deficit, the nation's health needs, the increasingly serious drug problem, and the growing incidence of crime. Among the leading issues identified by the public, *there was not a single foreign policy question.*[10] Except perhaps during periods of national emergency, for over two centuries the dominant tendency of the American people has been to be massively preoccupied with domestic concerns and pursuits. By contrast, the interest of citizens in external policy questions tends to be minimal and episodic; and their understanding of complex global issues is, for the most part, fragmentary and inadequate.

"BUCHANANISM"—THE ISOLATIONIST REVIVAL

Evidence to support these observations was supplied by the emergence of a contemporary version of the old isolationist credo, in the thought of a recent candidate for the presidency, Patrick J. Buchanan. His ideas—what we have called "Buchananism"—was perhaps the best example available indicating that the deep attachment of some segments of American society to the isolationist mind-set about America's international role.

Buchanan's views were not important in terms of his bid for the presidency. In the 2000 election, for example, as in earlier instances, he attracted less than 1 percent of the vote. Yet his version of isolationist thought quite clearly was more influential than voting statistics might indicate. For example, a number of labor unions openly supported his approach to American foreign policy. With Buchanan, they were convinced that the nation's attachment to a liberal trade policy since the New Deal had been highly deleterious to certain segments of the working population, causing unemployment, low wages, business failures, and other adverse economic conditions.[11]

Buchanan was born in Washington, D.C., in 1938, the son of a prosperous accountant. Buchanan has lived most of his life in or near the nation's capital. He was educated at Georgetown University and Columbia University; he had no military service; and he subsequently devoted his career primarily to serving as a national political commentator, consultant to public officials, and speechwriter for elected officials. Buchanan served as a special assistant to President Richard Nixon during 1969–1973 and was also a speechwriter for Vice President Spiro Agnew; for a brief period, he was a consultant to President Gerald Ford; and he held the position of director of communications in the Reagan White House.[12] In more recent years, he was a syndicated columnist whose views were given wide circulation throughout the United States.

Prior to becoming a presidential candidate, Buchanan could be classified as a "moderate conservative" in his approach to national policy questions. For example, he supported Washington's effort to defeat communism in Southeast Asia and in Central Africa. He also favored the Reagan administration's interventionism to defeat the pro-Communist Sandinista movement in Nicaragua. At one stage, Buchanan also enthusiastically commended President George Bush's expertise and active leadership in the foreign policy field, although he opposed the Bush decision to wage war in the Persian Gulf area. Buchanan also urged policymakers to take the steps necessary to bring about Russia's withdrawal from the Baltic region.[13]

But by the mid-1990s, Buchanan's position on foreign policy questions more and more bore the earmarks of traditional isolationist thought. In fact, Buchananism was perhaps the closest approximation to the classical isolationist frame of mind to command widespread public attention in the United States since World War II. It was more than coincidence perhaps that Buchanan's slogan of "America First" was also the name of one of the most influential isolationist movements during the 1930s.[14]

One commentary summarized Pat Buchanan's message to the American people by saying that, "You have lost control over your lives. . . . Who has power instead? Your enemies."[15] Or, as another commentator expressed it, Buchanan was extremely skilled at "tapping people's anxieties and offering a cathartic identification with [himself] as the cure."[16] The "average American's" enemies were variously identified by Buchanan as Jews, blacks, and gays; as "predatory" and anti-American governments abroad; as illegal (and sometimes, even legal) immigrants who threatened "American jobs" and did not share the society's basic values; as domestic and foreign corporations that were primarily interested in maximizing their own profits, to the detriment of the nation; as trade laws and international pacts (such as the North American Free Trade Agreement) that were, in Buchanan's view, injurious to the well-being of American workers and business firms; and as the United Nations and other international agencies that continually infringed upon the nation's sovereignty and its diplomatic freedom of action. In other words, to Pat Buchanan and his followers, the worst fears expressed by traditional isolationists were rapidly being realized: the future of the American democratic system was being dangerously threatened by ominous external and internal forces and developments that were inimical to its survival.

In the strongest possible terms, Buchanan urged citizens to reclaim the nation's power of independent decisionmaking before it was too late. Specifically, he called on policymakers to refuse to participate in multinational efforts designed to solve global problems (as illustrated by peacekeeping activities in the Balkans and other settings); to reduce substantially America's financial contributions to the United Nations and other global organizations; to refuse to place the nation's armed forces under foreign military command; to withdraw U.S. military units from actual and potential trouble spots around the world; to slash the nation's foreign assistance budget (already the lowest among the major industrialized countries), along with budgetary allocations for other international programs; to rely on the military establishment if necessary to halt illegal immigration into the United States and to place a five-year moratorium on legal immigration; and to modernize and strengthen the nation's military arsenal. After the government of Iraq took two American citizens hostage, Buchanan demanded that the Clinton administration use military force to gain their release.

At one stage, Buchanan proposed "a New World Order" to restore America's sovereignty and freedom of diplomatic action (although the details of Buchanan's unique version of this idea vis-à-vis the same concept advocated earlier by President George Bush were never forthcoming).

It was above all in the realm of national trade and commercial and financial policies, however, that Pat Buchanan was perhaps most forcefully outspoken. In his view, the position of American workers—and of the nation's economic system generally—was deteriorating rapidly, chiefly as a result of trade and commercial policies promulgated by successive administrations in Washington since the 1930s. To Buchanan's way of thinking, a fundamental cause of the problem was blatant discrimination against American-made products by other nations (prominent examples were Japan and China). Buchanan was convinced that ever since the New Deal (with the enactment of the reciprocal trade program), the nation's leaders had promulgated and adhered to trade policies that were extremely detrimental to America's workers and business firms—a problem greatly compounded by recent trade pacts, such as the North American Free Trade Agreement (NAFTA).

Time and again, therefore, Buchanan urged policymakers to take steps designed to protect the domestic economy from what he described as foreign "predators." Buchanan urged his fellow citizens to accept the fact that certain foreign nations (such as China, Japan, and the members of the European Community) "are rivals, competitors and . . . mighty adversaries" of the United States. Therefore, Washington has "got to start being very tough" in relations with them.[17]

As merely one example, Buchanan proposed the restoration of what was described as "the American system" of high tariffs on imports that existed for many years before the New Deal. Echoing the earlier views of such groups as the Populists and "Bryan Democrats" a century or so earlier, Buchanan vocally denounced certain business corporations for their trade and investment policies abroad that were regarded as injurious to the domestic economy. He was equally critical of the activities of foreign governments and lobbies within the United States, which, to his mind, exert an undue influence upon the formulation of U.S. foreign policy.[18] A recent example was afforded by the overtly interventionist role of the People's Republic of China in efforts to influence the outcome of national election in the year 1996.

As already indicated, from the perspective of the number of voters who were prepared to support Patrick Buchanan's bid for the presidency, his species of isolationism could be dismissed as of little long-range importance for the conduct of American diplomacy. As has been true of most political "splinter groups" in the American political system, Buchanan's bid to win the presidency failed. Studies of public opinion after World War II consistently showed that no more than 10 to 15 percent of the electorate could accurately be classified as "isolationist" in their approach to international issues.[19]

On both the political right and political left, Buchanan encountered massive criticisms for his foreign policy views. For example, despite his claim to the label "conservative," a number of other conservatives overtly repudiated Buchanan's ideas. One conservative spokesman, for example, described Pat Buchanan as "a woolly mammoth, frozen in Siberian ice" who was "a perfectly preserved specimen of the 1930's isolationism and nativism." Another prominent spokesman for conservatism today, William F. Buckley, severely criticized Buchanan for "perverting" and discrediting conservatism within the American society.[20] Buchananism, still another right-wing observer commented, exemplified "everything couth conservatives want to escape."[21]

Predictably, commentators within the liberal community were even more scathing in their denunciations of Buchanan's approach to foreign and domestic policy. As one liberal spokesman assessed it, Buchanan's base "is the shadowy realm of the religious right and the militia fringe." For the most part, his supporters were "anti-abortion fanatics, gun-toting social renegades, and anti–United Nations fanatics." More than one liberal commentator was convinced that at base Buchananism was anti-Semitic and anti-feminist in its approach to public policy questions. While purporting to "protect" the rights of citizens, in reality Buchanan's approach to internal and external issues actually jeopardized the rights of all Americans.[22] Other liberal commentators called attention to the patent contradiction between Pat Buchanan's repeated fulminations against the "Eastern Establishment" and his own establishment in a large and comfortable suburban home near Washington, D.C., where he could "write his columns, read poetry, and hobnob with his friends in the establishment worlds of politics and the media."[23] From the available evidence, it would not be inaccurate to describe Buchananism as a short-lived and eccentric political phenomenon, representing the diplomatic orientation of a very small but often noisy, newsworthy, discontended, and in many ways ignorant segment of the American population.

At the same time, Pat Buchanan's revival of traditional isolationist sentiments cannot be totally dismissed as unimportant. His viewpoints unquestionably expressed the deep-seated frustrations, dissatisfactions, and bewilderment pervasive among certain segments of the American population with regard to a broad range of foreign and related domestic policy questions. While the evidence clearly indicated that American people were not ready to abandon an internationalist approach to global problems in the new millennium, a minority of citizens doubtless shared many of Buchanan's discontents and concerns regarding certain aspects of America's role in international affairs. In the current phrase, Pat Buchanan's ideas "resonated" broadly throughout the American society and expressed a number of deep-seated public discontents and anxieties. In this sense, Pat Buchanan "sent a message" forcefully to policymakers in Washington regarding latent and actual concerns and apprehensions in the minds of the people.

Moreover—and this may well have been its most important consequence—the phenomenon known as Buchananism unquestionably had an impact upon the views and positions of other candidates for political office within the American society. As has not been an uncommon occurrence with splinter movements in the American political tradition, at times other candidates and spokesmen for both major political parties quite clearly echoed Buchanan's views on international issues. On some occasions, for example, even the views of President Bill Clinton and his principal diplomatic advisers obviously reflected ideas vocally expressed by Pat Buchanan.[24] In other words, Buchananism served as a reminder that the isolationist heritage still had an appeal for the American mind in dealing with international problems. As our later discussion of a pragmatic approach to external affairs in Chapter 6 will emphasize, incongruous as it might be, the American people and their leaders not infrequently exhibit both isolationist and internationalist tendencies concurrently in their attitudes and actions in the foreign policy field.

CHAPTER 2

CONSERVATIVE NEO-ISOLATIONISM

I N THE POST–WORLD WAR II PERIOD, TWO REASONABLY DIS-
tinct versions of "neo-isolationist" thought can be identified in the
American people's approach to foreign affairs: a conservative version
and a liberal one. We begin by examining neo-isolationist attitudes exhibited
by those approaching foreign affairs from a right-wing ideological perspective.

Late in 1995, the Republican-controlled House of Representatives passed a
bill (by a vote of 242–171) prohibiting the expenditure of funds to support
American military intervention in Bosnia. Sponsors of the measure contended
that American lives should not be endangered by participating in Bosnian
peacekeeping efforts because no evident diplomatic or security interests of the
USA were served by doing so.[1]

Earlier, Secretary of State James Baker was also outspoken in opposing
America's involvement in the crisis gripping the Balkans. In his expressive lan-
guage, Americans should stay out of that conflict because "we got no dog in
that fight"![2] In his bid for presidency in the first national election of the new
millennium, George W. Bush expressed a comparable judgment regarding
America's role in global affairs in the post–Cold War era. In his view, the
United States ought to inform its allies that, "If there's a conflict in your area,
you get to put troops on the ground, *you* get to keep the warring parties apart,
you get to be the peacekeepers."[3]

These observations introduce the central theme of this chapter: the concept
of right-wing neo-isolationism. At the outset, it is necessary to define the concept of "conservative neo-isolationism" as used in our analysis. The term is
employed here to describe a diplomatic orientation that seeks *to limit and scale
down America's international obligations* by relying upon a set of criteria advocated
by those on the ideological right wing of the political spectrum.

Taking the period from the end of World War II down to the late 1980s as
the standard of an "interventionist" (sometimes called a "universalist") ap-

proach to global problems, advocates of neo-isolationism accept two general propositions concerning the foreign policy of the United States after the Cold War. One is that the USA has inescapable global commitments and responsibilities. The crucial difference between the old and the new isolationism is that the latter acknowledges the reality that the United States is the world's only remaining "superpower," and this fact confers upon the nation a number of unavoidable obligations and responsibilities as a member of the international system.

The second general proposition common to the conservative neo-isolationist approach is that the USA must limit the commitments it assumes abroad and must exercise care in assuming them. Much as they might disagree about American policy toward specific international issues, conservative officials and commentators widely accept the idea that the USA must avoid "overcommitment" abroad. This means that the nation's leaders must exercise selectivity and discrimination in decisions to become involved in problems and crises abroad, doing so only when the preservation of national independence and security is clearly at stake.[4] In turn, this requirement necessarily presupposes the existence of a set of explicit or implicit criteria for determining when the United States will and will not become involved in a particular crisis or issue beyond its own borders. (As we shall see in the chapter that follows, the other species of contemporary neo-isolationist thought—what has been called "liberal neo-isolationism"—also advocates limiting the nation's commitments and responsibilities overseas. In most instances, the principal differences between these two approaches revolve around the criteria to be applied in making the decision to intervene or not to intervene.)

One conservative observer has called attention to a study by the Center for Defense Information showing that in the twentieth century, the USA has been involved in a total of two declared, and eight undeclared, wars and conflicts, in which over 600,000 lives have been lost, at a cost exceeding $5 trillion![5] Or from a still different perspective, according to another commentator, in the new era America's proper international role is to serve as the "balancer of last resort" in efforts to preserve global peace and stability. The nation's proper approach to global problems, therefore, lies somewhere between the extremes of classical isolationism and indiscriminate interventionism.[6]

Proponents of right-wing neo-isolationism are convinced that, as the results of the traumatic Vietnam War experience forcefully illustrated, policymakers must continually guard against the temptation to become "overextended" abroad.[7] This requires them to exercise the utmost care in the assumption of international obligations. In the future, policymakers must do what they have not always done in the past: tailor external commitments to the nation's own diplomatic interests and to the nature and scope of America's power.[8]

It is also necessary at this stage to underscore an idea that was emphasized in our earlier discussion of classical isolationist ideas about American foreign policy. Conservative neo-isolationists do not constitute a monolithic school of thought with regard to America's international role in the new post–Cold War era. Not infrequently, in fact, significant *disagreements* exist among conservative observers on this question.[9] The analysis that follows will provide examples of such divergent viewpoints. Meanwhile, an effort has been made to present what the authors believe is the dominant point of view prevailing among conservative neo-isolationists.

CONSERVATIVE TENETS AND DIPLOMATIC BEHAVIOR

A number of aspects of conservative thought combine to support a neo-isolationist approach to American foreign policy after the Cold War.[10] A hallmark of conservative ideology, for example, is the attitude of its devotees toward change in human society. Abraham Lincoln once said that conservatism has a "preference for the old and tried over the new and untried." A leading conservative spokesman in the contemporary period has said that conservatives are attracted to "custom, convention, and continuity" over radically new ideas and schemes for improving human society. He quoted the views of John Randolph to the effect that "Providence moves slowly, but the devil always hurries."[11] In the vast majority of cases, the conservative mind is dubious about the prospects for achieving beneficial change—especially rapid change—in political, social, and economic affairs.[12]

The conservative mind, Russell Kirk has said, rejects the principle of human "perfectability"; human nature is characterized by the existence of "grave faults" which are unlikely to be modified significantly. Or as another leading conservative commentator contends, "Human nature and human reality are never transformed."[13] And right-wing commentators are congenitally skeptical about the ability *of government* to improve the condition of human society, especially beyond America's own borders.[14]

As they assess it, more often than not interventionist efforts by the USA abroad not only fail to provide long-term solutions for the problems toward which they are directed, but in the end frequently result in deleterious consequences (in the form of internal political divisiveness, neglect of urgent domestic problems, and the waste of national resources) for the American society itself.[15] As we shall see in discussing specific aspects of post–Cold War American foreign policy, from Washington's attempts to encourage democracy abroad, to diplomatic activities directed toward "nation-building," to efforts seeking to resolve age-old conflicts in the Balkans, conservatives find little convincing evidence that an interventionist foreign policy by the United States pays real dividends.[16]

Conservative spokesmen have always viewed the global political environment in Hobbesian terms.[17] To their minds, the end of the Cold War has not basically altered the external political setting of U.S. foreign policy. While tensions between Washington and Moscow have unquestionably diminished, the global environment remains dangerous and unstable.[18] Thus, one observer late in 1996 referred to a number of "impending or actual international disorders with potentially severe consequences" for the United States. To his mind, such developments as ongoing political conflicts in the former Soviet Union and the uncertain state of Russian-American relations; China's economic emergence, its growing diplomatic assertiveness, and its obvious resistance to Western political ideas; Western Europe's progress in achieving economic and financial integration, which will in time pose a genuine challenge to the leadership role of the United States; the continuing deadlock in the Arab-Israeli conflict and the existence of other serious threats to the peace and stability existing in the Middle East; recurring violence and political upheaval in the Balkans—all these are newsworthy examples of global developments creating an unfavorable environment for the realization of American foreign policy goals.[19]

In the view of still another observer, contrary as it may be to their own ethos and cherished ideological values, the nation's citizens and leaders must come to terms with the reality that the prospects for effectively protecting human rights in foreign societies, implanting democracy abroad, and achieving a long list of other goals traditionally valued by Americans are extremely remote. Conservatives have cited the conclusions of a study by Freedom House, showing that throughout the world, the movement toward greater political freedom is "in retreat," while "violence, repression and state control are on the increase."[20] Or, in the words of another commentary, the international system has become increasingly "unreceptive, and ultimately more threatening, to the interests of the United States and its allies."[21]

Other conservatives have echoed Senator Daniel P. Moynihan's description of the world beyond America's own borders as "a dangerous place," no less in the post–Cold War era than before.[22] A leading conservative and policymaker during the Reagan administration became convinced that the Vietnam War experience provided a painful lesson for Americans; it underscored the dangers of "trying to be the world's midwife to democracy when the birth is scheduled to take place under conditions of guerrilla warfare." In this view, on a number of occasions in the past, unrestrained interventionist behavior by the USA abroad set the stage for "diplomatic disaster."[23] In the judgment of another conservative observer, the results of conflicts like the Vietnam War and Moscow's intervention in Afghanistan "should stand as an enduring testament to the pitfalls of interventionism and the limits of power."[24] In time, even ex-president Richard M. Nixon conceded that prolonged and massive American involvement in the Vietnam War had been a major diplomatic error by officials in Washington. Nixon concluded that democracies are not good at waging "protracted war," especially when the front is "half a world away." To his mind, the general lesson to be learned is that the USA must resist the temptation to solve the political and economic problems of other nations, especially when the society concerned shows little inclination or capacity to do so.[25]

Still another conservative spokesman has cautioned that all too often in the past officials in Washington have "overestimated their ability to influence foreign political movements." They have appeared to operate upon the premise that "it is possible to democratize governments, any time, anywhere, under any circumstances." Yet experience has provided convincing evidence to the contrary. In the vast majority of cases, these expectations are unrealistic and have led to a number of widely publicized policy failures.[26] Goals traditionally associated with the American way of life—such as democracy, human rights, and pluralism—confront formidable obstacles in what appears to be an increasingly chaotic and violence-prone international system.[27] To cite merely one example, in the view of a leading conservative commentator, "The U.S. Government doesn't have a clue how to resolve most of the world's ethnic conflicts, and never will." For most Americans, the "expertise, leverage, and political will" to deal with such problems successfully are totally lacking.[28]

In other words, as most conservatives are agreed, there is a fundamental difference between a nation's possessing vast power and its having *infinite* power.[29] The fact that the USA remains a superpower does not mean that it is omnipotent beyond its own borders. (For that matter, as conservatives often emphasize, the existence of certain increasingly critical domestic problems remind us that the federal government is not omnipotent even within its own boundaries.) As former secretary of state Dean Rusk used to point out, by definition of the term "*foreign* affairs," most of the world's problems lie outside the ambit of American law and beyond its effective jurisdiction.

As a general operating principle of U.S. foreign policy, modern-day conservatives are often prone to repeat the admonition enunciated by John Quincy Adams early in the nineteenth century. In its foreign relations, one of the nation's eminent political leaders observed, the United States "goes not abroad in search of monsters to destroy."[30] A modern translation of Adams's principle is: the American republic ought not to "look for trouble" abroad. Officials in Washington, conservatives are widely agreed, should always be vigilant in protecting the nation's own security and independence. But they should devote their time and efforts primarily to creating and safeguarding "the American way of life." This requires them to avoid becoming embroiled in foreign controversies and problems that are really none of America's business and concerning which, in most instances, they lack the power to resolve.

Conservative spokesmen advocate limiting America's global commitments for another reason having to do with the nature and scope of the nation's power. Nearly all conservative observers accept the idea that in the post–Cold War period, the United States is a superpower, the only one remaining in the international system. Admittedly, the power of certain other nations (such as the members of the European Community, Japan, and China) is increasing year by year.[31] Conceivably, in time these and other nations may join the ranks of the "superpowers." But that development lies many years in the future.[32] Meanwhile, with the collapse of the Soviet Union, from the perspective of global political decisionmaking, the USA is the only nation that can accurately lay claim to that title.

Impressive as American power is, experience has made abundantly clear that not even a superpower can assume an *indefinite number of global commitments*, with little serious thought devoted to the costs such obligations ultimately entail. Although he was not regarded as a "conservative" thinker during his career, the distinguished political analyst Walter Lippmann, whom right-wing proponents of neo-isolationism are fond of quoting, once likened foreign policy commitments to checks an individual might write on a bank account. If, when the time comes, nations are not prepared to "honor" these obligations— or, in other words, to pay the costs such commitments may ultimately entail— the inevitable result will be a condition of diplomatic "bankruptcy" that can have serious internal and external consequences.[33] Or, in a term that has been widely applied to American diplomacy since the Vietnam War, the nation's foreign policy is in danger of lacking "credibility."

For many conservatives in the contemporary period, too often in the past policymakers have written such diplomatic "checks" indiscriminately, without calculating the costs or implications involved. Then when such obligations ultimately had to be honored, and when public officials and the people alike finally realized that the cost of doing so would be extremely high, in a number of cases the commitments were abandoned as too expensive![34]

Such erratic and unpredictable behavior by the United States created the impression abroad of a nation whose conduct in global affairs was uncertain and of a society whose policymakers did not understand the elementary principle that overseas commitments entail costs—in money, in lives and military resources, in economic and financial losses, and in what might be called "psychological wear and tear" on the members of society. Or, for conservative neo-isolationists the underlying principle that ought to guide future American foreign policy is accurately described by the term "discriminating detachment" in dealing with global problems.[35]

Right-wing observers are also widely skeptical about a concept that has become fashionable among contemporary students of international politics, notably Kenneth Waltz. This is an approach known as "neo-realism"—a modified version of traditional *Realpolitik* as advocated by such classical thinkers as Machiavelli, Hobbes, Metternich, and Bismarck.[36] After World War II, leading American advocates of this approach were Walter Lippmann, Hans J. Morgenthau, and (at times, although not consistently) George F. Kennan. Key concepts in *Realpolitik* thought are national power, balance of power, spheres of influence, and the national interest. As the political realist sees it, nations pursue and use *power* to achieve their objectives; and in this perspective, the *balance of power* serves as an essential mechanism for preserving global peace and stability.[37]

In recent years, the "neo-realists" have adapted classical realistic thought to take account of modern conditions.[38] In the revised version of the concept, military and other coercive forms of power are de-emphasized in favor of economic and financial aspects; and the ability of the policymakers to create and maintain coalitions supporting American policies abroad is viewed as a key component of national power. As one proponent of this approach assesses it, the old *Realpolitik* concept of "geopolitics" has now been superseded by the concept of "geoeconomics," since economic factors have become the most influential determinants of national power.[39] Alternatively, another student of American foreign relations is convinced that a basic defect of classical political realism lies in ignoring a factor that has become increasingly influential in determining America's power overseas—the concept of political leadership. At times, this has quite clearly been a crucial element in determining the outcome of American diplomatic efforts.[40]

As devotees of the neo-realistic school of thought see it, a long list of novel and difficult challenges confronting the USA overseas—such as increasingly acute environmental problems, the global population explosion, the collapse of governmental authority in one state after another, and the demands of ethnic, religious, and tribal groups for greater political autonomy—have rendered older forms of power irrelevant for a successful foreign policy today.[41] From a different perspective, other advocates of neo-realism are persuaded that in responding to challenges likely to confront the United States abroad, the nation's "power" will consist chiefly of its ability to serve as a "rallier of nations" and as a successful advocate of a "community of interests" among nations, enabling them to solve global problems on a collaborative basis.[42] In turn, this means that "If there is to be burden sharing, there must be power sharing as well."[43]

Yet a goodly number of right-wing commentators remain unconvinced that the precepts of classical realism have become outmoded and should be discarded. In their view, after the Cold War no less than before, the military power of the United States matters.[44] For example, many of the goals advocated even by political liberals (such as "humanitarian interventionism") are often unlikely to be achieved without the actual or threatened application of military force by the United States and other nations. These and other ventures abroad often require a "shield" provided by overwhelming military might. (Indeed, in recent years officials of a number of foreign governments have sometimes been vocal in calling for outside *military* intervention to restore peace and stability to their strife-torn societies, as in Sierra Leone in the year 2000. Conservative observers remind the nation's leaders that "security is the precondition" for achieving almost all of America's overseas objectives; and in turn, the concept of security inescapably implies an ability to safeguard the nation's independence and its vital interests from actual and potential dangers abroad.[45]

Only a small minority of conservatives believes that the post–Cold War world has witnessed a significant decrease in the forces and tendencies endangering global peace and security. To cite merely one example: very few right-wing commentators are prepared to accept the idea that the global and regional behavior of "the new Russia" will be completely benign. The majority point to evidence indicating that the nation's leaders have not abandoned many traditional Russian goals in dealing with former members of the USSR and in relations with Moscow's neighbors in Eastern Europe, as in the ongoing conflict in Chechnya.[46] Many conservative neo-isolationists are also apprehensive that increasingly serious internal problems within Russia could induce its leaders to embark upon an expansionist course abroad. (Throughout history, national leaders have engaged in expansive or aggressive conduct abroad in order to divert public attention from the existence of crucial domestic problems. At times, the Clinton White House was accused of resorting to this tactic to divert attention from the president's scandalous behavior.) In brief, it would be totally unwarranted for American policymakers to assume that "the Russian threat" to Western security and independence has been now eliminated for all time.[47]

This is merely another way of saying, as many commentators over the years have pointed out, that the Cold War resulted not only from the threat posed by communism, but also from the Kremlin's pursuit of certain historic and deeply ingrained Russian diplomatic goals, most of which had no necessary relationship to communist ideology. Several conservatives observers question whether the latter objectives have really been abandoned by Russia's leaders and certain political groups within the society after the Cold War.

A corollary idea, espoused by a number of conservative neo-isolationists today, is that the United States must not only possess an adequate and modern military establishment, but under certain circumstances officials in Washington *must be prepared to use the armed forces at an early stage*, to avert serious threats to the nation's security and vital interests. For some conservative neo-isolationists, a salient lesson from recent diplomatic experience is that action *taken early* in responding to ominous developments abroad may make unnecessary a much more prolonged and costly application of American military power at a later stage.[48] The approach to American diplomacy known as conservative neo-isolationism, it needs to be emphasized, is no new phenomenon. For example, it emerged early in the post–World War II period and was exemplified by the ideas of ex-president Herbert Hoover and Senator Robert A. Taft (R–Ohio) during the 1950s concerning America's international role. Many of the ideas advanced by right-wing advocates of neo-isolationism today clearly embrace this earlier version of the concept.[49]

A leading idea central to the Hoover-Taft approach, for example, was the concept of "Fortress America." Even at this early stage, those advocating this diplomatic strategy called for a reduction in America's international commitments (this was the period, we need to remember, in which the Truman administration had recently adopted the containment policy.) As Hoover, Taft, and their followers assessed it, the USA should confine its efforts overseas chiefly to preserving the security and stability of the Western Hemisphere. (In effect, the concept of Fortress America was an effort to revive the historic non-interventionist principle, as enunciated in the Monroe Doctrine.)[50] In far too many instances in its diplomatic experience, proponents of this strategy contended, the American nation has embarked on "crusades" around the world, often with questionable, and sometimes harmful, results. Officials in Washington, therefore, ought to concentrate their efforts upon solving problems at home and within the New World. It is worth noting that during its heyday, the concept of Fortress America did not win majority support in Congress or among the American people.

To the minds of most conservatives in applying the nation's power abroad, policymakers must be guided by one transcendent principle. The dominant purpose of American foreign policy *is to protect the nation's security and to promote its own diplomatic interests*. (As we shall see in a later chapter, other conservatives disagree with neo-isolationists on the specific steps needed to achieve this broad objective.) Conservatives widely reiterate the old *Realpolitik* concept of "national interest" as the lodestar of U.S. foreign policy. As they view it, the end of the Cold War has in no way changed the centrality of the concept as a guide to external policy. Without apology, right-wing observers contend that the United States has a set of unique and fundamental interests; the paramount goal of the nation's external policy must be to promote and protect them.[51] At times, conservatives widely insist, the interests of the USA are to be distinguished from those of humanity at large; nor are they synonymous with the dictates of "world public opinion." Those approaching foreign affairs from this perspective are uniformly skeptical about the ability of the United Nations or other multilateral agencies to preserve global peace and stability and to deal effectively with threats endangering the security of the United States.[52]

Expressed differently, the dominant purpose of the nation's foreign policy is to create and maintain conditions under which citizens may devote themselves to preserving, strengthening, and enjoying "the American way of life." External, no less than internal, policy should contribute directly to the well-being, good health, and prosperity of the American society. Unless developments overseas directly impinge upon the American society's interests, therefore, policymakers should avoid massive involvement in them or assuming responsibility for their outcome.[53] Yet as one commentator has lamented, in recent years, impelled by what is described as "the call of conscience," the nation's leaders have widely engaged in diplomatic interventionism "in the near-total absence of substantive national interests." Or as another observer has expressed the idea, the nation's leaders have been driven by what often appeared to be a compelling urge "to do good in the world"; yet in the final analysis they were unwilling to pay the price that "doing good" inevitably entailed.[54]

Just as pre–World War II isolationists passionately believed, for many conservatives today, the most important contribution the United States can make to the improvement of the conduct of international relations is the power of its own example.[55] Far from serving as a model "city set on a hill" or as a "beacon for mankind," in the graphic words of one contemporary observer, in the eyes of foreigners today the American society often appears more like the South Bronx![56]

Implicit in these ideas is the belief that—despite the postwar emphasis upon multilateralism—the United States and all other nations remain devoted to the pursuit of their own unique interests in global affairs. The existence of the United Nations and other multilateral agencies has not fundamentally altered this basic reality. After a half-century or more, the UN, for example, is still an association of sovereign nations, not a world government. The resolutions of the UN General Assembly do not have the force of law for the United States or any other nation; they are merely policy recommendations or suggested guidelines that the members of the UN are free to accept or reject, as their interests dictate.

Among right-wing observers, the belief is pervasive that in the years after World War II, many of the actions (or in some instances, the inactions) and resolutions of the United Nations (most especially, of the General Assembly), and of several other multilateral agencies, have been contrary to the national interests of the United States.[57] Conservatives tend to be skeptical about certain multilateral agreements, such as the Chemical Weapons Convention (1993), designed to ban such weapons from the international system. As one commentator observed, since the agreement is basically unenforceable, America's participation in it does little more than foster a false sense of security and, for that reason, actually endangers the national diplomatic and security interests of the USA.[58] Similarly, as other conservatives evaluate it, America's participation in international trade agreements is in some degree responsible for the deterioration of its position in world trade and commerce.[59] As a general principle of external policy, another conservative analyst has concluded, it is neither necessary nor desirable for the United States "to act as the star player on a collective security team."[60]

In the light of their doubts and criticisms about the United Nations—and the concept of "multilateralism" generally—conservative individuals and groups believe that the United States must preserve the right of unilateral decisionmaking.[61] In effect, this school of thought remains devoted to the old concept of "the free hand" that was prominent in the period of classical isolationism.[62]

CONSERVATIVE NEO-ISOLATIONISM AND SPECIFIC GLOBAL ISSUES

A number of specific ideas concerning America's role in world affairs in the post–Cold War period are prominent in the thought of conservative neo-isolationists. There is the belief, for example, that while the United States remains the world's only superpower, the relative power position of the nation is declining.[63] Two nations in particular—Germany and Japan—are becoming increasingly powerful and, in the years ahead, may be expected to challenge America's once-dominant role in the international system. A number of other nations (sometimes called "regional influentials") are also gaining power, and it may be anticipated that their power will continue to increase. The interests of these nations do not always coincide with those of the United States. With a handful of exceptions, the American-led effort to promote the "development" of the Third World has failed.[64]

Similarly, efforts by the United States since World War II to promote democracy in other societies, to safeguard human freedoms, and to achieve lasting political stability beyond its own borders have also for the most part been unsuccessful. In one country or region after another—the Korean peninsula, Southeast Asia, Central America and the Caribbean area, Lebanon and several other Middle Eastern states, Somalia, and most recently the Balkans—as a general rule, American-led interventionist efforts have resulted in a complete or substantial failure to achieve Washington's announced goals. As many conservatives view it, the overall lesson to be derived from such cases is that there exists little convincing evidence to support the case for an interventionist foreign policy by the United States.[65]

A corollary belief of right-wing analysts is that "peacekeeping" operations by the United Nations and other multilateral organizations have, with very rare exceptions, also failed to accomplish their purposes. In most instances, they have done little to remove the underlying causes of conflict and violence abroad; and in some cases, such external interventionism has added a new source of violence and political instability for societies experiencing internal crises. It has proved extraordinarily difficult, for example, for multinational peacekeeping forces to remain neutral in foreign political controversies.[66] Almost inevitably (if, for example, they encounter resistance to their humanitarian efforts), foreign powers are forced to take sides in existing political contests. It is almost impossible, that is to say, for them to avoid *political intervention* in the prevailing conflicts. Experience, therefore, cautions strongly against America's participation in such ventures.

To those holding conservative political views, a basic tenet of liberal thought (identified historically with such thinkers as Immanuel Kant and Woodrow Wilson) has been brought into question by recent political developments. This is the belief that a direct correlation exists between the worldwide extension of democracy and the prospects for international peace and security. Today, as in the past, conservatives find little evidence to support this optimistic prediction. But even if it is true, conservatives discern little prospect for the rapid emergence of democracy throughout the world.[67]

With the end of the Cold War, conservatives have also raised fundamental questions about the value of most of the defense pacts and alliance systems to which the United States belongs. NATO and the other alliances sponsored by the United States during the height of the Cold War (at a time, critics charged, when officials in Washington appeared to be afflicted with "pactitis") were directed primarily against the threat of Communist expansionism. The collapse of the Soviet empire has greatly reduced that danger (even if, as a number of conservatives believe, the risk of future expansionist moves by Communist China and North Korea cannot be completely ruled out).

As many right-wing observers see it, NATO has now become largely obsolete; its relevance for the problems and challenges facing the USA in the post–Cold War world seems highly questionable. Despite a remarkable degree of allied unity during the Persian Gulf War—a phenomenon that conservatives widely believe is unlikely to be repeated—in the new era, the European allies are more and more inclined to promote their own security interests independently, through such mechanisms as the Western European Union (WEU) and the Conference on Security and Cooperation in Europe (CSCE), organizations in which the USA plays a very limited role.[68]

In other regions, formal military pacts created during the Cold War possess even less utility than NATO. Conservatives have long believed that the nation's allies can and should assume a larger share of the burden for solving global problems and for international peacekeeping operations, thereby relieving the United States of these burdens. Increasingly, many conservative commentators are convinced that America's continued military presence in other societies and regions (such as in Western Europe and in East Asia) serves as a major cause of anti-American sentiment and as an impediment to more cooperative relations with other countries.[69]

On the basis of the post–World War II diplomatic record, conservatives caution that policymakers must be on guard against another danger inherent in such alliance systems: a tendency to allow small and weak allies to determine the foreign policy of the United States. A conspicuous example of course was provided by the government of South Vietnam during the Vietnam War. But other examples of the phenomenon by actual or de facto allies—such as South Korea, Pakistan, the Philippines, Israel, Iran (before the shah's overthrow), Lebanon, and the Dominican Republic—also serve as cases in point. A number of conservatives, therefore, have called upon the president and Congress to "take back" the power of diplomatic decisionmaking from other governments—a crucial step in the preservation of America's national sovereignty.[70]

As already noted, in the period following the Cold War, conservatives widely have placed great emphasis upon the need for the nation's leaders to devote greater attention to the solution of domestic problems. For observers in this category, for example, it is imperative that officials in Washington take the steps required to improve the nation's position in world commerce and trade. In turn, achieving this goal demands solving or substantially alleviating a number of domestic problems and conditions impairing America's competitive position abroad, such as forging ahead in research and development, providing incentives to improve the productivity of American business enterprises, and undertaking long-overdue reforms and improvements in the nation's educational system.[71] As graphically illustrated by the movement known as "Buchananism" (discussed more fully in Chapter 1), the neglect of urgent internal problems—such as unemployment, labor discontents, and declining economic productivity at home—can give rise to, or reinforce, xenophobic sentiments directed against those foreign societies deemed (correctly or not) responsible for America's economic problems.

With regard to U.S. foreign policy toward Western Europe, several specific ideas are prominent in the thinking of conservative neo-isolationists. Nearly all observers belonging to this school of thought believe that today and in the future, no less than in the past, the European continent remains a region of high priority for the security and diplomatic interests of the United States. The American nation participated in two global wars, primarily because of a belief that threats to European security posed a direct and ominous danger to its own society. The containment policy enunciated in 1947—America's overall global strategy for some forty or so years thereafter—was promulgated by the Truman administration mainly in response to the Communist threat to Western security. In the years that followed, NATO served as the most important alliance system to which the USA belonged. The end of the Cold War has not changed the reality that the U.S.-European connection remains vital for American society.[72]

At the same time, many right-wing observers are equally convinced that in the post–Cold War era, European-American relations are changing fundamentally. The increasingly prosperous European allies have become more self-confident and assertive in pursuing their own diplomatic interests. They are less inclined than in the past to accept American diplomatic leadership docilely or to follow dutifully in Washington's diplomatic wake.[73] With the passage of time, Europeans are relying more and more on organizations like the European Union (EU) and the CSCE to protect, promote, and express their security interests.[74]

Under these new conditions, a number of conservatives have raised fundamental questions about the utility and rationale of the Western alliance system. Created to protect the West against expansive communism, NATO finds its usefulness after the Cold War widely debated.[75] To the mind of one commentator, in the years ahead NATO is destined to become "a bit player" in the European political drama; and at times it will have no part at all in shaping events within the region.[76] Pervasive doubts about the utility of NATO include

(1) the idea that the alliance is not well adapted to dealing with the kinds of problems and challenges confronting its members after the Cold War; (2) the belief among many Americans that for too many years, the allies have had a "free ride" at the expense of the USA in paying the high costs of Western defense efforts; (3) the conviction that America's membership in NATO sometimes inhibits policymakers from promoting the nation's best interests abroad; and (4) a belief that the postwar "bipartisan consensus" supporting a dynamic role by the USA in promoting European security has now collapsed, producing a low level of domestic support within the USA for this "entangling alliance."[77]

A related, and highly controversial, issue has been the question of NATO's "extension" to include the former Communist states in Eastern Europe and, according to some advocates of the idea, possibly in time even Russia itself. A number of right-wing observers vocally oppose this idea. They find no real need for, or value in, an "enlarged" NATO after the Cold War. They question what such an augmented alliance will accomplish; they are certain that Moscow is resistant to this idea; they fear that Russia's leaders would regard an expanded NATO as a provocation and would respond accordingly; they are apprehensive that an enlarged NATO would in the end prove to be a drain on America's military strength and other resources; and they fear that ultimately, the expansion of NATO would lead to new foreign policy obligations and commitments for the United States.[78] (A relevant lesson from World War II, applicable to this issue, is that Poland proved to be indefensible by the Allies. In the end, the country was defeated and occupied by both German and Russian forces.)

Another related question is NATO's assumption of "out-of-area commitments" (and a prominent example is the Persian Gulf area). For the first time, during the Persian Gulf War the members of the alliance collaborated in responding to a security threat lying outside NATO's geographical orbit. Western governments of course agreed that a prolonged shutoff of oil shipments from the Persian Gulf region would pose an extremely dangerous threat to the security and well-being of the NATO area, as well as to almost all other industrialized nations. Accordingly, the level of allied collaboration during the Persian Gulf conflict was extraordinarily high. Yet conservative observers also caution that such unanimity among the allies in responding to challenges arising outside of NATO's customary orbit was exceptional and most unlikely to be repeated.[79] In responding to future crises affecting their interests, the European allies are likely to pursue a course (or courses) independent from that of the USA in dealing with regional and global issues.[80]

A noteworthy example of such policy divergences is the issue of the differing approaches to Russia after the Cold War. In most instances, European officials tend to be more sympathetic to Moscow's position and demands than their counterparts in Washington.[81] Another outstanding example is provided by the continuing crisis in the Balkans. Fundamental differences could be discerned in the European and the American positions in responding to that difficult and complex challenge.[82]

In the light of this reality, many conservative observers are convinced, a high priority goal of U.S. foreign policy after the Cold ought to be promoting "burden-sharing" among America's friends and allies.[83] On Capitol Hill especially, the conviction has long been prevalent that the increasingly prosperous European nations, in company with Japan, are now able to shoulder much of the burden of meeting such international obligations as providing aid to needy Third World societies, responding to threats to the peace against societies experiencing external dangers, and preserving domestic peace and order within those societies confronted with international instability and upheaval.[84]

Our earlier treatment has called attention to the views of conservative neo-isolationists with regard to Russian-American relations in the new era. Without repeating that discussion, we may observe briefly that several ideas are prominent in this approach to the issue. Naturally, as leading advocates of the postwar effort to contain expansive communism, right-wing observers are elated at the outcome of the Cold War. To their minds, that result stands as full vindication of the containment policy and of the position of "peace through strength" that guided Washington's diplomacy after World War II. In hindsight, a number of conservatives believe, at times American policymakers tended to overestimate Russian military strength, leading them to exaggerate the danger that Moscow's behavior posed for the United States and its allies. Officials in Washington must be on guard against that tendency in the post–Cold War era.[85]

At the same time, conservatives are much less inclined than most political liberals to believe that the danger of Russian expansionism and interventionism has totally disappeared. Among certain segments of Russian society, the appeal of communism remains strong, and (if Russia's leaders are unable to solve the society's pressing economic and social problems) Communist forces within the country may well gain new converts.

Apart from the ideological dimensions of Moscow's foreign policy, many conservatives are not convinced that the Russian state has altogether abandoned its historic diplomatic ambitions in regions like Eastern Europe, the Middle East, and Asia—goals that, in some cases, have been pursued by the Kremlin for several centuries. For example, Henry Kissinger has urged policymakers to be vigilant that Russia's "traditional nationalism does not spill across its borders," jeopardizing the security of other countries and perhaps regional and global peace as well.[86]

The neo-conservative view of Russian-American relations in the new era may be summarized by underscoring three broad principles that ought to guide Washington's diplomatic efforts. One is the old diplomatic concept of "watchful waiting": policymakers in the USA need to follow developments in Russia very carefully, being diligent for any sign of a revival of hegemonial tendencies by Moscow. For an extended period of time, the Russian society and its former provinces are likely to be in the grip of what one observer describes as "nationalistic fanaticism, xenophobia, and intolerance."[87] Alternatively, one observer has urged that, as the Russian society once again experiences a "Time of Troubles," the United States must make every effort to avoid becoming deeply involved in the phenomenon.[88]

In the light of these conditions, another principle of American diplomacy ought to lie in exercising considerable caution regarding the prospects for democracy within Russia and most of the former Soviet republics. Conservative observers call attention to numerous obstacles that must be overcome before anything resembling Western-style democracy emerges within Russia and its former empire; and most right-wing commentators have serious reservations about the power of the United States or other foreign nations to ensure that outcome.[89] (Overt external interventionism to achieve the goal may in fact have exactly the opposite result of the purpose intended.)[90] As another study has emphasized, the contemporary world has witnessed the emergence of many different species of government claiming to be "democratic"; in too many cases, the *form* of a society's government has been viewed by the West as crucial, while the citizens of the society regard its *effectiveness* in solving pressing problems as the decisive issue. Or as another analysis has expressed the idea, many societies throughout the contemporary world will require a prolonged period of authoritarian government if they are to achieve national development. In many cases, during this long and often politically traumatic stage, their political systems "can pass for democracy, [only] if the observer is willing to close one eye and squint the other"![91]

Right-wing neo-isolationists generally favor a limited program of aid by the United States and its European allies to the new Russia. At the same time, outside assistance to the Russian society must be formulated with regard to America's own serious budgetary problems.[92] Aid from the USA should also be relatively modest in scope (much less than Moscow requests). Moreover, it should be clearly predicated upon Russia's continued progress in implementing reforms leading to a free-market economic system, in participating in schemes for promoting regional trade, and in opening Russia's borders to foreign in-

vestments. Yet even with external assistance, conservative neo–isolationists believe, Russia's political and economic future will be determined *by its own*
people, with the USA playing a marginal role in the outcome. As many analysts
in this group see it, in dealing with Russia and many other foreign societies,
policymakers in Washington must guard against a tendency to overestimate
their ability to determine the course of political events beyond America's own
borders.[93]

Along with most Americans, right-wing observers are convinced that the
United States has major diplomatic and security interests in the Middle East.
Well-informed observers of Middle Eastern affairs call attention to the increasing volatility of the region. Unless policymakers in Washington confront certain dangerous tendencies and formulate effective policies for dealing with
them, in the words of Henry Kissinger, "we had better prepare ourselves for
an inevitable blow-up" in this key region.[94]

Four specific aspects of U.S. policy toward the Middle East deserve brief
mention. One of these is America's long-standing ties with the State of Israel,
leading the USA on several occasions to take action designed to preserve Israeli
security. With the animosity of many Arab states and groups toward Israel remaining undiminished, this goal is likely to remain high on the list of Washington's diplomatic objectives.[95]

A second and closely related American interest is continuing to serve as instigator and facilitator in renewed efforts to resolve the Arab-Israeli conflict.
Most commentators on American foreign relations, including conservative
neo–isolationists, accept the reality that no other nation is in a position to discharge this obligation effectively.

A third goal of U.S. policy in the Middle East—highlighted by the Persian
Gulf War of 1990–91—is preserving access to the oil supplies of the region.
The dependence of the United States and its allies upon oil imports from the
Middle East remains high and (in the absence of an American energy policy) is
unlikely to decrease in the foreseeable future. In turn, this reality dictates that
the USA continue to play a leading role in maintaining the security and stability of the Persian Gulf region.[96]

A fourth objective of Washington's policy toward the Middle East is responding to terroristic movements directed against Americans. For many years,
policymakers have identified certain Middle Eastern nations—notably Libya,
Iran, Syria, and Iraq—as sponsors of terroristic activities aimed at the USA and
other Western nations. From the available evidence, that challenge also shows
no sign of disappearing in the years ahead.[97]

By contrast, conservative neo–isolationists do *not* believe that American-led
efforts to promote democracy throughout the Middle East is a compelling or

achievable diplomatic goal. From Morocco to Iran, the prospects for the early emergence of Western-style democratic institutions and processes appear to be remote; and attempts by the United States since World War II to foster this process have had few positive results.[98] At times, overly close association with the United States by some Arab governments has engendered *anti*-democratic tendencies (such as fostering Islamic fundamentalism). At the same time, many right-wing commentators emphasize that the absence of democratic institutions and processes throughout the Middle East is *not* a condition that endangers the foreign policy interests or well-being of the United States.[99]

Asia is another region with which the United States has had long-standing ties. For example, America's involvement in the region's economic and commercial affairs goes back to the late eighteenth century. Trade between the United States and China began before 1800; and as every student of American diplomatic history is aware, Washington played a key role in "opening Japan" to Western influence. Since World War II, the USA has assumed the primary obligation for maintaining peace and security in Asia; the U.S.-Japanese security treaty, for example, has been an essential instrument in achieving the goal.[100]

After the Cold War, several commentators are persuaded that U.S.-Japanese relations will be a key factor in preserving peace and stability in Asia.[101] Despite the outcome of the Vietnam War, officials in several Asian nations (including the People's Republic of China) have left no doubt about their belief that the United States still has a vital role to play in Asian affairs. Washington may anticipate that with the passage of time, Japan will play an increasingly independent role on the global stage. The smaller Asian nations look upon a continued American military presence (especially naval power) in Asia as indispensable in serving as a barrier against a revival of hegemonial tendencies by an economically dominant Japan.[102]

Nevertheless, conservative neo-isolationists also widely believe that opportunities now exist for scaling down America's involvement in Asian affairs. For example, a number of right-wing observers anticipate a substantial reduction in the American military presence within Asia in the years ahead.[103] They are certain that greater responsibility for preserving regional security can and should be accepted by Japan and by regional bodies like the Association of Southeast Asian Nations (ASEAN).[104]

Regarding American diplomacy toward the People's Republic of China, several ideas are prominent in the thought of right-wing neo-isolationists.[105] According to a leading conservative observer, formulating a successful policy for confronting "the rising dragon, China," may well turn out to be "the largest question of American life for a generation." The goal of U.S. policy must be "modulating the turbulence surrounding China's emergence as a superpower."[106]

A number of conservatives are impressed with the fact that with every passing year, the PRC is becoming more powerful economically; China maintains a formidable military establishment; and it is becoming increasingly self-confident and assertive on the diplomatic front. In the words of former secretary of state Henry Kissinger, China is "an incipient superpower."[107]

Observers in the conservative tradition also tend to be skeptical about the ability of the USA or other foreign governments to influence the Chinese regime's behavior at home and abroad.[108] A report dealing with congressional attitudes on the question of Sino-American relations after the Cold War underscored the fact that "the new Republican majority" was encountering considerable difficulty in arriving at a consensus on Washington's approach to the PRC.[109] As a group, conservatives exhibit little confidence in external efforts to dictate China's domestic policies or to determine the nature of its political system. In the future, as in the past, the Chinese people and their leaders remain extremely sensitive and resistant to efforts by foreigners to influence their conduct. Well-publicized attempts by American officials in recent years to "democratize" China and to influence the government's treatment of political dissidents have accomplished little beyond creating tensions in relations between Washington and Beijing.[110] Nor are right-wing observers optimistic that actual and potential economic reforms within Chinese society will necessarily be accompanied by rapid progress in democratizing its political system.[111] Many conservative neo-isolationists have advised that the most essential requirement is for Washington to maintain a continuing "dialogue" with Beijing.[112]

Another Asian challenge facing American policymakers is the ongoing conflict between North and South Korea. Ever since the Korean War, of course, the United States has served as a guarantor of South Korea's security in the face of repeated threats and provocations from the north. Recent efforts by North Korea to acquire a nuclear arsenal and improve its ballistic missile capabilities have ominous implications for the ongoing conflict on the Korean peninsula, as well as for the overall security of East Asia. With most Americans, right-wing observers believe that the U.S.–South Korean link remains vital; and they regard North Korea's efforts to join the nuclear club as a dangerous and destabilizing development. At the same time, commentators on U.S. foreign policy, including right-wing neo-isolationists, are divided on the question of the precise steps Washington ought to take to counter North Korea's nuclear ambitions.[113]

By contrast, for many years sub-Saharan Africa has been a zone of low diplomatic priority for the United States, and in the view of many conservatives that reality has not fundamentally changed since the end of the Cold War. As emphasized in our earlier discussion, right-wing observers caution against American attempts to achieve two goals on the African continent. One is engaging in "humanitarian interventionism," which (if it has any chance of being effective in the long run) inevitably leads to political intervention in the affairs of unstable and conflict-prone African societies. Judging by the results of recent experience—and U.S. intervention in Somalia provided a graphic case in point—such efforts have a very low probability of achieving their goals.[114] The other temptation is for officials in Washington to take active steps in efforts aimed at "democratizing" African societies. For the most part, based on experience in a number of cases since World War II, these efforts also have a minimum likelihood of success. In Africa, as in other regions, ultimately a society's political future will be determined by the indigenous people and their leaders.[115]

Finally, as has been true historically, conservative observers are keenly interested in the foreign policy of the United States within the Western Hemisphere. Ever since the early nineteenth century—as illustrated by the celebrated Monroe Doctrine—officials in Washington have viewed the New World as a zone in which developments impinge directly and crucially upon the diplomatic and security interests of the United States.[116] As merely one example illustrating the point, the most dangerous military encounter between Washington and Moscow—the Cuban Missile Crisis of 1962—occurred in this region.[117]

For most conservatives, the end of the Cold War has not altered the fact that hemispheric policy remains a vital dimension of Washington's diplomacy. Today, as in the past, the United States remains the dominant power within the hemisphere and the ultimate guarantor of regional peace and security. Efforts by several administrations in Washington to find a substitute for the power of the USA, for example—such as the creation of a multilateral peacekeeping force under the auspices of the Organization of American States (OAS)—have had few positive results, except on an ad hoc basis and for brief periods of time. No evidence exists indicating that such a force is likely to be established in the foreseeable future, and this means that the USA continues to bear the primary responsibility for regional security.

At the same time, most conservative spokesmen are dubious about Washington's efforts to promote national development and to implant democratic institutions and processes south of the border.[118] Conservatives widely believe that in most respects, the "Alliance for Progress"—launched by the Kennedy administration and widely viewed as a "Marshall Plan for the Americas"—

failed to achieve its principal goals.[119] Similarly, another project aimed at stimulating Latin American development—the Reagan administration's "Caribbean Basin Initiative"—also had only limited success. In more recent years, the emphasis in Washington has been to depend upon private investment and programs, and on the expansion of trade, to accomplish the goal. In a number of Latin American states, economic and social conditions are still at a low level; the gap between upper- and lower-income groups is widening; and these conditions in turn foster ongoing political instability and upheaval.[120]

Ever since they became independent, the other American republics have expressed a strong commitment to the democratic ideal. And in some societies, in recent years progress toward the goal has undeniably been noteworthy. At the same time, most Latin American societies have a highly variable record in their quest to create stable democratic systems; and from time to time, these societies have tended to retrogress in achieving the objective. From Mexico to Chile, civilian governments have often been severely challenged to solve the society's deep-seated problems. Historically, and down to the present day, military elites have played a crucial role in Latin American political life.

In their observations regarding the nation's hemispheric policy, conservatives tend to emphasize two major admonitions. One is the idea that interventionist efforts by the USA in Latin America's political affairs are both widely resented and seldom accomplish their purpose. To the minds of citizens in the other American republics, interventionist behavior by "the North American Colossus" is viewed as the primary *danger* threatening their independence. A second admonition is that regional institutions—especially those charged with the preservation of peace and stability within the hemisphere—remain weak and only minimally effective. This reality means that for the indefinite future, officials in Washington must be prepared to act unilaterally when necessary to discharge the nation's historic mission of maintaining the peace and security of the Western Hemisphere.[121]

CHAPTER 3

LIBERAL NEO-ISOLATIONISM

D URING HIS CAMPAIGN FOR THE PRESIDENCY IN 1992, BILL CLINTON promised a "more modest role" for the United States in international affairs. To the voters, he pledged to devote primary attention to "America's internal renewal." The Clinton campaign team found relatively little support among the people for a policy of active American "engagement" abroad.[1]

This chapter is devoted to an analysis of the counterpart of conservative neo-isolationism: liberal neo-isolationist thought. Political liberals, no less than conservatives, believe there are a number of sound reasons for curtailing the activities and commitments of the United States abroad. They part company with those advocating the right-wing version of neo-isolationism primarily with reference to the criteria relied upon by each group for keeping America's diplomatic commitments limited.

Several diverse terms have been employed to describe the liberal neo-isolationist orientation in external affairs, including the concept of "a more modest foreign policy," "constructive disengagement," "low-profile diplomacy," "selective engagement," more "discriminating detachment" in dealing with international issues, and "the new idealism."[2] The distinguished student of American diplomacy George F. Kennan advocated a more "modest and relatively self-effacing" role for the USA abroad, one that reflects a "less ambitious and grandiloquent" approach to external problems.[3] In turn, this diplomatic reorientation dictates a "curtailment of [America's] external undertakings and involvements," accompanied by "the avoidance of . . . new ones."[4]

Or, as another observer has put it, officials in Washington must abandon the idea that the United States is called on "to run the world." To his mind, too often in the past the real goal of U.S. interventionism was to impose "a global liberal economic regime" or capitalistic system on other societies. Events have shown that this objective is unattainable, and in the post–Cold War era it should be dropped from America's diplomatic agenda.[5] Still another study has urged officials in Washington to forgo a role of "global leadership" for the USA, since in effect such a policy differs little from the kind of "imperial" approach to international problems identified with Great Britain and other European powers in the eighteenth and nineteenth centuries.[6]

The common denominator of these observations is the conviction that in the wake of the Cold War, the United States must avoid a policy of indiscriminate "internationalism" or "globalism," by scaling down its overseas obligations and commitments. The USA, said a former member of President John F. Kennedy's foreign policy team, cannot serve as "the policeman of the world" or even, for that matter, "of a given region."[7] To the mind of another commentator, the end of the conflict between Washington and Moscow provides the USA a long-awaited opportunity to "disengage" from many global trouble spots around the world. In the future, toward most problems and conflicts arising beyond its borders, America's position ought to be one of "benign neglect."[8]

A leading student of American diplomacy has identified a number of specific problems toward which the United States might be prone to follow an interventionist policy. In every instance, this commentator believes, interventionist behavior by the USA would be unwise or infeasible.[9] Another study finds that liberal opinion in the United States has become widely disillusioned with the nation's foreign policy, which, it is believed, has increasingly lost touch with reality in the contemporary world. Or, as still another observer concludes, the "reduced world power base" of the United States within the international system requires that it curtail its global commitments significantly.[10] The USA, according to another analysis, should hereafter disclaim any right of intervention in the affairs of other nations in the post–Cold War era, except for the most compelling reasons of self-defense.[11]

From a different perspective, a longtime observer of Middle Eastern affairs has cautioned American policymakers that there is a fine line between devotion to democracy and an "imperial" foreign policy. In this view, with the end of the Cold War there is no longer any justification for interventionism by the USA in the Middle East.[12] Similarly, another commentator has cautioned national officials not to exaggerate threats to America's security and diplomatic interests posed by events and tendencies within the Third World. In this view, relatively few such developments in this zone impinge directly upon the vital interests of the USA.[13] Or, as another study of recent American diplomacy concluded, Washington's reliance upon interventionist and confrontational policies abroad actually *prolonged* the Cold War, making the differences between Washington and Moscow more difficult than ever to resolve.[14] To the mind of another observer, policymakers in Washington ought to concentrate on achieving "real security" for the nation. This requires that after the Cold War the concept of "national security" be redefined, primarily in economic and social, rather than military, terms. In a word, American foreign policy must be "demilitarized." Washington should depend mainly upon collective security efforts to deal with threats to global peace and stability.[15]

According to another study, the militant opposition to communism exhibited by successive administrations in Washington after World War II proved to be highly inimical to the rights of American citizens. For example, it enabled national leaders to stifle dissent, to curtail information given to the media and the people, to give intelligence agencies virtually free rein to undertake any activities they desired (often to the detriment of the nation), and to expand the powers of the president vis-à-vis Congress in the foreign policy process.[16] An analysis of the activities of the CIA and other members of the "intelligence community" reached comparable conclusions. It concluded that the intelligence agencies of the U.S. government were ill prepared to deal with the problems of the post–Cold War era. The report was highly critical of the growing "militarization" of national intelligence operations. In far too many instances, intelligence agencies relied upon expensive technological devices to provide insight into developments abroad, instead of depending upon informed human judgments. As a result, intelligence estimates in recent years have often been of little use to the president and his advisers in arriving at sound and accurate judgments about developments around the world. The report concluded that in the future *diplomats,* not spies, ought to play the key role in analyzing developments overseas and in recommending America's response to them. For these reasons, the report advocated substantial reductions in the size and activities of the intelligence establishment.[17]

A different evaluation of American diplomacy after the Cold War has called on policymakers to abandon the interventionist impulses—often evident in the views of liberal organizations, citizens, and policymakers—that have motivated the nation's external policy since the late 1940s. In this view, the American republic possesses no mandate to serve as "the world's leader," in efforts to impose a "new world order" upon the international system. Such interventionist behavior by the USA is merely a contemporary version of an "imperial" policy, analogous to Great Britain's global role in the nineteenth century. Illustrative of the interventionist mentality was the contention of Secretary of State Dean Rusk during the 1960s. To his mind, the American society was safe and secure only to the degree that "its total [global] environment is safe." In effect, such thinking was tantamount to a kind of global "domino theory," or the erroneous idea that political upheavals and conflicts anywhere in the world pose a threat to the peace and security of the United States. In brief, after the Cold War the nation's decisionmakers must avoid a policy of "virtuous omnipotence" in dealing with the outside world. They must abandon the vision that many Americans have of a "perfectible" international order that can be created by dynamic and forceful American diplomatic activity. In reality, the post–Cold War international system will likely prove to be even less "perfectible" than was true under conditions of bipolarity.[18]

From a different perspective, an analysis of America's approach to the Third World concludes that intensive efforts to promote the economic development of nations throughout this zone have, with rare exceptions, demonstrably failed and ought, therefore, to be abandoned.[19] To the minds of other critics, private agencies are much more likely to succeed in efforts to contribute constructively to the development of backward societies than are governmental programs. In the future, American foreign aid programs ought to rely primarily on such private efforts and should give the recipients a decisive voice in their formulation and administration.[20]

According to another liberal observer, with the end of the Cold War, there has been a significant decline in the American people's willingness to support an interventionist policy abroad. He found a "growing contradiction" between official professions of the need for America's global leadership, on the one hand, and the willingness of the people to bear the burdens of such a role, on the other. This observer raises serious questions, therefore, about whether Americans "are politically and economically capable" of supporting an active role by the United States abroad.[21]

A different spokesman for a neo–isolationist position contends that after the Cold War, three important principles ought to guide Washington's diplomatic behavior. First, national leaders and citizens alike must "recognize our limitations" abroad. Second, the policymakers should be constantly aware of "the vanity of trying to remake the world in our image." And third, decisionmakers must keep uppermost in their minds a long-standing tenet of the liberal political credo: the need to restore "the promise of our neglected society."[22]

A number of tenets of the liberal credo support the idea of a more limited role for the United States in foreign affairs following the Cold War. Before World War II, liberals who supported the isolationist position nearly always contended that a "strong" or interventionist foreign policy endangered freedoms and constitutional rights within the American society. On the basis of more recent postwar experience, many liberals are convinced that a major consequence of interventionist diplomacy has been the emergence of the "imperial presidency," with a corresponding decline in the influence of Congress and public opinion in the decisionmaking process.[23] In the liberal view, a related danger (another fear expressed by pre–World War II isolationists) is growing military influence in American life.

As a rule, liberals also oppose unilateral American actions abroad. They believe that today, more than at any time in the nation's history, the solution of urgent and complex global problems requires multinational efforts. Conversely, recent diplomatic experience offers little ground for believing that unilateral interventionism by the USA to achieve this goal will be successful.[24] To the contrary, as often as not unilateralism strengthens anti-American sentiment overseas, weakens the nation's ties with its allies, deepens political divisions within societies subject to such intervention, in the end wastes American lives and resources and engenders intense partisan debate, dissensus, and political unrest within the United States.[25] As other commentators view it, even interventionist activities undertaken chiefly for humanitarian reasons must inevitably lead to political intervention in the affairs of the society concerned, in misguided efforts to deal with the underlying social and economic conditions that made external intervention for humanitarian reasons necessary.[26]

A close identification between political liberalism and isolationist precepts can be traced far back into American history. During the Revolutionary War period, for example, Thomas Paine was one of the earliest proponents of an isolationist approach to foreign affairs; Thomas Jefferson advocated "no entangling alliances" as a fundamental axiom of American diplomacy. Around 1900, the Populists and "Bryan Democrats" nearly always objected to what was called a "strong" external policy. Down to the late 1930s, President Franklin D. Roosevelt supported the isolationist position.

Early in the Truman administration, Secretary of Commerce Henry Wallace criticized Washington's increasingly militant opposition to the communism abroad.[27] Similarly, as the years passed a long list of "revisionist" historians and commentators denounced the containment policy. Their basic contention was that, in many key respects, Washington was as much to blame for perpetuating the Cold War as Moscow and Beijing.

Revisionists were by no means agreed, however, concerning the basic causes or sources of America's interventionist impulses. One school of thought, for example, attributed them to economic forces, such as the influence of business corporations and the need to secure and obtain overseas markets. Another group believed that the impulse to dominate other countries was an outgrowth of America's nuclear monopoly in the early postwar period. Still other commentators identified the source of the nation's interventionist behavior as stemming from the influence of a powerful "military-industrial complex" upon American life. An alternative explanation was that, consistent with their dedication to a capitalistic economic system, Americans exhibited an irrational fear, or phobia, concerning "international communism" and were inclined to attribute nearly all global problems to Communist machinations around the world.[28] As another recent study lamented, the preoccupation of officials in Washington with the Communist challenge *prolonged* the Cold War, making Soviet-American differences much more difficult to resolve.[29]

Perhaps the most widely publicized revisionist interpretation of recent American diplomacy can be found in the views of J. William Fulbright, who as a Democratic senator from Arkansas had served for many years as chairman of the Senate Foreign Relations Committee. Fulbright concluded, for example, that it was primarily "the arrogance of American power" that led the nation to become embroiled in the Vietnam War and other (usually unsuccessful) instances of interventionism abroad. As he assessed it, America's hegemonic tendencies exemplified an all-too-familiar behavior pattern, exhibited at one time or another by all powerful (or "imperial") nations throughout history. Fulbright was persuaded—and liberal spokesmen in the years that followed frequently echoed his views—that in the vast majority of cases, massive American involvement in the affairs of other societies was unjustified, and it had a highly deleterious impact upon them. For example, it aggravated existing political tensions and intensified conflicts within the society involved.[30] It also tended to make foreign governments dependent upon the United States.

The effects of an interventionist policy upon the American society itself were no less serious and unfortunate.[31] In another of Fulbright's often-quoted phrases, an external policy of indiscriminate interventionism turned the United States into "a crippled giant," whose power and influence on the global scene were declining, and whose domestic problems, meanwhile, were becoming progressively more critical. Together with other liberal spokesmen, Fulbright was persuaded that Washington's addiction to interventionist behavior was a serious distraction, gravely weakening the nation's ability to solve internal problems.[32] Moreover, an interventionist foreign policy jeopardizes traditional constitutional principles and endangers freedoms long enjoyed by the American people.[33]

President John F. Kennedy cautioned his fellow citizens against "the illusion of American omnipotence," and throughout the years that followed liberals discovered many reasons to recall Kennedy's admonition. (Critics of the Kennedy administration charged of course that JFK frequently failed to heed his own admonitions in dealing with external problems, as in his escalation of America's involvement in Southeast Asia!) The trauma of the Vietnam War gave new and strong impetus to neo-isolationist impulses, especially by members of the liberal community.

Liberals were usually at the forefront of the anti-war movement; and they played a prominent part in identifying certain "lessons of Vietnam" that ought to serve as guidelines for foreign relations in the future. President Lyndon Johnson's ambitious domestic program to achieve the "Great Society" was a casualty of the conflict in Southeast Asia; and the war resulted in a noteworthy decline in public confidence in the nation's political leadership (especially the presidency).

From the Vietnam War experience, many liberals derived the lesson that vast as America's power might be, a wide variety of global problems are not amenable to solution by the United States.[34] Another lesson was that the USA must avoid becoming allied with non-democratic governments abroad which often oppress their own citizens and whose policies lack popular support. Still another lesson of the war in Southeast Asia was that the American nation's diplomatic and security interests are not directly threatened or involved in the outcome of every regional and local conflict erupting within the international system. Moreover, the Vietnam War experience raised serious questions about whether the American people are willing to support prolonged, costly, and inconclusive military engagements overseas.[35] Many liberals have also derived the lesson that interventionist moves by the USA abroad are unlikely to be successful unless they are part of a larger, multinational operation under the auspices of the United Nations or regional bodies.[36]

A number of liberal observers believe that in the new millennium, Americans must keep in mind two key facts about the power of the United States. One is that, although it remains a superpower, the USA confronts a host of novel and complex problems abroad which often are not susceptible to solution by the traditional instruments of statecraft, especially military power. This list includes what appears to be an epidemic of religious, ethnic, and tribal conflicts throughout the globe; civil wars and boundary disputes; the phenomenon known as "failed states" or the inability of incumbent governments to make their authority effective within the state's boundaries; and pervasive conditions of disease, ignorance and illiteracy, malnutrition, and overpopulation south of the equator.[37]

The second key fact about the power of the United States is that from a relative perspective, it is declining. This is quite clearly the case insofar as economic power is concerned. Other centers of global power have emerged, notably Japan, China, Germany, and the European Community.[38] And as their power continues to increase, they will be less disposed to follow American leadership in dealing with a wide range of global and regional issues.

Liberal neo-isolationists also emphasize an idea that has long been a central axiom of the liberal tradition: the belief that a direct correlation exists between the prospects for global peace and stability, on the one hand, and the world-wide extension of democracy, on the other hand. This idea was prominent, for example, in the views of the nineteenth-century philosopher Immanuel Kant; and it has been reiterated time and again by more recent spokesmen for the liberal cause, such as Woodrow Wilson, Franklin D. Roosevelt, and Jimmy Carter.

The logical application of this general principle to foreign affairs means that policymakers in Washington ought to accord highest priority to promoting and strengthening democracy abroad.[39] In turn, adhering to this principle requires that national officials differentiate between those foreign governments that accept and practice democratic norms and those that do not. As one liberal commentator has expressed it, toward governments in the latter category, America's position ought to be one of "silence tinged with indifference."[40] Or, as an earlier study of U.S. policy toward Latin America expressed the idea, dictatorial regimes should receive a polite and formal "handshake" from Uncle Sam, while democratic governments could expect a cordial "embrace." This fundamental difference should be reflected tangibly, in such undertakings as U.S. foreign assistance and arms-aid programs.[41]

In the contemporary period, liberals favoring a neo-isolationist position also often reiterate another basic axiom of classical isolationist thought. This is the idea that ultimately America's future and destiny will be determined by its success in solving domestic problems, a number of which have become progressively more critical in recent years (owing in no small measure to their neglect during the Vietnam War and other interventionist episodes in recent diplomatic experience).[42] As Ronald Steel has expressed the idea, "A sick civil society is the sign of a weak nation."[43] A corollary belief of liberal neo-isolationists is the long-standing conviction that the power of the American example remains the most potent instrument available to national policymakers for influencing the course of events abroad.[44]

A related idea is the perception of many liberals regarding the role of military power in solving global and regional problems after the Cold War. Liberal observers are widely attracted to the concept of "neo-realism," one of whose tenets is that military force has lost much of its utility as a diplomatic instrument in the contemporary period.[45] The distinguished commentator on the nation's foreign diplomacy George F. Kennan has called on officials in Washington to formulate "a modest and relatively self-effacing foreign policy" for the USA, allowing them to concentrate on solving domestic problems "with a minimum of outside interference and distraction." Once they adopt this diplomatic strategy, the nation can then maintain a military establishment that is geared to "a less ambitious and grandiloquent" international role by the USA.[46]

Along with Kennan, other liberal observers have been outspoken in proposing massive reductions in the national defense budget, with the resulting "peace dividend" being allocated to the solution of domestic problems. Several spokesmen for this view became outspokenly critical of the Clinton administration's failure to reduce military spending substantially.[47] Not only would this step make more funds available for domestic programs, but it would also reduce the influence of "the military-industrial complex" on the nation's external policy. To the liberal mind, this powerful interest group is prone to discover threats to the nation's security abroad where none actually exists.[48] A related belief is that in the new era, the scope of the nation's military alliance system can and ought to be drastically reduced and, in some cases, terminated altogether.[49]

LIBERAL NEO-ISOLATIONISM AND
SPECIFIC DIPLOMATIC ISSUES

Turning now to views of liberal neo-isolationists on specific global issues, we begin by examining the question of America's participation in multinational institutions. As every informed student of modern international politics is aware, liberal individuals and groups were at the forefront of movements leading to the establishment of the League of Nations, the United Nations, the World Court (or International Court of Justice) and a long list of other multilateral agencies. The nineteenth-century philosopher Immanuel Kant envisioned the establishment of "a league for perpetual peace." President Woodrow Wilson took the initiative in formulating and establishing the League of Nations. A generation or so later, President Franklin D. Roosevelt was the moving force in planning for and establishing the United Nations; its location on American soil was tribute to the role of the USA in its existence. After World War II, it is fair to say, more often than not the financial and diplomatic support of the United States was a crucial element in the UN's successful operations. America's role was similarly decisive in the creation of a number of other multinational institutions, such as the International Monetary Fund (IMF), the World Bank, the European Community, and, most recently, the North American Free Trade Agreement (NAFTA).[50]

Liberals have also been active in the movement advocating sweeping reforms of the United Nations, with a view to making it a more effective institution and of meeting a number of criticisms that have been leveled at the UN since 1945. Most liberals concede that the UN and certain other global and regional organizations need to be "revitalized," making them more responsive to existing international problems. As George F. Kennan assessed the matter, once that occurs, the United States can and should turn over some of its international obligations (and this applies especially to peacekeeping obligations) to a reinvigorated United Nations.[51]

Yet it is also true that in recent years, liberals have become critical of and disillusioned with the United Nations and certain other multinational institutions. If criticism from liberal sources does not usually reach the level of that from right-wing groups, there has unquestionably been a decline in liberal support for the United Nations and some of its activities. (The UN General Assembly's periodic condemnation of Zionism and certain actions of the State of Israel provide a noteworthy example.)

From a different perspective, some liberal observers have become outspokenly critical about a tendency by officials in Washington to view the UN and other international agencies as merely an arm of the State Department and to rely upon them chiefly to impose America's sense of law, justice, and its preferred political system upon the world. For example, some liberal analysts have objected strongly to the action of the United Nations, under intense pressure from the USA, in imposing an embargo upon the Republic of Iraq (viewed by officials in Washington as a "rogue state"). In this view, such a policy is misguided and inhuman, primarily because it ignores the effects of the embargo upon the women and children of Iraq.[52]

Regardless of their political orientations, most well-informed students of American foreign policy accept the idea that a sense of regional priorities must guide the nation's diplomatic activities. In brief, some regions are more important to the United States than others. (Before World War II, it ought to be remembered, nearly all advocates of isolationism agreed that developments within the Western Hemisphere were crucial for the security and well-being of the USA.) In the post–Cold War period, the salient question is: Which regions should be high on the scale of American diplomatic priorities? Even among liberal neo-isolationists (as is equally true, of course, of conservatives), there is little unanimity on this question.[53]

All informed students of the American diplomatic record are aware of course that throughout the twentieth century the European continent has played a central role in the nation's diplomatic experience. By many criteria, European-American relations would qualify as the most important dimension of U.S. foreign relations. During the period of World War I, the contribution of the United States was decisive in preserving the independence of the European allies. (Even earlier, many diplomatic historians are convinced, the "special relationship" that had developed between the United States and Great

Britain was a key reality of international politics. For many years, for example, London's support of the Monroe Doctrine was an essential element in its enforcement.) President Franklin D. Roosevelt once said that America's military frontier was now the Rhine River. After World War II, the North Atlantic Treaty became the foundationstone of Western security in the face of the Communist challenge. And today, many commentators continue to view Western Europe as a region with which the USA has vital diplomatic and security links.

Yet while they recognize the key importance of the European continent for American diplomacy, many liberal neo-isolationists also believe that fundamental changes have occurred in European-American relations and that these must be reflected in Washington's approach to developments abroad after the Cold War. Many commentators are convinced that the European nations are becoming collectively more influential in global decisionmaking. This reality calls for a more limited role by the United States in European affairs.[54] According to one analysis, the end of the Cold War has seriously called into question "any rational basis for U.S. involvement in European security affairs"; and it has "undermined shared interests" between the USA and its European allies outside the NATO area. In this view, the Europe that is now emerging "looms primarily as a series of traps and dangers that could bog down American forces in hot spots having no bearing on U.S. security interests." According to this assessment, Europe has come to rival the Middle East as a zone of insecurity. With the passage of time, the differences between the United States and its European allies on major regional and international issues have become more and more pronounced.[55] Another study has concluded that, with the reunification and continued economic progress of Germany, Berlin is playing a progressively more influential role in regional and global affairs. This is regarded as a highly significant and favorable development for the United States, since it permits the American society to "get on with its own post–Cold War domestic agenda."[56] At the same time, a number of liberals harbor deep-seated apprehensions about the implications of an increasingly powerful Germany, fearing that the German nation *still* has territorial ambitions outside its own borders.

In the opinion of several observers, these problems have been underscored by differing American and European approaches to the conflict in the Balkans (a subject discussed at greater length in Chapter 6.) At times, the complex and continuing crisis in that region highlighted basic divergences between policymakers in Washington and in European capitals on the question of how to respond to the challenge. In light of this fact, it proved extraordinarily difficult—not to say at times impossible—to forge a common Western strategy toward the Balkans problem.[57] As one liberal observer complained (in an updated version of Senator Fulbright's earlier views), Washington's main interest in the Balkans appeared to be supporting authoritarian and anti-democratic forces in the region's ongoing political contests.[58] Or as another commentator concluded, by intervening in political contests in the turbulent Balkans, the Clinton administration set itself an impossible diplomatic goal. Washington's active involvement in such conflicts only intensified existing problems, since the evidence has made clear that the people of the region really do not *want* to create a single unified state.[59] Given such realities, another observer proposed that an urgent goal of American diplomacy ought to be devising an "exit strategy" for disengaging from the Balkans as soon as possible.[60]

George F. Kennan is but one among several liberal observers who believe that, with the end of the Cold War, the time has come for the total or substantial withdrawal of America's armed forces from the European continent. Moreover, he opposed American membership in any new regional security organization that is initiated by the European allies.[61] As another commentator analyzed the matter, after the Cold War America's continued military involvement in Europe makes no positive contribution toward solving the problems likely to confront the region in the years ahead.[62]

Liberal neo-isolationists were often outspoken in opposing two specific aspects of U.S.-European relations. One of these was the proposed enlargement of NATO, to include the former Communist states of Eastern Europe, and, in time, possibly Russia and some of the former Soviet republics. Several commentators concluded that such a step would be an unwise—not to say dangerous—development.[63] It would almost certainly entail new and unforeseeable, and quite possibly major, commitments by the United States (for example, in defending an expanded NATO against future threats).[64] It would result in a significant increase in defense spending by the United States. In time, it could lead to deep divisions among the European nations.[65] And it would unquestionably be viewed by officials in Moscow as a provocative act, thereby engendering new tensions in Russian-American relations.[66]

Another specific issue in U.S. foreign policy toward Europe is the continuing quest for European unity. Within American society, liberal opinion tends to be divided on this question. On the one hand, some spokesmen are convinced that, as in the past, Washington ought to use its influence to encourage European unification, in the belief that a united Europe is a more secure and politically stable region.[67] Yet other commentators have serious reservations about this goal. They question whether the objective is even attainable. And some observers point out that the real purpose of Washington's efforts to promote European unity is to impose America's own capitalistic system upon the unwilling Western allies.[68]

Regarding relations with "the new Russia," liberal neo-isolationist thought emphasizes several ideas. One of course is the hope and expectation that, at long last, the Russian society has been launched on the path of genuine democracy—a goal of American diplomacy since the czarist period.[69] Liberals have often been vocal in calling on national policymakers to do everything possible to accelerate and strengthen democratic tendencies within contemporary Russian society. (This is a conspicuous case of a tendency by neo-isolationists along the entire range of political opinion to *advocate* interventionist behavior by the USA in behalf of their own preferred causes.) Throughout modern history, liberals have contended that a vital correlation exists between the extension of democracy abroad and the prospects for global peace and security.[70] On that assumption, they encourage the emergence of democracy within the former Soviet empire as a high-ranking goal of American diplomacy.[71] Other liberal observers have emphasized the idea that, as a result of the outcome of the Cold War, Russia is no longer America's adversary and should not be treated as one.[72] More generally, in Europe, in the Middle East, and in other regions, many liberals are persuaded that Washington and Moscow ought to concert their policies in behalf of international peace and stability.

Another region in which the United States has vital diplomatic and security interests is the Middle East. In the opinion of several well-informed commentators, the period following the Cold War will continue to be characterized by political upheaval and violent conflicts. Both within most Middle Eastern nations, and in relations among them, political tensions and conflicts may be expected to keep the region in a state of political turbulence and instability. Even if certain Middle Eastern societies succeed in achieving (or moving toward) greater "democratization," this process is apt to set in motion powerful and often destabilizing political forces engendering internal instability and turmoil. Any tendency toward a more democratic political order in several Arab states, for example, will almost certainly encourage separatist movements by groups seeking greater political autonomy. Moreover, in a number of Arab societies, Islamic Fundamentalism—a movement that is often overtly anti-American—is becoming an increasingly influential and active political force.

Ever since the creation of the State of Israel and the issuance of the Truman Doctrine early in the post–World War II period, the USA has been deeply involved in the affairs of the Middle East.[73] Liberals were prominent among those urging policymakers in Washington to support the Zionist cause and, after Israel's establishment in 1948, to protect its security from threats by the Arab states. American military, financial, and diplomatic support of Israel, it is fair to say, has been a crucial factor in the state's survival and economic advancement.[74]

It is no less true, however, that in recent years there has been some erosion in liberal support for the Israeli cause within the United States. For example, President Bill Clinton was openly critical of Israeli officials for their unwillingness to make territorial concessions in order to provide new momentum to the peace talks with the Arabs. While liberal opinion toward the State of Israel remains basically favorable, those advocating a more limited American role in the Middle East adduce several reasons why Washington ought to scale down its commitments to Israel. One of these is that, if the USA is to serve as an effective mediator in the Arab–Israeli conflict, it must give greater credence to the Arab cause than has often been true in the past. Some commentators are convinced that to date, Washington has totally failed to convince Arabs that it is capable of serving in the role of impartial peacemaker.[75] Another reason is that some of the actions of the government of Israel (e.g., in displacing Palestinian Arabs from their historic homes and in refusing to carry out the provisions of peace agreements reached with Arab governments) have evoked criticisms from all segments of American opinion.[76] As the largest beneficiary of U.S. foreign assistance, Israel has also suffered from reductions in the foreign aid program.

A different dimension of U.S. foreign policy toward the Middle East that has evoked criticism from liberal neo-isolationists is Washington's approach to what are often labeled "rogue states," such as Iraq, Iran, and Libya. A number of liberal observers have questioned whether a confrontational policy toward these states really pays dividends for the USA and whether it is ethically and morally justified.[77] They doubt, for example, that the long boycott of Iraq has really done anything constructive to change the regime's behavior at home and abroad; and they are concerned about the effects of coercive measures applied to Iraq upon the nation's civilian population.

Toward another Middle Eastern regime—the government of Afghanistan—liberal critics believe that a major (if unintended) result of interventionist American efforts directed against Soviet influence in Afghanistan was to strengthen the grip of Islamic fundamentalism upon the society—a movement that in time became overtly anti-American in its foreign policy orientation.[78]

Still another aspect of America's Middle Eastern policy that is of keen interest to liberal neo-isolationists is the quest for democracy within the region. Since the Persian Gulf War, liberals have been outspoken in urging officials in Washington to exert initiatives designed to strengthen democratic tendencies in such states as Kuwait, Saudi Arabia, and Jordan—nations that have maintained close ties with the USA for many years. A number of well-informed commentators on Middle Eastern affairs are disturbed that progress toward political modernization in these states and elsewhere within the region has been minimal; and they are genuinely concerned that, unless movement toward greater democracy occurs, new waves of political unrest will almost certainly engulf the area.

The Kingdom of Saudi Arabia provides a graphic and important case study of the problem. Saudi Arabia has long been regarded by successive administrations in Washington as a key to the stability and security of the region; and after the Persian Gulf War, Saudi Arabia and Kuwait continue to be vital sources of petroleum products for the United States and the other industrialized nations. Yet as some liberal neo-isolationists view it, new technological developments offer promise at long last of solving the "energy crisis," thereby permitting a significant reduction in the American society's long dependence upon Middle East oil supplies. In turn, this will make possible a significant reduction in Washington's diplomatic and military commitments within the region.[79]

Ruling political elites in these traditional societies have shown little inclination to relinquish their hold on the levers of political power, despite undeniable evidence of mounting internal ferment and agitation aimed at bringing about fundamental political changes. In a phrase popular with critics of Washington's diplomacy in the region, in the absence of sweeping political changes Saudi Arabia is destined to become "the next Iran."[80] At the same time, there is little agreement among liberal neo-isolationists—who, as a matter of principle, oppose overt political interventionism in the affairs of other countries— concerning the specific steps that American policymakers ought to take to achieve the desired goal.

With the end of the Cold War, the United States is provided a number of opportunities to reduce its diplomatic and military involvement in Asia. As one liberal interpreter views it, America's "deep engagement" in the region since World War II has been a major obstacle to solving a number of Asian problems.[81] Senator Fulbright and his followers believed that the USA actually had very few security interests in Asia justifying the maintenance of a large military presence on the Asian scene. (Ironically, Fulbright and other liberal neo-isolationists often echoed the view of an arch–political *conservative*—General Douglas MacArthur—to the effect that the USA should carefully avoid becoming deeply involved on "the Asian mainland.") They were further convinced that in most instances, the existence of U.S. military bases throughout Asia contributed to the existence of political tensions within the region and was at times a source of serious controversy and misunderstanding between Washington and Asian governments, as illustrated by the sharp deterioration in America's relations with the Republic of the Philippines.[82]

Japan provides another instance in which substantial opposition exists toward a large U.S. military presence within the society.[83] President Jimmy Carter suggested that the USA ought to scale down the size of its military contingent within South Korea, but this move encountered formidable opposition on Capitol Hill and was abandoned.[84] With the end of Vietnam War, the Southeast Asian Treaty Organization (SEATO)—designed as a kind of Asian counterpart to NATO—became moribund.

Asia is also a key area involving attempts by the United States to implant democracy beyond its own borders. As explained more fully in Chapter 6, the United States has been involved in the affairs of China ever since the late eighteenth century. The Open Door Policy—whereby the USA in time became committed to the principle of preserving the "territorial integrity" of China from foreign intruders and aggressors—ranked as a foundationstone of U.S. foreign policy for almost fifty years after 1898.[85]

Every administration in Washington since World War II has endorsed the ideal of democratic government on the Chinese mainland, although none has compiled a record of conspicuous success in achieving the objective. Ever since the rapprochement in Sino-American relations—initiated by the Nixon administration, and consummated by the Carter White House—Washington has depended mainly upon diplomacy and maintaining "a dialogue" with China's leaders to accomplish its purpose.[86] Although during his campaign for the presidency in 1992, Bill Clinton championed coercive measures by Washington in dealing with Beijing, in time the Clinton administration basically adopted this same policy toward the PRC, in the belief that a hard-line approach would in the end make little positive contribution to promoting the cause of human freedom and democracy within the PRC.[87] As our later analysis will demonstrate, it cannot be said that this policy was conspicuously successful in influencing the political behavior of the China's leaders. By the new millennium, Sino-American relations remained one of the most controversial aspects of contemporary American foreign policy.[88]

A former American ambassador to Indonesia has observed that, as a general principle, interventionism by the USA to promote democracy abroad is a questionable diplomatic strategy. Based upon the policy's lack of positive results in one country after another, he advocates that Washington practice "low-profile diplomacy" in Asia and elsewhere. Specifically, the USA should reduce its diplomatic posts throughout Asia; it should endeavor at all times to act in close concert with its friends and allies in solving regional problems; and it should extend foreign assistance to Asian societies through multilateral agencies.[89]

Toward another region—sub-Saharan Africa—liberals have frequently urged policymakers in Washington to engage in "humanitarian intervention" for the purpose of relieving human suffering on the continent and of laying the groundwork for the ultimate emergence of democracy within African societies. Yet on the basis of recent experience, a number of liberal observers have become disillusioned with Washington's foreign aid efforts designed to promote national development within African societies and other Third World settings. With rare exceptions, judging by prevailing economic, social, and political conditions on the continent, it is difficult to identify many positive benefits from such aid programs in Africa (as is no less true of course at times in other regions). In the light of such evidence, one observer has recommended that after the Cold War the USA ought to be highly "selective" in extending assistance to African governments; aid from Washington should be extended on the basis of clear evidence of economic performance by incumbent governments. In other words, African regimes must demonstrate an ability to use American aid more constructively than has often been true in the past.[90]

For many years, successive administrations in Washington have expressed their devotion to the cause of human rights and democracy in sub-Saharan Africa—an objective, needless to say, enthusiastically endorsed by many liberal groups and individuals.[91] At the same time, certain liberal critics have raised fundamental questions about elevating the promotion of human rights to a high level on America's foreign policy agenda. Some commentators entertain doubts about the sincerity of official policy declarations on the subject; from time to time, they accuse officials in Washington of being less than zealous in actually pursuing their proclaimed goals. Observers in this group were especially negative, for example, concerning the Reagan administration's close ties with several authoritarian (in some cases totalitarian) African regimes, whose principal attraction for Washington appeared to be their proclaimed opposition to communism. The end of the Cold War removes that policy incentive for the USA, and in the liberal view it provides an unprecedented opportunity for a new impetus in the quest for democracy among African societies.[92] (For many years, American foreign policy toward Africa has no doubt been influenced significantly by the civil rights movement within the United States.) From a different perspective, other liberal critics have expressed the view that Washington's advocacy of human rights, as the concept is understood in Western societies, is in reality an ethnocentric policy that takes little account of the widely differing traditions and values of African and other Third World societies.

From yet another perspective, a number of liberal neo-isolationists are apprehensive that an American-led efforts to promote democracy on the African continent will almost certainly aggravate a number of existing problems encountered within the region. These include suspicions and conflicts among rival religious, tribal, and ethnic groups, often leading to separatist political movements on the African scene. In Africa, the Wilsonian concept of "self-determination" can lead, and has led, to separatist political movements whose members seek to gain their ends by violent means. Such developments confront officials in Washington with difficult policy choices—as in responding to pervasive human suffering and the need for programs of refugee relief—in efforts to respond to critical African problems.

In another key dimension of U.S. foreign policy—diplomacy toward Latin America—liberal neo-isolationists call for fundamental changes in the nation's approach to this region, as well.[93] With the end of the Cold War, liberals have renewed their long-standing demand that Washington cease "supporting dictators" south of the border and that it avoid involvement with military-controlled governments in Latin American societies. For a number of liberal commentators, Washington's military aid to Latin American governments has deliberately or indeliberately contributed to enhancing the political power of military elites throughout the region.[94] As in other regions, policymakers in Washington have time and again been urged to accord high priority to promoting democratic institutions and processes south of the border.

Yet it might also be noted that a number of liberal neo-isolationists are severely critical of efforts by agencies of the U.S. government to intervene in Latin America's political affairs on behalf of political movements deemed acceptable by officials in Washington. In this view, such interventionist efforts have nearly always had more negative than positive results, and they have intensified anti-Yanqui sentiment in the other American republics.[95]

Another specific aspect of Washington's Latin American policy that has evoked widespread criticisms by liberal neo-isolationists is the nation's diplomacy toward Castro's Cuba. For well over a generation, Cuban-American relations have remained tense and unproductive. Beginning with President Dwight Eisenhower, successive chief executives have been outspoken in condemning the Castro regime and in seeking its ouster. To accomplish the goal, officials in Washington relied on a variety of measures—from sponsoring a military invasion of Cuba, to covert intervention by the CIA in Cuban affairs, to diplomatic ostracism, to boycotts and other economic sanctions. Yet by the end of the 1990s, many critics of U.S. policy had concluded that it was time for officials in Washington to admit that these measures have failed to accomplish their purpose. Castro's regime remained firmly in power—despite the existence of severe economic and financial problems within Cuban society.

Meanwhile, as one commentator assessed it, repeated attempts to oust Castro's regime have hurt the USA more than they have injured Cuba.[96] Washington's diplomatic moves against the Cuban government have increasingly isolated the USA from its friends and allies. As one study of the issue concluded, the principal result of coercive policies toward Havana has been "to make life miserable for the people of Cuba."[97] Another study found that U.S. policy toward Cuba had not only failed to achieve its objective, but it had in fact actually *strengthened* Castro's hold on political power. (Throughout modern history of course, it is a familiar phenomenon that the existence of a visible external enemy is an extremely useful instrument for maintaining authoritarian or totalitarian governments in power.)[98] Or as another student of U.S.-Cuban relations has expressed the idea, after the Cold War officials would be well advised "to ignore" Castro's Cuba, since the Castro dictatorship is not a threat—but merely "an annoyance"—to the United States.[99]

Some neo-isolationist critics believe that U.S. policy in responding to terrorism around the globe also requires re-examination after the Cold War. One commentary in this vein, for example, contends that to a significant degree, terrorist activities directed against Americans at home and abroad are a reaction to Washington's support of right-wing regimes and political movements abroad and of America's opposition to such movements as Islamic fundamentalism. A beneficial step toward reducing the incidence of global terrorism, therefore, would be for officials in Washington to avoid "Rambo rhetoric" in their approach to external problems.[100] Another study asserts that America's military establishment is itself guilty of terrorism on a wide scale, since no other nation "can match our record of slaughter around the globe."[101]

Mention may be made once more of the view of liberal neo-isolationists regarding a major tenet of the liberal political tradition: a conviction that the expansion of democracy outside the United States is an essential step in the promotion of global peace and security. The growth of democracy around the globe, one advocate of this viewpoint contends, is the "best guarantee of world peace." Therefore, a paramount American diplomatic objective must always be to promote "the spread of freedom" throughout the world.[102] For many observers in this category, the new era in Russian-American relations offers unprecedented opportunities for American policymakers to pursue the goal—in the former Soviet empire, in Eastern Europe, and generally throughout the Third World.

Yet it is equally true that other liberal observers have become increasingly skeptical about the feasibility of this diplomatic objective for the United States. Despite the natural attraction of the goal for citizens and leaders in the USA, judging by recent experience in a number of cases, they entertain strong doubts about whether the U.S. government is actually *capable* of promoting democracy beyond its own borders. They find relatively little convincing evidence that policymakers in Washington really understand the complex and difficult problem of "democratizing" societies within the New World and other regions; and even if they do, a number of commentators question whether officials in the USA possess the diplomatic skills and instruments required to accomplish the goal.

Moreover, as we have already noted, it can be questioned whether policy-makers in the USA are aware of, and well informed about, many collateral problems that often accompany the movement toward greater democracy overseas. As mentioned earlier, one major result of democratization in foreign societies is to intensify existing conflicts among rival ethnic, tribal, and religious groups which take advantage of a freer political atmosphere to express their demands, sometimes by violent methods. Or as another study concluded, the "real problem" politically within most Third World societies today and in the future is the conflict between "the modernists and the traditionalists." Americans possess very few applicable insights into this source of ongoing political upheaval.[103] A study of U.S. intervention to promote democracy in Zaire concluded that the attempt was basically unsuccessful. In time, America's conspicuous presence within the country quite clearly *aggravated* existing political tensions and allowed anti-American forces within Zaire to strengthen their position against a foreign intruder.[104] In the same vein, another study concluded that overt U.S. intervention in Indonesia to advance the cause of democracy in that key Asian state did little in the long run to achieve the objective.[105] Similarly, most of the contributors to a symposium on U.S. policy toward the Middle East were critical of Washington's intervention in that region's political affairs. Such diplomatic behavior has paid few dividends for the USA.[106]

After many years of diplomatic service and reflection on the nation's diplomatic record, George F. Kennan became increasingly dubious about America's efforts to promote democracy and human rights beyond its own borders. He condemned a policy "of looking sharply down the nose [at a foreign government] to see whether its handling of domestic affairs meets with our approval." In more general terms, Kennan observed: "I know of no evidence that democracy . . . is the natural state of most of mankind." To the contrary, democracy has a "relatively narrow base in time and space," being limited mainly to northeastern Europe and North America.[107]

The logical corollary of such doubts was highlighted by the political slogan of one candidate for Congress in the early 1990s, whose watchword was: "Come Home America." Another candidate campaigned on the slogan, "It's time to take care of our own."[108] More than one study of post–Cold War American foreign policy has reiterated John Winthrop's widely quoted description of the USA as "a city upon a hill." Another frequently used metaphor is that the American republic serves as a "beacon for all mankind."[109]

After the Cold War, no less than in the past, many liberals remained convinced that the destiny of the American society will ultimately be determined by its ability to solve pressing *internal* problems. Achieving this goal of course demands that the nation's leaders protect the security of the USA from foreign threats; and in the new era of Russian-American relations that danger has been considerably reduced. After the Cold War, very few of the challenges confronting the United States abroad call the nation's security and independence into serious question. Given that reality, in effect many liberals have reiterated the maxim that was popular during the long isolationist era: "Foreign policy begins at home." As many liberals have long viewed the matter, this means that America's diplomatic efforts must be founded on a solid domestic base or they will almost certainly fail.[110] A corollary belief today, as in the period of classical isolationism, is the idea that ultimately American society's example to the world will prove to be the most crucial factor determining its power and influence within the international system.[111]

CHAPTER 4

CONSERVATIVE INTERVENTIONISM

D URING THE PRESIDENTIAL ELECTION OF 1996, GOP CANDIDATE Bob Dole attacked the diplomacy of the Clinton White House. Dole contended that President Clinton and his foreign policy team were "still suffering from post-Vietnam syndrome" in responding to developments abroad; in far too many instances they appeared to be motivated (specifically in relations with Moscow) by "misguided romanticism" in dealing with global problems. The Republican candidate urged the people to repudiate a Democratic leadership that "doubts American power, questions American purpose, and cannot fulfill American promise."[1]

In the same period, a leading conservative commentator called on the Republican Party to avoid such extremes as isolationism and "paranoid nativism" in its approach to foreign affairs. Instead, he urged the GOP to adopt a policy of "responsible internationalism" in dealing with global issues. To his mind, the defeat of the Soviet Union in the Cold War did not mean the end of American leadership in solving international problems. On the contrary, what was needed was a revival of "the hardheaded Republican realism of Theodore Roosevelt" in the foreign policy field.[2]

Still another conservative political leader called on citizens to reject such approaches to foreign affairs as pacifism, "America First-ism," isolationism, and neo-isolationism. Americans must resist the temptation to adopt a foreign policy based upon "nostalgia." Instead, the USA must exercise global leadership by pursuing a policy of "constructive internationalism."[3] According to the findings of a Republican Party study group, a reversion to isolationism by the United States was "impossible" after the Cold War. The preservation of global peace and stability required "a worldwide [projection] of American power"; and the "hour of decision can no longer be postponed."[4] Referring to the experience of the Persian Gulf War, another commentator drew the general conclusion that "only the United States can organize and lead the international community's response to a major regional military threat."[5] In brief, as another recent study of America's global role phrased it, the United States is required to serve as "the reluctant sheriff" of the international system.[6]

According to former president Richard Nixon, officials in Washington ought to exercise decisive leadership in a concerted effort to "remake the world." In modern history, the American society led the way in technological innovations. By the same token, America is required to demonstrate leadership in the attempt to transform international politics by implementing a "strategy to achieve real peace."[7] To Nixon's mind, "It is clear that there is no substitute for American leadership [in global affairs]. What is not clear is how the United States should lead."[8] Far from dividing the American society, in his view responding to major challenges overseas will tend to *unite* the people; Nixon cited the example of America's response to the challenge posed by the Soviet Union's Sputnik to prove the point. By contrast, as he saw it, the American society's "greatest enemy" since World War II was its "own self-defeating pessimism" and doubt concerning the nation's role and future.[9]

From a different perspective, another commentator was convinced that America's commitment to an avowedly interventionist foreign policy was a crucial factor in accounting for the outcome of the Cold War.[10] Or, as still another observer expressed the idea, in the new era of international relations "neither order nor lawfulness is likely to flow from any other sources than American power and leadership" in the global arena.[11]

These are diverse expressions of an approach to American diplomacy that can be described by the term "conservative interventionism."[12] As was pointed out in Chapter 2, some right-wing individuals and groups have advocated a neo-isolationist approach to foreign affairs since the Cold War—a diplomatic orientation emphatically rejected by the school of thought being examined in this chapter.[13] If the former group is concerned about the deleterious consequences of America's overinvolvement in the affairs of other societies, those in the latter category are equally apprehensive about the implications of failure by the United States to use its power abroad in response to circumstances and developments likely to prove damaging to its security and well-being. It was President George Bush, after all, who called for an American-initiated "new world order" after the Persian Gulf War. While the details of Bush's diplomatic blueprint were not always clear, no doubt existed that he envisioned a dynamic, and often decisive, leadership role by the United States in behalf of international peace and security.

For the conservative interventionist, the new stage in Russian-American relations is of course widely applauded. But despite optimistic expectations in some quarters, for most observers in this group the end of the Cold War does *not* automatically usher in a new age of peace, stability, and goodwill around the world. Instead, a different—and often extremely difficult, complex, and dangerous—set of challenges now confronts the United States beyond its own borders. Some of these will unquestionably require an overtly interventionist response by policymakers in Washington.[14] One study has underscored the fact that, from the standpoint of intelligence upon which to base sound foreign policy decisions, the USA is poorly equipped to deal with international problems arising after the Cold War.[15] Or, as another commentator observed poignantly, since the end of the conflict with Moscow, officials in Washington were perhaps surprised to find that "undesirable regimes continued to thumb their noses at the United States."[16]

CONSERVATIVE IDEOLOGY AND INTERVENTIONISM

Several tenets of conservative ideology logically support an interventionist approach to foreign affairs. There is, for example, the well-known preference of conservatives for security and stability over freedom and liberty. Right-wing observers often emphasize the idea that the attainment of every goal of the American society at home and abroad presupposes the continued existence of the United States as an independent and powerful nation. In turn, successfully preserving national security demands that policymakers respond (or at least be prepared to respond) to a wide variety of actual and potential threats posed by developments abroad. After the Cold War, no less than before, conservatives widely subscribe to the old Roman maxim *Si vis pacem, para bellum* (If you want peace, prepare for war!).

Conservatives have always tended to view the international system as essentially Hobbesian in nature, and the end of the Cold War has not essentially altered that reality. For nations that are neither willing nor able to recognize and to confront a variety of external dangers, life can be "nasty, brutish, and short."[17] One commentator has depicted "the natural state of the world" as "a fragile temporary . . . situation" in which the maintenance of global peace and security depends upon "high levels of American power, influence, and engagement."[18] Or, as another observer has described it, the contemporary international system is characterized by the proliferation of "teacup wars" (as in Bosnia, Somalia, Rwanda, and Haiti). These are conflicts of "national debilitation" that were undermining a number of "fragile but functioning nation-states" and are "gnawing at the wellbeing" of more "stable nations."[19] Another commentator has taken note of what he calls "new antagonisms" that have come into prominence within the international system, some of which could produce intense conflict in the North-South encounter.[20]

From a different vantage point, former president Richard Nixon urged the American people and their leaders to abandon certain long-standing "illusions" about the outside world. One of these was the notion, shared by many Americans, that conflicts among nations are "unnatural." Nixon was convinced that the contrary was true, that conflict is the natural and normal condition of international affairs, and difficult as it might be for Americans to accommodate themselves to that reality, they must do so. As Nixon expressed the idea, "international conflict has been a constant throughout the centuries."

Another persistent illusion, as conservatives assess it, is the notion that people around the world "are basically alike"—that is, that they have the same values, accept common ethical and moral principles, and share the same goals. (The logical implication of this idea, also pervasive among Americans, is that conflicts existing within the international system are caused by *governments*, whose leaders are "out of touch" with the desires of the people.) Nixon found very little evidence to support such conceptions. Nor, citing another widespread illusion, did he subscribe to the view that tensions and conflicts in global affairs derived mainly from a lack of "understanding" among the people of the world. (As merely one example of this fallacy, the more leaders and citizens in the West "understood" the regional and global ambitions of Hitler's Germany, the more they came to doubt whether a just and durable peace with the Third Reich was possible.) In the former president's view, the liberal community's age-old vision of "perpetual peace," advocated by philosophers such as Immanuel Kant, "will never be achieved, except at diplomatic think tanks and in the grave"![21]

In other words, in the conservative conception, after the Cold War the global political environment remains highly unreceptive to the external goals and purposes of the United States, such as peace, respect for international law, co-operation among nations, and the worldwide extension of democracy. The new era in Russian-American relations has witnessed the emergence or intensification of several forces and developments that are directly or indirectly hostile to America and, in some instances, pose serious obstacles for the realization of its diplomatic goals. This includes such phenomena as the emergence of what are called "rogue states" or "radical weapons states"—those nations that defy established norms of international law and conduct and are attempting to build up a formidable military arsenal for use in pursuit of their external goals.[22] A related and extremely dangerous tendency also—identified by some conservative commentators as possibly the most ominous threat to global peace and security in the contemporary period—is the continuing proliferation of nuclear armaments and other weapons of mass destruction, as illustrated by the nuclear competition between India and Pakistan in the late 1990s.[23]

Still other developments eliciting deep concern among conservative observers are "Islamic Fundamentalism" and certain other phenomena—such as continuing waves of migration across national frontiers—that often impinge directly upon American diplomatic and security interests;[24] growing reliance upon terrorism by some individuals and groups abroad to achieve their objectives;[25] a number of potentially dangerous tendencies and developments within the former Soviet empire; the emergence of an increasingly independent, powerful, and possibly aggressive China; the reappearance of an economically powerful, prosperous, and united German nation, whose influence in regional and global affairs is bound to increase; the likelihood that, in the not too distant future, Japanese diplomatic influence will reflect that nation's enormous economic power; continuing threats to the security of the Persian Gulf region; and anarchistic tendencies, critical social and economic problems, and "failed states" encountered widely throughout the Third World.

Conservatives who advocate a forceful role of global leadership by the United States have used several terms to describe their approach. For example, one observer characterized the foreign policy of the Bush White House as one of "containment plus." In effect, Bush's call for a "new world order" amounted to a policy of global interventionism.[26] Another observer described President George Bush's approach to foreign affairs as one of "selective internationalism."[27] Former president Richard Nixon used such terms as "benevolent leadership" and "enlightened world leadership" to describe the nation's proper role on the global scene after the Cold War. Other commentators have depicted the desired approach to diplomatic questions by such terms as "constructive internationalism," "responsible internationalism," "self-confident engagement," "preventive diplomacy," "cautious interventionism," "preventive engagement," and "conditional engagement."

Advocating a "broad role" for the USA in global affairs, this school of thought rejects both classical isolationism and more recent varieties of "neo-isolationism"; neither provides adequate guidance for the nation's diplomatic activities in the new era.[28] Or as one of America's most respected conservatives has expressed the idea, with the end of the Cold War, the USA now has no rival in terms of global power and influence; and it will face no real competition in this regard for many years ahead. This means that the twenty-first century (not the twentieth century, as some believed) will turn out to be "the American Century."[29]

The impulse for diplomatic interventionism advocated by right-wing groups derives also from a number of ideas about the power of the United

States in the post–Cold War period. A fundamental conviction, for example, is the belief that after winning the contest with the Soviet Union, the United States is left as the only superpower in the international system. As one study expressed the idea, in contrast to the dire predictions of the "declinists," in reality the USA is "the only nation in the world that [can] claim to be simultaneously militarily powerful and economically robust—in short, the only real superpower" existing on the global scene.[30] Other potential power centers— such as the European Community, Germany, Japan, India, China, and Brazil— have emerged; with the passage of time, their power has increased and no doubt will continue to expand; at some stage, American policymakers will have to admit their governments to a share in decisionmaking involving the solution of global problems.[31] Or as another interpreter has expressed the idea, unless the USA wants to assume the burden alone of serving as the world's policeman, it must work diplomatically in close concert with other increasingly powerful nations on the global scene.[32] While in the course of time, the world may witness the emergence of other superpowers, meanwhile, from a global perspective the power of these nations is largely potential; as a rule, they exercise influence beyond their own borders mainly on a regional basis.

Very few conservatives accept the pessimistic predictions of the "declinist" school of thought about the power of the United States.[33] They find little convincing evidence, for example, for believing that, like the Spanish or British empires in earlier eras, America's star is setting and that this is an irreversible process. Today and for the foreseeable future, the solution of most major international problems requires the active participation of the United States.

As the world's only superpower, it follows that the USA has certain inescapable obligations and interests beyond its own borders. We have already emphasized that for most conservative observers, in the new diplomatic era the transcendent goal of U.S. foreign policy is to preserve the security and promote the well-being of the American society. In opposition to the views of those in the liberal community, in the conservative perspective officials in Washington must avoid embracing what is sometimes called the "new paradigm" for America's role in global affairs that involves "flight from the national interest."[34] Or, as former senator Dole expressed the idea, officials in Washington must be prepared at all times to defend the nation's sovereignty. In his judgment, this is not a responsibility that can be "subcontracted" to the United Nations, regional bodies, or other external sources.[35] No less today than in the past, the United States *has* its own set of unique interests abroad; and the nation's leaders must understand, pursue, and defend them conscientiously.[36] This is not only essential for the future and welfare of the American republic; it is viewed as a vital prerequisite for maintaining the peace and stability of the international system.

Will adequate steps be taken to prevent the eruption or escalation of war and conflict in countless trouble spots abroad? Once violence has erupted, will it be contained, and will international peacekeeping efforts have any prospect for success? Will societies throughout the Third World be able to develop economically and socially? Will a host of problems affecting nearly all nations on the globe—threats to the environment, conditions of famine, epidemics, and pervasive poverty, the inadequacy of educational systems, the plight of millions of refugees around the globe, the removal of barriers to world trade—be solved? As many conservatives assess it, if the international community is able to discover answers to such difficult and complex questions (and admittedly, that may not always be possible) the process will inevitably demand the active participation of the United States. In other words, as a superpower the USA will necessarily *be deeply involved* in efforts to find the necessary solutions, and to apply effective remedies, for such pervasive international problems. This is a different matter, however, from saying that, vast as its power may be, the United States is capable *alone* of solving a long list of complex problems existing throughout the world.

Many conservative students of international affairs are also dubious about what has been called the "new realism"—a central tenet of which is the idea that military force has largely lost its utility as an influential component of national power.[37] As in the past, most right-wing observers subscribe to views of the nineteenth-century Prussian general Carl M. von Clausewitz, who called attention to the crucial relationship between military force and diplomacy.[38] Reflecting Clausewitz's theories, conservatives believe that today, no less than in the past, a strong military arsenal remains essential for the preservation of national security and the achievement of other important foreign policy objectives.[39]

To the minds of many right-wing observers, the outcome of the Cold War could be attributed primarily to one key factor: the United States' buildup of a position of military superiority over the Soviet Union. As one commentator expressed the idea, Russia's defeat in that contest basically stemmed from the fact that Washington "outgunned" Moscow.[40] Or, as another observer concluded, U.S. interventions to counter Soviet machinations in the Third World were a crucial development in the outcome of the Cold War.[41] More-recent and well-publicized examples were provided during the mid-1990s, when the need arose for Washington to provide a demonstration of America's power in responding to new threats in the Persian Gulf area and in East Asia (in response to renewed threats against the independence of Taiwan by mainland China).[42]

Several corollary ideas derive from the conservative conception of national power. As already emphasized, those in the conservative tradition believe that the United States must at all times possess a modern, well-trained, and highly mobile military establishment capable of responding to a variety of major and minor threats arising within the global environment.[43] One prominent conservative analyst has deplored what he calls "the demilitarization of the [American] military." Against the views of most liberals (who look forward to a large "peace dividend" from reducing military expenditures), this observer points out that under the Bush and Clinton administrations, the USA sent more troops abroad than it did in twenty years following the Nixon presidency. By the late 1990s, because of reductions in the size and strength of the armed forces, however, the USA would be unable to engage in a single major regional conflict "unless it withdrew from most of its international commitments."[44]

A number of right-wing commentators believe also that, in the euphoria gripping the nation since the end of the competition with Moscow, the nation's military power has declined alarmingly. Moreover, they are convinced that America's military establishment has not been adapted to meet the new and difficult challenges arising abroad since the Cold War. In other words, the nation has *the wrong kind* of military arsenal for responding to conditions and problems existing in the contemporary world.[45]

Conservative interventionists emphasize that policymakers must not only possess the requisite military power needed to achieve the nation's objectives abroad, but must also be prepared to use armed force when necessary to achieve American diplomatic goals beyond the nation's borders. A number of key diplomatic failures in recent years can be attributed to the lack of will-power among the people and their leaders in pursuing the nation's objectives abroad.[46] Another commentator has cautioned national policymakers about an all-too-frequent tendency to engage in "Hamlet-like soliloquies on the moral dilemmas of action" when they confront challenges arising abroad. When indecision, ambiguity, and endless soul-searching characterize the decision-making process in Washington, "the world will seek its political models elsewhere."[47]

Expressed differently, sooner or later Americans must come to terms with the inescapable reality that carrying out their global responsibilities will at times demand the application of military force—a process that will inevitably involve casualties.[48] At the same time, it is equally imperative of course that America's goals and purposes abroad be clear and consistent.[49]

In the period following the Cold War, one conservative observer is convinced that the USA must adhere to a foreign policy of "robust and difficult interventionism." The Reagan administration's overt intervention in Nicaragua, in an effort to defeat the pro-Communist Sandinista movement, was one conspicuous example of this approach. In that case, the USA openly supported the Nicaraguan peasants in a successful campaign to break the political power of the Sandinistas.[50] Or, as another analysis of the Nicaraguan crisis concluded, America's failure to intervene at an early stage in an effort to contain Communist advances within Central America meant that in time, the political crisis in Nicaragua became acute and ultimately required a concerted and costly effort by the USA to defeat the Sandinista regime.[51]

Several years later, another model was provided by the Bush administration's response to Iraqi aggression in the Persian Gulf area and, after military victory in that contest, to the president's call for a "new world order" initiated by the United States.[52] Late in 1995, Senator Bob Dole stated, regarding President Clinton's decision to send American military units to Bosnia, that he would support the White House in this undertaking.[53] Other analysts called on policymakers in Washington to act decisively in order to prevent the dangerous proliferation of nuclear weapons throughout the international system.[54]

Conservative interventionists do not conceal their conviction that in responding to challenges abroad, at times the United States must be prepared to act unilaterally to prevent foreign threats from endangering global peace and security.[55] Under certain circumstances, in other words, officials in Washington must engage in "preventive diplomacy," designed to keep a potential threat from posing an ominous danger to America's security and diplomatic interests.[56] A familiar, and still relevant, example in the annals of diplomacy is "showing the flag" to nations bent on intimidation of, or aggressive behavior toward, their neighbors.[57] An analysis of American diplomacy toward the crisis in the Balkans arrived at a comparable conclusion. Judging Washington's policy toward that issue a "failure," the study asserted that the United States and its allies should have intervened in the Balkans conflict at a much earlier stage, to prevent the disintegration of Yugoslavia. Several months later, some commentators called on Washington to provide modern weapons to the Muslim Bosnians, in order to prevent a genocidal conflict in the Balkans. The general conclusion reached on the basis of these examples is that at times the United States must act *before a problem or condition becomes critical;* otherwise, America and the international community is likely to confront conditions that are highly inimical to global peace and security.[58] From a different perspective, another study finds that the concept of "low-intensity conflict" will play a central role in American foreign policy after the Cold War. Actually, the concept is a modern variation on the earlier strategy of "counterinsurgency" identified with the Kennedy administration. With certain adaptations, this approach is viewed as applicable to a number of challenges confronting Washington in foreign affairs after the Cold War.[59]

In the new stage of American diplomacy, asserts one conservative spokesman, the USA must avoid the temptation of relying on "naive multilateralism," or what GOP presidential candidate Bob Dole denounced as the "dreamy pursuit of an international order" to solve critical global problems.[60] Former president Richard Nixon called attention to the fact that the twentieth century witnessed two great experiments in international organization designed to achieve and maintain global peace and security. In his judgment, both of these experiments proved to be "tragic failures." Since World War II, many of the activities of the United Nations have been "heavily prejudiced" against the USA.[61]

Most right-wing commentators concede that at times there are no doubt advantages to multinational efforts designed to solve global problems.[62] (Conservative voices, for example, have been outspoken in demanding greater "burden-sharing" by America's friends and allies!) Yet it is equally true that at times serious obstacles exist to achieving effective multinational co-operation, especially in peacekeeping ventures. Accordingly, policymakers in Washington must never relinquish the right to engage in unilateral decisionmaking.[63]

A number of right-wing observers underscore another idea that should be kept uppermost in mind by the nation's leaders in dealing with international problems arising after the Cold War. In fact, this is one of the central tenets of conservative interventionism: the conviction that a fundamental distinction exists between the "core interests" of the United States abroad and an almost infinite number of entries on the American society's diplomatic "wish list."

Regarding items in the former category, conservative thought often emphasizes two important ideas. In the first place, this category of goals consists of those that are directly related to the preservation of the nation's independence, security, and well-being. It is imperative that these primary objectives be carefully defined, articulated, and understood by the American people.[64] In the second place, it is no less essential that, when the nation's leaders are pursuing these high-priority goals, they bring to bear the power necessary to achieve the objectives successfully.

With respect to items in the second category, one conservative observer has said that the United States cannot serve as "the Mother Teresa" of the international community.[65] Or as the idea has been expressed, officials in Washington must at all times resist the impulse to engage in "international social engineering."[66] Needless to say, the entries on the American society's diplomatic wish list are far more numerous than the objectives in the former group; and this fact can lead to what conservatives describe as a foreign policy of "enlargement" or indiscriminate interventionism overseas.[67] Illustrative goals on the diplomatic wish list include achieving lasting peace on a global basis; successfully resolving deep-seated political controversies within other societies; creating stable democratic systems around the globe; and eliminating poverty, disease, illiteracy, and ignorance in Third World societies.

Conservatives have also become increasingly skeptical about the benefits to be realized from what is sometimes called "humanitarian intervention" in societies experiencing internal upheavals and conflict (a concept dealt with more fully in Chapter 6.) The record clearly indicates that the gains from intervention undertaken for humanitarian purposes are in most cases highly debatable; and in many instances, they appear almost non-existent.[68]

As conservatives assess it, distinguishing between these two categories of external goals implicitly requires that the American people and their leaders accept a transcendent reality: there are some international problems that not even a superpower can solve.[69] As one conservative has warned, difficult as it is, the American people and their leaders must come to terms with the fact that "much of the world's disorder *cannot* be solved."[70] Given these limitations, indiscriminate interventionism by the USA is an almost certain recipe for diplomatic failure, for dissipating the nation's resources in behalf of hopeless causes overseas, and for ensuing public disillusionment with the leadership provided by the president and Congress. In the end, unrestrained interventionism abroad is likely in time to trigger a new wave of isolationist and neo-isolationist sentiment within the American society.[71]

SPECIFIC DIPLOMATIC PROPOSALS AND CONCEPTS

Those advocating an interventionist course from a conservative ideological perspective propose a number of specific goals for American foreign policy in the new era. Although many aspects of European-American relations are changing as a result of the West's victory in the Cold War, most conservatives believe that the USA remains deeply involved in the region's affairs.[72] Since World War II, Europe has been—and it remains today—the region with which the United States has the closest security and diplomatic ties.[73] NATO was, and it still is, America's most important alliance system. Moreover, much of the impetus for European unification since World War II has come from Washington. American officials were convinced that a unified Europe—especially one capable of restraining a possible German resurgence—would be an increasingly secure and prosperous region.[74] Some right-wing observers also believe that the momentum in moving forward toward greater European unity has been slowed; only Washington's vigorous leadership is likely to supply the impetus needed to revive the movement. This step is viewed as essential in achieving another longtime American objective: greater "burden-sharing" by the nation's prosperous and stable allies.[75]

Against those who believe that NATO has become "outmoded," conservatives widely contend that the alliance must in fact be retained and strengthened. The Western defense structure needs to be renovated and adapted to meet the challenges likely to confront the allies in the new era.[76] This requires extending the compass of NATO eastward, to include at least some of the former Communist states of Eastern Europe. An "enlarged" NATO would provide insurance against a resurgence of Russian expansionism and a possible revival of efforts to intimidate its smaller neighbors.[77] At the same time, on all sides conservative voices are heard calling for greater "burden-sharing" by the prosperous European allies in the effort to achieve common goals.[78]

The Clinton administration, contended GOP presidential candidate Bob Dole in mid-1996, was guilty of "misguided romanticism" and of "terminal mumbles" in dealing with the former Soviet Union—a complaint widely echoed by other conservative voices. In his view, taking steps to guard against a revival of Russian designs on its neighbors had to be ranked among Washington's leading foreign policy objectives.[79]

Among this group, considerable anxiety also existed about developments within the once vast Soviet empire. While conservatives naturally are virtually unanimous in their enthusiasm about the collapse of communism and the outcome of the Cold War, at the same time many have serious doubts that Russia's external behavior will *remain* peaceful and benign.[80] After all, the Communists received the second-largest number of votes in Russia's national election in 1997, in which Boris Yeltsin's regime retained power; and a number of observers are apprehensive that (as internal problems mount throughout Russian society) the outside world will once again witness a new wave of militant Russian nationalism and hegemonial tendencies abroad.[81]

Despite the expectations of many liberals, conservative interventionists are skeptical that internal economic and other reforms (which of course they applaud) within the Russian society have been successfully and permanently implemented. Still less do they believe that such reforms will necessarily lead to a "softer" or more co-operative external policy by the regime in Moscow.[82] To the mind of another experienced observer, Washington's goals in dealing with Moscow must be directed toward achieving the "three Ds": democratization of Russia's political system; decentralization of its former empire; and "de-statization" of its collectivized economic system.[83]

Conservatives also widely believe that a position of Western military strength—anchored in a powerful and revitalized NATO—is required for the indefinite future in relations with Moscow. Policymakers in the USA will need to devote close attention to developments within Russia and its former domain. Implementing far-reaching changes within Russian society will no doubt demand a significant degree of American involvement in its affairs, in an attempt to achieve a more open political system and to promote economic stability and progress.[84]

Some conservative observers believe that American aid programs and investments in the Russian society should be directly conditioned upon Moscow's benign behavior abroad, as for example, in accepting the independence of the Ukraine, in refraining from using armed force against separatist movements within the former USSR, and in refraining from "mischievous" intervention in the Balkans.[85] Or, as a prominent Republican legislator is convinced, American policymakers ought to inform the Kremlin in no uncertain terms that any Russian efforts to suppress independence movements within the former Soviet empire and Eastern Europe will encounter firm American opposition and will endanger collaborative Russian relations with the West.[86] Other conservative voices have been heard calling for a special effort to develop a close relationship between policymakers in Washington and Russia's military leaders. In this view, this step is needed in order to prevent a possible nuclear disaster involving Moscow's arsenal of nuclear weapons.[87]

With regard to another European challenge—America's role in the crisis gripping the Balkans—conservative interventionists believe that Washington must accept a share of the blame for the genocidal and seemingly endless conflict in that region. As this group sees it, American policymakers waited far too long to become involved in efforts to resolve the conflict, with the result that it reached crisis proportions before the USA and other nations finally decided to take steps designed to bring an end to the violence. In the conservative indictment, the Clinton White House was guilty of serious neglect in responding to events in the Balkans; it allowed aggressive behavior to go unchecked for too long. Because of failure to act earlier, America and its European allies ultimately confronted an extremely difficult and intractable challenge in the Balkans—one that has thus far defied peaceful resolution. As a number of conservative observers assess it, belatedly the USA should support the Muslims in their efforts to establish and maintain an independent state.[88]

With respect to American policy toward the Third World generally, conservative interventionists exhibit mixed feelings on the subject. On the one hand, as Richard Nixon and other commentators have emphasized, with the end of the Cold War the strategic importance of the Third World generally for the

USA has unquestionably declined. Moreover, progress in many Third World societies has been seriously impeded by the existence of a number of pervasive and deep-seated problems, such as corrupt and inept political regimes and "disastrous economic policies" followed for many years by Third World governments. Based upon experience in a long list of cases, it is clear by now that the USA cannot "solve" most of the endemic problems existing in the vast majority of Third World nations.

At the same time, after the Cold War no less than before, Washington is required to *help* Third World societies find solutions for their critical internal problems, since failure to do so will unquestionably pose a number of difficult challenges and choices for the American people and their leaders. (A noteworthy example is provided by the challenge of dealing with the tide of refugees seeking to gain entry into the United States from poverty-stricken Third World countries.) If the United States quite clearly cannot "carry" the Third World on its back, neither can it avoid playing at least a limited role in multilateral efforts to assist in solving Third World problems.[89]

The Middle East—and especially, the Persian Gulf area—is another region in which the United States has developed vital security and diplomatic interests, and that reality has not changed as a result of the outcome of the Cold War.[90] Today and for many years ahead, continued access to the oil reserves of the area will be accorded high priority on America's foreign policy agenda.[91] The allied victory in the Persian Gulf War did not signify the end of future threats to regional security by ambitious governments.[92] Accordingly, Washington must be prepared to use its power to deal firmly with any new outbreak of aggression aimed at the region and to preserve stability within key Persian Gulf states.[93]

Regarding other dimensions of American foreign policy toward the Middle East, conservative interventionists call for an active role by Washington in responding to conflicts and tensions within the region. One study concludes, for example, that the Middle East is facing "one of the most unstable periods" in its history. In addition to the still unresolved Arab-Israeli imbroglio, internal conflicts within Middle Eastern societies are becoming more intense. A poignant example is provided by developments within Turkey, where Islamic fundamentalism has become increasingly influential; its adherents have left no doubt that they intend to change the secular nature of Turkey's political system existing since the era of Atatürk. In turn, this movement is firmly opposed by the Turkish military, which in recent history has served as the custodian of the nation's secular political order and has intervened several times to preserve it.[94]

Moreover, as a number of right-wing commentators see it, the USA must be diligent in opposing expansionist, disruptive, and destabilizing behavior by countries like Iran and Iraq. Some observers believe that for an indefinite period in the future, the USA will be required to act as the guarantor of peace and stability in the Persian Gulf region. In turn, successfully pursuing this goal will of course require that American policymakers have requisite military power at their disposal for accomplishing the task.[95] This quest will also dictate that the USA take steps to oppose attempts by Syria to acquire a modern missile arsenal from countries like South Africa and other sources.[96]

Since World War II, the United States has had close relations with the government of Saudi Arabia—the site of the largest oil reserves on the globe.[97] Officials in Washington should also exert pressure on the government of Saudi Arabia to counteract terroristic activities directed at Americans and to carry out reforms directed toward achieving a more open and pluralistic political system. Otherwise, the Saudi dynasty is in danger of suffering the same fate as the shah's regime earlier in Iran.[98]

As has been true since World War II, the United States remains committed to support the independence and security of the State of Israel, in the face of still-intense Arab opposition. By the new millennium, the prospects for a peaceful resolution of the Arab-Israeli conflict did not appear promising. Some conservative commentators also believed that Washington should make an effort to persuade Israel's leaders to adopt a more flexible and conciliatory approach to the Arabs, in the interests of breaking the Arab-Israeli deadlock. Even while they remained reluctant to compromise their differences, the parties to the conflict believed that Washington's role in efforts to break the existing impasse was nothing less than essential. If and when a peace accord is reached, the USA will no doubt be required to accept continuing responsibilities for preserving peace in the region and for extending economic assistance to both sides.[99]

For well over two centuries, the United States has been actively involved in Asian affairs, and nearly all conservative interventionists are agreed that this state of affairs will continue in the post–Cold War era. By the 1990s, for example, Asia had become the USA's largest trading partner, and American firms had investments exceeding $60 billion in the region.[100] By the late 1990s, the economic difficulties besetting a number of Asian nations sent tremors throughout the American stock markets, adversely affected the demand for American-made products in the Asian market, and generally affected the economy of the United States for the worse.

In his analysis of the global challenges facing the United States, former president Nixon repeated the prediction of Douglas MacArthur (when he was a junior-level officer in the U.S. Army) to the effect that, "the future and, indeed, the very existence of America, were irrevocably entwined with Asia and its island outposts."[101] As another commentator has predicted, in the years ahead new crises will almost certainly erupt within the Asian setting. Some of these will involve the interests of the USA and may well jeopardize regional, or even global, peace. For that reason, Washington must continue to exercise leadership in solving Asian problems.[102] If it fails to do so, America risks "getting dragged into messy shooting wars on matters of peripheral importance to U.S. interests."[103]

Commenting on the existence of regional disputes and conflicts erupting in Asia after the Vietnam War, William F. Buckley was convinced that the United States had an obligation to intervene militarily if necessary in order to prevent genocidal conflict in Cambodia. In his view, Washington's unwillingness to act would be analogous to America's failure many years earlier to prevent the Holocaust.[104] Or, as another leading conservative source expressed the idea, after the Cold War no less than before, the USA had a continuing obligation to "maintain stable peace and stability among North Korea, South Korea, Japan, and China."[105]

For most conservatives, the presence of a large, well-equipped, and modern American military establishment in Asia is essential to protect the nation's diplomatic and security interests.[106] This includes the maintenance of an American "nuclear umbrella" to preserve regional peace and stability.[107] Similarly, as has been true since the end of World War II, the USA must continue to preserve close military ties with Japan.[108] The key to Japanese security remains its alliance with the USA; and military collaboration between the two nations continues to be a prerequisite for the existence of peace and stability throughout the entire Asian region.[109] In addition, as some right-wing observers see it, an American military presence in Japan is needed to serve as a deterrent against the possible formation of a new Sino-Japanese axis, with disturbing implications for regional peace and security.[110]

China has always occupied a special place in the annals of American diplomacy, and Sino-American relations will almost certainly remain a key dimension of the nation's external policy after the Cold War.[111] (Relations between Washington and Beijing under the Clinton administration are examined more fully in Chapter 6.)

Conservative interventionists are agreed upon several major propositions about America's relations with the People's Republic of China in the new era. One of these is that the PRC is making impressive economic progress, significantly enhancing its influence in regional and, with the passage of time, no doubt global affairs. At the same time (with a population, according to some estimates, of over two billion people), from a per capita perspective the Chinese economy remains weak, even by Asian standards. In the view of some students of Chinese affairs, this fact operates as a major constraint on a policy of diplomatic activism and adventurism by the PRC.[112]

If mainland China is far from being a superpower, it is what one observer calls "a rapidly developing economic giant." And as Napoleon feared, the Chinese giant "is [now] awake" and "he is ready to move the world."[113] Moreover, China's leaders continue to build up a modern and formidable military establishment that is available to support their external goals.[114] In light of this reality, Asian spokesmen have expressed genuine concern about whether Washington is prepared after the Cold War to maintain its long-standing commitment to the preservation of Asian security.[115]

Increasingly, China's leaders are pursuing policies dictated by their national interests, rather than by ideological considerations. In the words of one conservative spokesman, "For China's leaders, freedom has historically meant its independence as a nation, not individual rights."[116] And in the post–Cold War era, the world was to witness a number of demonstrations of Chinese "independence" in regional and global affairs. As many right-wing students of international politics view it, this fact will almost certainly lead to fundamental disagreements, and possibly even conflicts, betweeen Washington and Beijing.[117]

The revival of mainland China's long-standing determination to bring Taiwan under its jurisdiction provides a recent illustration of this tendency. Conservative opinion is virtually unanimous in support of the idea that Washington must continue to adhere to the position it has taken since the end of the Chinese civil war: the United States must exhibit firm opposition—not excluding reliance on armed force—to counter Beijing's designs on Taiwan.[118]

The PRC has also claimed jurisdiction over certain offshore oil reserves in the South China Sea. Other issues evoking American opposition include the PRC's sale of ballistic missiles and the components for making nuclear weapons to other countries, some of which are avowedly anti-American; repeated instances of political repression within Chinese society; the "piracy" of copyrighted material and other intellectual property; discriminatory trade policies by Beijing; and the continuing suppression of religious freedom (especially for Christian congregations within Chinese society).[119] To the minds of some conservatives, an ominous potential danger is, as pointed out earlier, the prospect of a new Sino-Japanese axis that would be highly inimical to America's diplomatic and security interests within Asia and globally.[120]

Yet in contrast to the views of many political liberals, few right-wing interventionists urge policymakers in Washington to adopt a confrontational approach to the PRC because of its internal political problems. Along with most Americans, conservatives naturally applaud any tendency toward greater democracy on the Chinese mainland. A number of observers in this group have pointed out that steps in the direction of political liberalization have in fact been taken within China since the death of Mao Tse-tung, despite a number of well-publicized instances of the regime's continuing repression of political dissidents. A leading conservative commentator has urged policymakers in Washington to bear in mind that, in dealing with moral and ethical questions, Americans always like to occupy the "high ground" in relations with China and other nations. Yet the American people and their leaders must always keep in mind that, "catharsis is not a national interest" of the USA in its relations with China and other states. In approaching the PRC, "one should be skeptical of a foreign policy that makes one feel good." Castigating Beijing and subjecting the Chinese society to coercive economic policies and other sanctions actually do little in the end to restrain objectionable behavior by its political leaders or to advance America's objectives generally in Asia.[121]

In the view of most conservatives, the democratization of China's political system will be a very long, involved, and uneven process, heavily conditioned by the society's economic progress. A crucial step in turn is likely to be China's integration into the global economic system and its evolution toward a free-market economy. American-led trade boycotts, efforts to "isolate" China, or other measures designed to coerce or intimidate Beijing are likely to make little positive contribution toward achieving the goal.[122] For this group, the most effective means of giving momentum to greater democracy within China is to maintain a "dialogue" or at least minimally co-operative relations with authorities in Beijing.[123] It is in Washington's interests to encourage Chinese economic growth, to create new opportunities for expanding Chinese trade, and to open the door for growing foreign investments within the Chinese society. Policymakers in Washington are cautioned to avoid "grandstanding" American diplomatic gestures directed toward the PRC, that in effect put the Chinese regime "on trial" and humiliate its government before the world.[124] Right-wing observers also call attention to the fact that in efforts to solve several major Asian questions, the United States urgently needs the co-operation of the PRC if effective solutions are to be found. Or, as one analysis of Sino-American relations concluded, policymakers in Washington must formulate policy on the principle: "Better a strong friend than a strong foe."[125]

Nothing in Chinese history lends credence to the expectation that a hard-line American policy in dealing with Beijing is likely to succeed. Historically, the Chinese society has time and again shown itself resistant to pressures brought by outside nations (often referred to by the Chinese as "the Barbarians") to undertake internal reforms. As one student of Chinese affairs sees it, momentum in the direction of a free-market economy and a more open political system is *not* likely to be maintained by "frightened political dictators," who constantly face American-led efforts to coerce them because of their record in the human rights field. As some commentators view it, with the passage of time China's leaders will become increasingly preoccupied with their society's critical domestic problems. In the words of one observer, the most likely scenario is that the Chinese nation—subjected to mounting internal stresses and pressures—will *fail* in its effort to join the ranks of the superpowers. In the expressive words of one observer, a more likely prospect is that instead China will become "a supernova, a huge star that increases tremendously in brightness as it burns up."[126]

Another challenge to American policymakers arising in the Asian context is posed by North Korea's determination to join the nuclear club. Governed by one of the most oppressive Communist dictatorships on the globe (the nation has still not "de-Stalinized" its political system), North Korea has amassed an unenviable record of ongoing political oppression and steady economic decline internally, coupled with a militant policy abroad.[127] At a time when the nation is unable to feed itself, North Korea's leaders appeared determined to construct a formidable military establishment, based on the possession of a nuclear arsenal.[128] Their test of advanced missiles in August and September 1998 provided eloquent evidence of North Korea's devotion to this objective.

Conservative interventionists are also genuinely concerned that new aggressive moves by North Korea across the 38th Parallel cannot be ruled out. Even a half-century after the Korean War, the USA and its Asian allies must remain constantly vigilant against that danger. As in the past, the still-ominous threat posed by North Korea demanded that the USA preserve close military ties with South Korea, and that it continue to maintain an Asian military presence capable of responding to any new conflict erupting on the Korean peninsula.[129]

Toward another longtime adversary—the government of Vietnam—many conservatives believe that the time has come to heal old wounds and inaugurate a new era in relations with this key Southeast Asian nation. Its leaders are now focusing their energies primarily on internal development; they urgently need American and other external sources of capital and investments; the regime appears to be playing a constructive role in regional affairs; and the government has taken steps to create a more open political system. Accordingly, the USA ought to do what it can to encourage such favorable tendencies by entering into more co-operative relations with the government of Vietnam.[130]

As has been true since the issuance of the Monroe Doctrine in 1823, right-wing observers remain convinced that the United States has unique diplomatic obligations within the Western Hemisphere. Traditionally, this group has been among the enthusiastic supporters of the Monroe Doctrine. A leading example was President Theodore Roosevelt, who added a significant "corollary" to the doctrine, proclaiming the New World "off limits" to foreign powers and implicitly assigning the responsibility for preserving hemispheric peace and stability to the USA.[131] (It will be recalled from Chapter 2 that even followers of the Hoover-Taft school of conservative neo-isolationism accepted the idea that the USA had unique and inescapable responsibilities for preserving hemispheric peace and stability.)

To date, regional bodies (such as the Organization of American States) have demonstrated no real capacity to deal effectively with threats to the peace arising within the hemisphere. As in the Dominican crisis of 1965, the most they have been able to accomplish in this respect is to assume responsibility for enforcing conditions designed to preserve peace and stability that have been created initially by the armed forces of the USA.[132] The end of the Cold War has not altered the reality that today, no less than in the past, the power of the USA still serves as the ultimate guarantor of regional peace and security.[133]

With regard to another dilemma confronting policymakers in the United States—the existence of non-democratic governments within the Western Hemisphere—most conservatives are persuaded that in the last analysis, only the people of Latin America can determine their political future. Diplomatic experience since the New Deal—including a number of cases since World War II—indicates that the quest for genuine and durable democratic systems in the other American republics still faces formidable obstacles, few of which can be removed by the United States.[134]

Moreover, on the basis of post–World War II experience in Latin America, the role of the USA in deciding the political destiny of its hemispheric neighbors is at best marginal.[135] Indeed, the evidence provides strong reason for believing that, as often as not, overtly interventionist behavior south of the border by the "North American Colossus" is counterproductive; it can actually *hinder* the emergence of democratic institutions and processes within the hemisphere.[136] By the end of the twentieth century, policymakers in Washington appeared to possess no more real insight into how to implant and maintain stable democratic political systems within the other American republics than they had demonstrated in earlier periods of diplomatic history. In the end, Washington's abortive attempts to do so as often as not produced more diplomatic losses than gains for the United States.[137] For example, to this day, relations between the United States and Mexico are often crucially affected by the consequences of Washington's earlier attempts to intervene in its neighbor's political affairs.

Toward another longtime regional challenge facing policymakers in Washington—relations with Castro's Cuba—many conservative interventionists have changed their position on the issue. After supporting a hardline American approach toward Castro's government for a generation or so following the Cuban Missile Crisis of 1962, today many conservative voices are heard calling for a fundamental change in Washington's relations with to Havana. Despite American-led boycotts of Cuban commerce and other coercive measures (moves that many friendly governments and allies of the USA usually ignored), Castro's Marxist regime is "still there" and shows no sign of collapse. Washington's uncompromising opposition has failed to dislodge the regime. Instead, the principal result appears to be widespread hardship and privation for the Cuban people.

The end of the Cold War offers possibilities for a new chapter in Cuban-American relations. A key development of course is the substantial reduction in Soviet military and economic aid to Havana, along with a cessation of Moscow's support and encouragement of Cuban revolutionary activities abroad. Based upon recent evidence, Havana *has* significantly curtailed its interventionist activities on a wide front—from the African continent to the Western Hemisphere. With its internal economic problems mounting, and the termination of subsidies from Moscow, it appears highly unlikely that Castro's government will be in a position to engage in aggressive and destabilizing behavior beyond its own borders. Consequently, many conservatives believe that the American-instigated embargo against Cuba ought to be abandoned; and an effort should be made to expand Cuban-American economic ties. As in the nation's approach to Russia and China, as a number of conservatives assess it, such steps offer promise of opening the oppressive political environment in Cuba to "the winds of freedom."[138]

For many conservatives, problems on the African continent epitomize those existing widely throughout the Third World. Since World War II, sub-Saharan Africa has occupied a low place on America's diplomatic agenda. Generally speaking, most conservatives are agreed that after the Cold War the African continent offers an unpromising field for the achievement of American foreign policy goals. In recent years—and despite intensive foreign aid efforts by the United States and its European allies—social and economic conditions within the region continue to deteriorate; and no early reversal of that process is indicated. One study, for example, refers to the economic and political "marginalization" of Africa.[139] For many societies on the African continent, internal conditions at the end of the century were unquestionably worse than they were a generation earlier. The eruption of widespread violence in Sierra Leone at the end of the 1990s provided a graphic example of the political turbulence and instability existing widely throughout Africa. In that and other cases, the United States and its allies, along with the members of the United Nations, appeared to be at a loss to know what to do to resolve such crises.

Corrupt, oppressive, and inept governments; unwise (in some cases, ruinous) economic policies; high levels of spending for modern armaments by African regimes (sometimes encouraged by the USA, Russia, and other outside countries); mounting external debts and unfavorable trade balances; highly adverse climatic and weather conditions; pervasive and increasingly critical problems of ill health, poor sanitation, and malnutrition; the eruption of widespread ethnic, tribal, and religious conflicts—these conditions pervade contemporary Africa. In the light of this reality, few right-wing interventionists favored active or deep involvement by the USA in African affairs after the Cold War. On the African continent, as in other Third World settings, policymakers in Washington have yet to discover the key to implanting democratic political systems and ensuring their future under what are often extremely adverse and unfamiliar conditions.[140]

As might be anticipated, those approaching foreign policy questions from a right-wing perspective favor a dynamic American role in promoting trade, commerce, and investment abroad. Conservative business groups, for example, advocate "a multi-national, free-trade orientation" for U.S. foreign policy.[141] Washington, one conservative commentator lamented, was "retreating from its traditional leadership" in endeavoring to expand free markets overseas.

In this view, the expansion of global trade and commerce is not only a worthwhile goal in its own right; it is no less an essential step in promoting political freedom in Eastern Europe and Russia, in China, and throughout the Third World.[142] According to another observer, the extension of democracy overseas and the expansion of international trade and commerce were "the same revolution," which Washington ought to spearhead abroad.[143] Still another analyst is convinced that America's own prosperity and economic well-being can be maintained only by promoting sound economic policies within the international system. Achieving this objective ought to rank among the highest goals of American diplomacy.[144] And to the mind of another conservative, today business and economic interests "drive" U.S. foreign policy, fully as much as political goals. In the words of Richard Nixon, the well-being of the American society "is inextricably bound to a world trading system." For example, some 11 percent of the nation's gross national product is exported—a figure that will almost certainly rise in the years ahead. Therefore, Americans should look forward to and relish the challenge of "achieving excellence by competing with others." Along with other conservatives, Nixon had no doubt that free trade is a force that will "spark reform in the developing nations."[145]

As was pointed out in Chapter 2, a number of conservatives are doubtful that the United States can or should make the promotion of democracy abroad a high-priority goal on the nation's foreign policy agenda. For this group, the objective does *not* rank among America's diplomatic vital interests. Admittedly, some conservatives disagree with this view. President Ronald Reagan, for example, called for a "democratic revolution" around the world, and he pledged his administration to support the undertaking. To Reagan's mind, the global movement toward democracy was "gathering new strength"; and it had received a renewed impetus from the outcome of the Cold War.[146] In the same vein, Secretary of State George Shultz once declared that "freedom is not the sole prerogative of a chosen few [nations]." Consequently, America's global mission must be "to nourish and defend freedom and democracy and communicate these ideas everywhere we can."[147] Referring to the defeat of communism in Nicaragua, Secretary of State James Baker declared confidently that "beyond containment lies democracy."[148]

Yet much as they might endorse the abstract goal of promoting democracy throughout the world, conservative interventionists are far from agreed about how to achieve the objective. Nor do the American people and their leaders exhibit deep understanding of the long-range consequences and responsibilities involved in efforts to promote democracy in foreign societies.

As our earlier treatment has emphasized, for the most part conservatives are not sanguine that overt interventionist efforts by the USA, for example, will be successful in installing and maintaining stable democratic political systems within foreign societies. Conservatives are broadly agreed that, in the final analysis, such an outcome will be determined primarily by the actions taken (or not taken) by the indigenous peoples to shape their own political future. Overtly interventionist efforts by foreign powers like the United States, on the other hand, can and often do cause widespread resentments abroad and place new barriers in the path of the emergence of a stable democratic political system.

One of the nation's eminent political leaders, who served for a time as secretary of state, Daniel Webster, once defined what he viewed as America's "true mission." It was "to teach by example and show by our success, moderation, and justice, the blessings of self-government and the advantages of free institutions." In the new era of international relations, conservatives widely express the view that domestic affairs ought to have first claim on the nation's resources, time, and energy.

As one contemporary observer has expressed the idea, today the nation's citizenry believes that it has "earned the right to address its societal ills by having borne the expense of containment for so long."[149] A Gallup poll in the winter of 1995–96 found that only some 2 percent of the American people ranked foreign policy high on the list of national concerns![150] Many conservatives are persuaded that after the Cold War, no less than in the past, the American society's ability *to solve its domestic problems* is a vital element in achieving diplomatic success. Therefore, in the words of one conservative observer, the president and Congress must devote sustained attention to such critical internal problems as "a disabled dollar, [a] results-absent education strategy, and undisciplined deficits."[151] Or, as Richard Nixon expressed the idea, the success of the nation's diplomatic efforts ultimately depends directly upon the "renewal" of the American society internally.[152]

According to another observer, the people want to see direct and tangible domestic benefits from active involvement in the world's problems.[153] From another vantage point, a different student of the nation's diplomacy believes that the resentment and sense of "rage" exhibited by the people toward their elected leaders serves as a strong deterrent against supporting an active foreign policy, that seems to suggest "overconcern for foreigners at the expense of American taxpayers."[154] The American people, another study has asserted, are not prepared to make major commitments abroad when they perceive the society at home as being in a state of considerable "disorder." In this view, the nation's diplomatic success arises "within our society."[155] In brief, beset as they are with a multitude of serious domestic problems, citizens have little incentive to support a foreign policy of "international heroics" by the United States.[156]

Yet much as they might be inclined to agree with such general propositions, some conservative spokesmen have also expressed an admonition regarding them. Americans, Richard M. Nixon lamented, exhibit an "almost hypnotic contentment because we are at peace abroad"; at times, they display a "myopic preoccupation" with their domestic problems."[157] As he and other conservative observers readily concede, across the nation there exist a number of critical internal problems, genuine concerns, and unfulfilled needs. To Nixon's mind, however, this fact must not be construed to mean that the USA should revert to an isolationist stance or that it should play a weak or passive role in international affairs. Nearly all nations (including America's possible rivals as a superpower) have domestic problems that are equally or even more critical. Despite the necessity for policymakers to devote attention to deteriorating conditions at home, the reality remains unchanged that the USA is the world's only superpower. This fact dictates that America continues to be actively and centrally involved in efforts to preserve global peace and stability and to solve a broad range of international problems.

CHAPTER 5

LIBERAL INTERVENTIONISM

A T THE END OF MAY 2000, AN EVENT OCCURRED WHICH DRAmatically illustrated the basic theme of this chapter. In Aachen, Germany, President Bill Clinton was selected to receive the International Charlemagne Prize because of his contributions to the cause of European unity and regional co-operation. Within recent years, fundamental changes had occurred—and were still taking place—on the European continent. European leaders believed that the Clinton administration deserved recognition for its role in providing "a new vision" for Europe, at a time when it was feared that the United States would withdraw from the region's affairs after the end of the Cold War. Instead, officials in Washington continued to take the initiative in bringing about such changes, even after Europe's own leaders sometimes faltered in doing so.[1]

While, as explained in an earlier chapter, some liberal observers and groups advocate a reduction in America's overseas commitments in the post–Cold War era, others favor exactly the opposite course: an approach to international issues that we have designated "liberal interventionism." One account of President Bill Clinton's first term analyzed his assessment of the crisis existing in the Balkans by saying that in his view, if the United States failed to take the lead in responding to it, "nothing will happen."[2] Similarly, an analysis of the views of Clinton's secretary of state, Warren Christopher, described his approach to global issues as exhibiting "dedication to earnest, international liberalism." Christopher believed that when he had been put in charge of the State Department, he "had been picked to create a new, lasting global foundation." At his Senate confirmation hearings, Christopher declared that, "We need to design a new strategy for protecting American interests by laying the foundations for a more just and stable world." In responding to developments abroad, the nation's policymakers needed to exhibit "practical idealism" and "responsible liberalism."[3]

As he began his second term in office, President Clinton called the United States the world's "indispensable nation" that had a crucial role to play in solving global problems. In his view, "the world is broadly supportive of what we do" overseas.[4] On another occasion, Clinton declared that, "at the dawn of a new century we can make the twenty-first century an American century." In its approach to international problems, America "must be driven by something that is bigger than ourselves." A major goal of U.S. foreign policy would be to "make people triumphant in the face of change."[5]

A former national security adviser to President Jimmy Carter defined America's mission abroad as countering "the global tendencies toward chaos" and leading the way in constructing a "community of developed nations."[6] From a different perspective, another liberal observer asserted that—contrary to the views of many commentators—after the Cold War, the United States still needed to engage in "covert" operations abroad from time to time. If it failed to do so, Washington might soon discover that adversaries had placed the nation at a serious disadvantage when it finally had to respond to challenges abroad.[7] Alternatively, many liberals believed that with the end of the Cold War fundamental changes occurred in the concept of "national security." If it was the case that American society no longer faced a Soviet threat, it *did* face a number of other, and often dangerous, external challenges to its security and well-being. And in some respects, these could prove to be even more formidable and difficult for Washington to meet successfully than the former Communist challenge.[8] Still another liberally oriented interpretation contends that American diplomatic leadership is imperative, if a more secure and peaceful international order is to follow in the wake of the Cold War.[9]

In describing the approach of the Clinton administration to foreign policy issues, another commentator used the term "a strategy of enlargement" to characterize its diplomatic orientation. Clinton's major goals appeared to be strengthening the bonds among the "major market economies" of the world; promoting democracy in the former Soviet Union; halting the proliferation of nuclear weapons throughout the world; and relying more heavily on the United Nations and other multinational institutions in achieving America's external goals.[10] Or, as another student of the nation's diplomacy has defined the objective of external policy, it is to create a viable community of democratic nations, in which war "is unthinkable."[11] Still another analysis of America's approach to international issues after the Cold War advocates a strategy of "preventive diplomacy" by the USA in dealing with global problems. Based upon an examination of several recent cases, this commentary concluded that intervention by the United States and other advanced nations *at an early stage* is required in order to avert the eruption of major regional and global conflicts.

With dynamic and timely diplomatic leadership by the United States, one study concludes, the prospects for international peace and security "should be closer now to realization than at any previous time in modern world history."[12]

This introduces us to the next approach to American foreign policy after the Cold War to be considered. We have described it by the term "liberal interventionism"; an alternative term would be "liberal internationalism." This is an orientation to international issues exhibited by those who approach global problems from the perspective of liberal ideology. Identified with such political leaders as Woodrow Wilson, Franklin D. Roosevelt, Harry Truman, John F. Kennedy, Jimmy Carter, and Bill Clinton, liberal interventionism occupies a prominent place in the annals of American diplomacy. And according to several studies of public opinion, despite memories of the Vietnam War, the concept of "liberal interventionism" perhaps comes as close as any term available to describing the approach of a majority of American citizens to many foreign policy issues following the Cold War.[13] It should be noted also that intensive pressure is sometimes exerted upon policymakers in Washington *by foreign governments* to pursue an interventionist course abroad.[14]

As is no less true of conservative opinion, it must be borne in mind that liberal thought is far from monolithic in approaching diplomatic questions.[15] Several developments in U.S. foreign policy during the late 1990s—as the diplomacy of the Clinton White House toward the Persian Gulf area, Bosnia, and China quite clearly illustrated—provided graphic examples of this reality. In these and other instances, the approach of the Clinton administration could be described as illustrating a policy of "moderate" or "limited interventionism" abroad. From Latin America to East Asia, executive policymakers relied on a series of moderate or controlled diplomatic and military responses to challenges facing the USA overseas. And in nearly all instances, President Clinton's diplomacy encountered discontent and opposition, not merely as might be expected from his avowed political opponents but also from liberal critics, many of whom demanded at times that the White House take more forceful steps, not excluding decisive military action, to promote and protect the nation's interests overseas.[16]

One of America's well-known Revolutionary War leaders once said that "the cause of America is in a great measure the cause of all mankind."[17] During World War I, President Woodrow Wilson observed that the nation's flag was not only the symbol of the American republic, but the flag "of humanity as well."[18] And in World War II, during Great Britain's darkest hour, Prime Minister Winston Churchill declared that his nation would fight alone against Hitler's Germany "until in God's good time the New World with all its power and might, sets forth to the liberty and rescue of the Old."[19]

After America entered the war, its leader, President Franklin D. Roosevelt, soon emerged as the acknowledged spokesman for the Allied cause; FDR and his advisers served as the source for most postwar planning and reconstruction. Roosevelt envisioned this new global conflict as something more than a military confrontation between the Axis powers and the Allies, caused by *Realpolitik* calculations. To his mind, it was an epochal struggle to remake the world and to usher in a new era of international peace, security, and well-being. Roosevelt's celebrated "Four Freedoms" epitomized his mind-set and provided a poignant illustration of the dynamic role he envisioned for the United States in creating a new and peaceful international system.[20]

For some two centuries, liberal individuals and groups have advocated an interventionist foreign policy for the United States.[21] During the heyday of isolationism, time and again liberal voices were raised in behalf of interventionist moves by the USA in responding to a broad range of problems and conflicts abroad. The isolationist era, in other words, was interspersed with numerous interventionist episodes frequently championed by liberal groups. Thomas Jefferson and his followers, for example, left no doubt that their sympathies lay with France in its ongoing struggle with Great Britain; and they openly espoused many of the principles of the French Revolution. (It might be noted, however, that many Jeffersonians also joined with Federalists in refraining from honoring the alliance with France, requiring the USA to give active military support to the French cause. There were, in other words, quite clearly limits upon the steps America should take to intervene in France's behalf.)

Several times during the nineteenth century, liberal opinion in America supported efforts by groups abroad to acquire greater political freedoms and to promote the cause of democracy against despotic governments. A celebrated case was the Greek rebellion against Turkish rule erupting in 1821. According to one diplomatic historian, American public opinion was gripped by "Greek fever"; policymakers in Washington faced mounting pressures to intervene directly in behalf of the struggle for Greek independence. (Once again, however, reiterating the nation's declared isolationist policy, policymakers stopped short of overt intervention to support the Greek revolt, and in the end the rebellion against oppressive Turkish rule failed.)[22]

One of the epochal developments in American foreign policy—the issuance of the Monroe Doctrine in 1823—can also be regarded as a conspicuous example of liberal interventionism.[23] The doctrine embodied two key ideas. One of these—expressing America's determination to avoid involvement in Europe's political quarrels and conflicts—was a forceful reiteration of the isolationist principle, explained more fully in Chapter 1.

The other idea was more relevant to our discussion of liberal interventionism. It warned the European powers against expanding their colonial empires in the New World. As the meaning and implications of Monroe's celebrated message were expanded in the years ahead, this admonition became broadened into a prohibition against the extension of foreign *political influence* within the Western Hemisphere. As a number of commentators on the Monroe Doctrine pointed out, the inescapable implication of this injunction was that, shielded by the growing power of the United States, the New World was destined to witness the emergence of democratic governments within the newly independent nations south of the border. The Monroe Doctrine, in other words, provided eloquent evidence of the prevailing view of citizens of the USA that their democratic system served as a model for foreign societies. And indeed with the passage of time, a number of Latin American republics did base their systems of government and politics on the model offered by the United States.

The years 1830 and 1848 witnessed a number of revolutionary upheavals on the European continent. As always, the sympathies of Americans were on the side of popular efforts to expanding political freedoms against restrictions by despotic government. A prominent case illustrating the point was provided by the visit of the Hungarian revolutionary leader, Lajos Kossuth, to the USA in 1851. Sometimes called "the George Washington of Hungary," Kossuth was given an overwhelmingly enthusiastic reception by the American people, who exhibited what was described as "Kossuth fever" during his travels within the USA. (Kossuth and his followers left the USA deeply disappointed and frustrated, however, because officials in Washington were *not* prepared to translate existing popular enthusiasm for his cause into tangible American support for the Hungarian people's revolutionary struggle against oppression by authorities of the Austro-Hungarian Empire. Along with others on the European continent, the revolutionary movement in Hungary soon collapsed.)[24]

A comparable episode occurred in the mid-1860s, when Italians were seeking to become politically unified and to establish a republic. Typifying foreign political figures who have looked to Washington for tangible support, Italy's great leader Giuseppe Mazzini described the USA as the "representative" of democratic forces throughout the world. Mazzini bluntly declared that the American republic served as "a Nation-Guide, and you must act as such." He urged American officials to aid "morally, and if necessary materially, your republican brethren everywhere the sacred battle is fought."[25] "Nation-guide" or not, the American society gave overwhelming moral support to Mazzini's cause—but little else.

Another dimension of American diplomacy before World War II illustrating the concept of liberal interventionism was Russian-American relations. For many years down to 1917, liberal opinion in the United States was outspokenly critical of the oppressive czarist regime, viewing it as the antithesis of democracy and as an especially objectionable species of despotism. Russia's appalling Gulag system for dealing with political dissidents, after all, had its origins in the czarist period.

Criticism of czarism within American society was spearheaded by a number of political commentators and organizations, including the popular lecturer and writer George Kennan, who pledged to lead a movement whose aim was to topple the hated czarist autocracy.[26] Kennan and his followers publicly advocated American support for violent resistance against czarist rule. One of America's most eminent literary figures—Mark Twain—supported this cause, declaring that "If such a government cannot be overthrown otherwise than by dynamite, then, thank God for dynamite"![27] Time and again Russian officials protested to Washington about the activities of such anti-czarist individuals and groups, but to no avail. (Throughout modern history, foreign governments have had difficulty distinguishing between the acts of private individuals and groups within the American society and the actions and official positions of the U.S. government in the foreign policy field.)

A related dimension of American diplomacy during the late eighteenth and early nineteenth century was interventionism in behalf of Jewish people abroad, especially those subject to anti-Semitic practices and policies in Russia and Eastern Europe. On several occasions, officials in Washington expressed their opposition to discrimination against the Jewish people to Moscow and other capitals—usually without avail. (For some inexplicable reason, America's solicitude about the condition of the Jews abroad did not extend to tangible steps designed to assist them during one of the darkest hours in their history —the Holocaust, or Nazi Germany's attempt to solve "the Jewish problem" once and for all.)[28]

When the czarist regime was finally overthrown in the revolution of 1917, President Woodrow Wilson did not conceal his enthusiasm for this turn of events. Wilson was certain (and one wonders on what evidence he based his conclusion) that the czarist political establishment had never really "represented" the will of the Russian people; and the president had great confidence that, at long last, Russia's new revolutionary government would soon join the ranks of the world's democracies.[29] (As every student of modern history is aware, after a few months the revolutionary regime led by Alexander Kerensky was in turn overthrown by the Bolshevik movement led by V. I. Lenin, marking the beginning of the Communist dictatorship that was to rule Russia for some three-quarters of a century thereafter.)

During the Wilson administration, another episode in the annals of American diplomacy serves as a dramatic example of liberal interventionism: relations with Mexico. Beginning in 1877, Mexico was governed (or the correct term perhaps was *misgoverned*) by one of the most oppressive and exploitive dictatorships in the history of Latin America, led Porfirio Díaz. During the long era of what was called "Diazpotism," political oppression, corruption, and flagrant mismanagement of Mexico's affairs were rife. The hated dictator was finally ousted in the long-awaited Mexican Revolution of 1911. Woodrow Wilson and other liberals in the United States were ecstatic: at long last, it was widely believed, one of the largest and most influential states within Latin America would take its place among the democratic nations of the world—an event that ought to have a beneficial impact upon other societies south of the border. But the new revolutionary government in Mexico had a short life span. Early in 1913 it was in turn toppled by a coup, and a new regime under Victoriano Huerta seized power. In effect, this regime proved to be a new form of "Diazpotism"—or perhaps even worse.

Denouncing the Huerta regime as "a government of butchers," President Wilson and other liberals vocally condemned its behavior and openly called for its ouster. (Wilson actually approached several European governments with a plan to intervene with armed forces to accomplish the objective, but the European nations showed little enthusiasm for the undertaking, leading the White House to abandon his project.)

Yet the lack of foreign support to accomplish his purpose did not deter President Wilson from taking other steps to determine Mexico's political destiny. One instrument his administration relied upon to achieve the goal was a new recognition policy. Reflecting Wilson's deep conviction that the Huerta regime lacked popular support, as long as he remained in the White House President Wilson refused to extend official American "recognition" to it. (Under traditional international law, recognition was customarily extended to new governments that were stable, were in fact governing their society, and were prepared to honor their international commitments.) In the years ahead, the Wilsonian doctrine of recognition—in effect, requiring that new governments abroad adhere to the principles of democracy before they were officially recognized by Washington—was relied upon time and again by American officials in the conduct of foreign affairs. Conspicuous examples were the refusal to grant recognition to the Communist government of the Soviet Union for many years after 1918; unwillingness to extend recognition to Communist-ruled China after 1948; and Washington's opposition to establishing normal diplomatic relations with Castro's Cuba after 1959.

Frustrated in his attempt to overthow the Huerta regime, finally President Wilson resorted to even more forceful measures—initiating one of the strangest and most traumatic episodes in the American diplomatic record. At length, in April 1914, supported by an enthusiastic Congress, President Wilson ordered the U.S. Navy to shell the city of Veracruz, with the obvious intention of forcing the overthrow of the obnoxious Huerta regime. After this act, open warfare between the United States and Mexico was averted only by the successful mediatory efforts of other Latin American nations. If anything (and it was a not unfamiliar phenomenon in other settings), U.S. military intervention in Mexico actually *strengthened* the Huerta regime's hold on political power. Irrespective of their feelings toward the existing dictatorship, the Mexicans deeply resented this effort by "the North American Colossus" to determine their political future. To this day, the ill-fated "Veracruz Crisis" casts a dark shadow over Mexican-American relations and has shaped Mexican attitudes about co-operation with the United States in behalf of interventionist undertakings within the hemisphere.[30]

This episode also illustrates another important principle often relied upon by liberals in their approach to foreign policy issues. This is the distinction, made by President Wilson in the Mexican case (as well as in responding to the actions of Imperial Germany during this period), between the aggressive or unlawful *actions of governments* abroad and *the attitudes of the people* in foreign societies with respect to international questions. Supposedly (and again a basic question exists concerning the evidence Wilson and his followers relied upon in drawing the distinction), in contrast to the actions of their political leaders, the ordinary citizens of societies abroad entertain only peaceful, friendly, and co-operative intentions toward other countries. In more general terms, for many liberals it was an article of faith that "people are the same the world over." On that premise, a primary cause of wars and international conflicts is the "lack of understanding" among the peoples around the world. It follows that the prospects for global peace and security will be significantly enhanced if peoples all over the world "get to know each other better."

Another important chapter in American diplomatic history that furnishes numerous examples of liberal interventionism is Sino-American relations.[31] As was pointed out in Chapter 1, the isolationist principle did not govern the policy of the United States toward Asia. Throughout much of the nineteenth century, American missionaries were engaged in winning converts to Christianity in China; and their activities were often directly or indirectly supported by officials in Washington. (The "Old China Hands" who played an extremely influential role in making U.S. foreign policy toward China and other Asian states during and after World War II often consisted of former missionaries or the children of missionaries to China.)

The basic premise of the missionary campaign of course was that a backward and misgoverned Chinese society needed and welcomed America's guidance in its quest for modernization. In brief, China came to be regarded as a kind of "ward" of the United States government, which served as China's mentor, benefactor, and protector from adverse forces at home and abroad. The ties that bound the United States and China were viewed as unique and strong. American opinion was enthusiastic about what was widely viewed (in large part, erroneously) as significant progress toward democracy in China.[32] This frame of mind by the American people and their leaders in large part explained why the belief existed that the USA had "lost China," when the Communist movement won the civil war in 1949.[33]

Before World War II, the most important principle governing America's diplomatic behavior in Asia was the "Open Door Policy," initially issued in 1899; the policy was reiterated and reinterpreted at frequent intervals down to World War II.[34] Initially, the Open Door concept meant that the United States pledged to maintain the "territorial integrity" of China, which was governed by a corrupt and ineffectual dynasty that was finally overthrown in 1912. Over the course of time, however, the Open Door concept became broadened into an American guarantee of Chinese political independence.

By the early twentieth century, the most ominous threat to the Open Door principle was posed by Imperial Japan's expansionist ambitions. For example, during World War I (taking advantage of the West's preoccupation with Imperial Germany's ambitions in Europe) Tokyo presented a list of "Twenty-one Demands" (or an ultimatum) to the new, but extremely weak, revolutionary government of China. As officials in Tokyo were amply aware, China's acceptance of these demands would have amounted to reducing the nation to a Japanese satellite. When he learned of Tokyo's action, President Wilson was incensed; and he demanded that the Japanese government rescind its ultimatum. Faced with adamant American opposition, Japan's rulers reluctantly complied.[35] (Tokyo's imperial ambitions of course were not abandoned; they were renewed several years later when Japan instigated the "Manchurian Crisis" of 1931–32, regarded by many observers as the opening phase of World War II.) Typically for liberal interventionists before the Second World War, most of those who enthusiastically endorsed the Open Door principle were extremely reluctant to translate their endorsement of the policy into tangible measures of support needed to attain the objective.[36]

Although isolationism remained the rule of American foreign policy down to World War II, as the Axis powers engaged in expansionism and intimidation of weaker nations, the sympathy of Americans were nearly always with the victims of international lawlessness. With each Axis advance at the expense of other nations, a rising tide of opposition began to sweep across America, gradually undermining the nation's historic isolationist stance. Hitler's absorption of Austria in 1938; Germany's incorporation of Czechoslovakia in 1939; Japan's aggressive moves against China, Korea, Indochina, and other countries in Asia—by the late 1930s, these developments had turned opinion in the USA against the Axis powers. Finally (and the passage of the Lend-Lease Program of aid to the Allies in 1941 may be taken as the turning point) the Roosevelt administration adopted an overtly interventionist approach in responding to the global political crisis.[37]

Following the Japanese attack against Pearl Harbor on December 7, 1941, and America's declaration of war against the Axis powers, the USA soon emerged as the leader of the Allied coalition, with President Roosevelt widely acknowledged as the spokesman for the Allied cause. In what might be viewed as the epitome of the liberal interventionist mentality, FDR informed British prime minister Winston Churchill that "There is in this global war literally no question, either military or political, in which the United States is not interested."[38] A conspicuous example of FDR's diplomatic initiative during the war was his firm opposition to European colonialism and his determination to liquidate Western colonial empires. Some commentators believe that Roosevelt regarded Western imperialism as a greater threat to postwar peace and stability than Soviet-led communism.[39]

During the war, the Roosevelt White House served as the center for the planning of a new, peaceful, and stable international order following the defeat of the Axis powers.[40] The establishment of the United Nations and other multinational institutions, such as the World Bank and the International Monetary Fund; the unconditional surrender, followed by the democratization, of Germany and Japan; the wartime attempt to maintain co-operative relations with Moscow; the decision to treat France and China as "great powers" for the purpose of postwar planning; the decision to develop the atomic bomb (followed by the decision of the Truman White House to use nuclear weapons against Japan)—these and other major wartime developments bore President Roosevelt's imprint.[41]

After victory in World War II was achieved, FDR's successor, Harry S Truman, continued most of his policies and engaged in new diplomatic undertakings requiring interventionist activities by the USA. For example, the Roosevelt and Truman administrations decided to support Chiang Kai-shek's Nationalist Party in China in its contest with the Chinese Communist Party for control of the government. Led by Mao Tse-tung, the Communist side ultimately won the civil war, despite massive material, diplomatic, and moral assistance by the USA to the Nationalist cause.[42]

Repeated efforts by the Truman administration to compel Moscow to respect the political rights of the people of Eastern Europe provide another example of the same tendency.[43] In more general terms, in the words of Secretary of State Dean Acheson, under the Roosevelt and Truman administrations, there occurred a "complete revolution in American foreign policy" vis-à-vis the isolationist era. In co-operation with its allies, the United States had created "such power that chances of peace would be immeasurably improved"; but if war should erupt again, "we had a first class chance to win it."[44] Other observers referred to the period following World War II as "the American century," in which the power of the United States would prove to be the decisive force in global politics.[45]

Yet the diplomatic undertaking that perhaps best exemplified the concept of an interventionist foreign policy occurred early in 1947, when (in connection with the Greek-Turkish Aid Program), the Truman administration adopted the "containment" strategy directed against the international Communist movement led by Moscow.[46] As envisioned by its instigator, George F. Kennan, the ultimate goal of containment was to bring about fundamental changes in the Soviet political system and its external behavior (Kennan called it the "mellowing" of the Soviet state).[47] By the early 1990s, with the collapse of Russia's Marxist system and the disintegration of its vast empire, it could be said that the fundamental objective of the containment policy had finally been achieved.

In 1948, the Truman White House proposed, and Congress passed, the multibillion-dollar European Recovery Program (or "Marshall Plan") providing American assistance for the reconstruction of war-torn Europe.[48] Then the following year—again largely upon Washington's initiative—the North Atlantic Treaty Organization (NATO) was established to provide security for Europe and North America.[49] NATO became the most important military pact to which the United States belongs. As we shall see, by the 1990s the "enlargement" of NATO had become a high-priority item on the American diplomatic agenda. The Truman administration also initiated the "Point Four Program" of aid to developing countries. Designed to promote the modernization of needy societies, Point Four was modified and reorganized a number of times in the years ahead, but in effect it remained a key component of U.S. foreign policy for a half-century or so thereafter.[50]

LIBERAL TENETS AND INTERVENTIONIST DIPLOMACY

Several basic tenets of liberal thought support an interventionist approach to American foreign policy.[51] For many of those approaching international issues from this perspective, as the only superpower left in the international system, the United States cannot insulate itself from problems and developments beyond its own borders. Inevitably, the well-being of American society itself is affected by the course of events abroad. As the experience of World Wars I and II forcefully illustrated, for example, sooner or later the security and well-being of American society are directly influenced by crisis conditions overseas. As merely one example, the Japanese warlords realized that in order to achieve their imperial ambitions, they would eventually have to confront the principal obstacle in their path—the United States. This realization led Japan's leaders to launch their epochal attack against Pearl Harbor. Hence America's painful discovery that it was impossible for it to live an insulated existence, safely protected within an isolationist shell from adverse developments abroad—if for no other reason than that other nations would not allow the USA to remain isolated from, and unaffected by, events beyond its own borders.

By the same token, in the liberal view the end of the Cold War permits no reversion to isolationism by the American nation. As many liberals widely assess it, in the future as in the past, the nation's failure to exercise global leadership can—and almost certainly will—lead to major external crises involving the nation's security and its diplomatic vital interests. To the minds of some liberal observers, America's mission in global affairs after the Cold War is to lead the way in creating a more "pluralistic" international system; alternatively, as another study defines it, America's diplomatic efforts should be directed at "satisfying basic human needs on a global scale."[52] What is demanded after the Cold War, another observer has contended, is forceful diplomatic initiatives by officials in Washington aimed at achieving nothing less than worldwide "democracy under American leadership."[53]

As in earlier periods, many liberals today reiterate their long-standing conviction that a cause-and-effect relationship exists between the spread of democracy throughout the world and the prospects for international peace and security. According to this theory, to the degree that democracy takes firm root outside the West, the prospects for peaceful and co-operative relations among nations are greatly enhanced. In order to achieve the goal, Washington must engage in "preventive diplomacy" designed to resolve regional and global crises at an early stage.[54]

Liberals believe that human nature is essentially benign, peacefully inclined, and receptive to beneficial change. Typically, liberal opinion is sanguine about the possibility of successfully reforming human institutions, such as existing economic and political systems; and as a rule, liberals are found in the vanguard of such reform movements.[55] To the liberal mind, change is not only inevitable; in most cases it is highly desirable and can be expected to lead to positive results. Moreover, in modern history political liberals have also exhibited great confidence in the ability of government to solve a long list of human problems.

Liberals nearly always subscribe to a rational approach to problem-solving at home and abroad. One of President Lyndon B. Johnson's favorite phrases, "Come now, let us reason together," describes the liberal mind-set in responding to challenges in both foreign and domestic affairs. With this state of mind, it is often difficult for liberals to accept the reality that foreign governments, political leaders, and political movements abroad often do *not* exhibit rationality (at least as those in the Western political tradition define it) in efforts to solve existing problems.[56] Consequently, those in the liberal tradition are often unprepared for the reality that a variety of irrational forces and influences in fact determines the diplomatic actions and policies of governments (including no doubt at times the actions of the USA).[57]

Another long-standing article of the liberal faith is the conviction that "the march of democracy" throughout the world is irresistible.[58] In this view, from a political perspective the natural political state of mankind is democracy. As the world's oldest democratic nation, the American republic not only serves as a beacon for others seeking to democratize their political systems, but bears the obligation to assist foreign societies in reaching the goal.[59] The primary objective of U.S. foreign policy, one analysis has concluded, must be to "extend democracy" on a global basis.[60]

The liberal mind also believes that there is a fundamental connection between the expansion of democracy throughout the world and the prospects for international peace and security. Liberal observers are fond of repeating their long-standing conviction that democratic nations do not wage aggressive war or intimidate their neighbors, and democratically elected governments are more inclined to settle their differences by peaceful means.[61] It follows that an essential step in bringing into being a peaceful and secure world is American leadership in promoting the concept of democracy around the globe.

A closely related tenet of liberal thought is devotion to the cause of human rights and freedom beyond America's borders.[62] Liberals are dedicated to "the rule of law," both within and outside of national boundaries.[63] Historically, they have been at the forefront in imposing restraints upon the actions of government and in expanding the rights of citizens. Those in the liberal tradition have played an active part in efforts to expand and strengthen international law. Customarily, they exhibit a high degree of confidence in international legal pacts and agreements, or what are often viewed as "contracts" entered into by governments throughout the world. And they are incensed when (as Adolf Hitler once said of a treaty, that it was a mere "scrap of paper") such legal obligations are not honored. (Perhaps no development did more to cause resentment, anxiety, and mounting opposition among Americans toward the Soviet Union after World War II than the unwillingness of Stalin's government to honor what Washington regarded as solemn and binding agreements requiring the Kremlin to respect the rights of the people of Eastern Europe. To President Harry Truman, the Soviet-dominated satellite system—maintained by the might of the Red Army—provided irrefutable proof that Moscow could not be trusted and was indicative of the Kremlin's aggressive intentions toward other countries.[64])

As emphasized earlier in our discussion, on the assumption that "people are the same the world over," liberals nearly always favor removing obstacles hindering "international understanding," which they view as a vital step in preserving global peace and stability. People-to-people movements, educational and cultural exchange programs across national boundaries, the elimination of barriers to expanding communication and travel across national frontiers—these are measures routinely favored by liberals as essential in making progress toward a peaceful and stable international system.[65]

Implicit in our discussion thus far is the rejection by liberals of the idea that war and conflict are the "natural" condition of international relations. To the argument that throughout history nations have been addicted to war, liberals answer that is a propensity that can and must be changed. The inclination to engage in war and violence has often brought once-powerful nations low—a prospect that faces the USA, unless it breaks the age-old pattern of behavior.[66] The United States, one study of its post–Cold War diplomacy has concluded, must lead the way in "delegitimizing war and the unilateral use of military force in relations among states."[67]

A pervasive liberal view is that war and conflict among nations are an outgrowth of poverty and the lack of "development" throughout the world, especially in societies south of the equator. Accordingly, the USA must take the initiative in overcoming these obstacles to global peace and security.[68] Immanuel Kant's blueprint for achieving a condition of "perpetual peace" has always had a powerful attraction for liberal minds.[69]

Liberal opinion is nearly always favorable toward steps by the United States and other nations to eliminate what are sometimes called the "indirect" causes of war and violence among nations. As liberals assess it, these include such conditions as pervasive poverty in most Third World nations; a high incidence of disease, epidemics, and other forms of ill health pervasive in societies south of the equator; famine, widespread malnutrition, and inadequate dietary levels in foreign societies; adverse social and economic conditions produced by natural calamities; and public attitudes of despair and hopelessness engendered by unproductive economic systems, low levels of employment, and inadequate incomes in societies abroad.[70] Such conditions can and do give rise to regional and international tensions and conflicts. With reference to domestic violence (which of course can sometimes involve outside countries), another major contributing factor is widespread and growing political disaffection and unrest, stemming from mounting opposition to the activities of despotic and corrupt governments abroad.[71]

At the same time, even while they advocate an active role by the United States abroad, most political liberals also recognize the need for certain constraints upon an interventionist American policy overseas. Since the Vietnam War, a frequently expressed admonition—a maxim endorsed by most segments of American public opinion after the Cold War—is that the United States cannot serve as "the policeman of the world." (Yet in many instances, this extremely general caveat lacks specific content. In practice, as we shall see, it often means that officials in Washington should refrain from engaging in interventionism in behalf of causes that are disapproved of by liberal and left-wing groups.)

Another constraint was underscored by President Bill Clinton's lament (after witnessing repeated and unsuccessful efforts to stabilize the Balkans) that, "I don't think the international community has the capacity to stop people . . . from their civil wars."[72] In other words, to Clinton's mind, some global problems are not susceptible to solution by the interventionist efforts of other nations. Indiscriminate interventionism abroad, Ronald Steel has asserted, is also incompatible with sound domestic policy. It distracts the attention of the nation's leaders from critical internal problems and needs, and it diverts resources that ought to be used at home to a variety of questionable undertakings throughout the world.[73]

At the same time, most liberals *do* accept the idea that the USA can and must "police" parts of the world. Washington is required to exercise police powers in responding to certain kinds of regional and global problems. For example, one study concluded that for the Clinton White House, the major problem confronting the USA abroad was the challenge arising out of adverse conditions in the global economy.[74] Or, as another study has expressed the idea, after the Cold War it is incumbent upon officials in Washington to engage in "less costly" and more "politically correct" forms of interventionism than has been true in the past.[75]

A wide variety of terms has been used to describe the approach favored by liberal spokesmen to global problems in the new era. These include "prudent internationalism," "selective engagement," "stringent selectivity," "cautious internationalism," and a foreign policy of "controlled moderation."[76] The individual who was in time to become President Clinton's secretary of state advocated a policy of "assertive multilateralism" for the United States after the Cold War.[77]

Most liberal interventionists acknowledge (in many instances, with evident reluctance) that military force is still an important component of national power.[78] (The Clinton administration, for example, relied upon military power to prevent new eruptions of violence in the Balkans and to "discipline" Saddam Hussein's regime in Iraq for using force against the Kurds.) Late in 1997, President Clinton ordered a major buildup of American military force in the Persian Gulf area in a confrontation with Baghdad over UN inspections of Iraqi territory for evidence of illegal weapons.

At the same time, many liberals were also persuaded that the utility of military force in solving global problems was declining. As a general principle, armed force should be relied upon by America's leaders to promote and protect its diplomatic interests only as a last resort.[79] If at times it becomes necessary for policymakers to project military power abroad, they ought to do so with more discrimination and selectivity than they have displayed in the past.

Another constraint upon American diplomatic activity after the Cold War is the need to act in close collaboration with the nation's allies and friends, and under the auspices of multinational and regional organizations. In the new era, one observer has contended, the United States must abandon its "autocratic style" in the foreign policy field. Instead, America must seek true "partnership" with other nations in its efforts to solve regional and global problems.[80] (The concept of "partnership" no doubt was given considerable impetus by the high degree of unity exhibited by the USA and its allies during the Persian Gulf War.)

Closer collaboration between the United States and other nations will contribute to two desirable results: it will impart greater "legitimacy" to America's use of force in efforts to achieve its diplomatic objectives; and it will go far toward ensuring that the costs of interventionist undertakings abroad will not be borne exclusively or mainly by the American people.[81]

SPECIFIC GLOBAL ISSUES

For those approaching postwar diplomatic issues from a liberal perspective, the European-American axis has long been the most important dimension of the nation's external policy. The end of the Cold War has not changed that fundamental reality.

With respect to U.S. policy toward the European continent, liberal interventionists advocate a number of specific undertakings for the United States. Few officials and observers in this group, for example, question the idea that the USA *remains* deeply and inextricably involved in European affairs. In the wake of the Cold War, Washington confronts a multitude of new problems and challenges in this dimension of its foreign relations, such as deciding the future of NATO; continuing the momentum toward European integration; dealing with the implications of a unified, economically powerful, and diplomatically assertive Germany; formulating a new policy toward non-Communist Russia; and responding to the ongoing crisis in the Balkans.[82]

Some liberal spokesmen believe that in the new era, the very concept of "Europe" must be redefined to include not only the nations of Western Europe, but also east-central Europe, Russia, and at least some parts of its former empire. Some observers are convinced that, realistically speaking, the concept of "Europe" must now be understood to embrace the United States and Canada. As one analysis has expressed it, the goal of Washington's European policy ought to be the creation of a new "community of nations" from Vladivostok to Vancouver.[83]

Similarly, the purpose (or purposes) of the North Atlantic alliance needs to be re-examined. Normally, alliances are directed against an identifiable "enemy" or threat. Now that the Cold War is over, who or what is the "enemy" confronting the members of NATO? What specific "threats" do its members face, and is there basic agreement on the subject among the NATO allies? What contribution can the Western alliance make in meeting such challenges as continuing upheaval and violence in the Balkans, conflicts and tensions between Russia and the former members of the USSR, and recurrent threats to the peace and stability of the Middle East?

Liberal voices have been loud in calling for the "extension" of NATO eastward by the admission of new members, perhaps in time even including Russia.[84] In July 1997, President Bill Clinton renewed his call for NATO's extension eastward, declaring that it would presage the emergence of "a democratic, peaceful, and undivided Europe for the first time in all of history."[85] In 1999, Poland, Hungary, and Czechoslovakia were admitted to membership in the alliance. On the issue of NATO's expansion, the concept was given significant impetus by the lobbying activities of ethnic minorities within the American society (a conspicuous case was the Polish-Americans), who pressured officials in Washington to extend NATO's security guarantees to "the old country."[86]

As has been true since the end of World War II, liberals widely support the concept of European regional integration and urge policymakers in Washington to give momentum to the movement. Progress to date in achieving the goal unquestionably owes much to American diplomatic initiatives.[87] As liberals assess it, organizations like the European Community (EC), the Western European Union (WEU), and the more recent Conference on Security and Cooperation in Europe (CSCE), play indispensable roles in preserving regional stability and security; and they look forward to even greater contributions by such organizations in the future, enabling the United States to reduce its activities (particularly its military contribution) on the European continent.[88] In this respect, many liberals join with conservatives in calling for greater "burden-sharing" by an increasingly prosperous and unified European continent.[89]

Similarly, liberals widely believe that Washington has an essential role to play in determining the political destiny of Eastern Europe after the Cold War. In the liberal view, with the collapse of their Marxist regimes, societies in this zone now have an unprecedented opportunity to install stable democratic governments; and the USA has an inescapable obligation to assist in achieving this goal. In turn, this will necessitate assistance by the USA in solving serious and often deep-seated economic problems which most Eastern European societies are experiencing in the transition from communism to democracy. Diplomatic and moral support by the United States, limited financial aid, the extension of NATO eastward, and admonitions to the Kremlin against future threats to the newly gained independence of its Eastern European neighbors—these are among the major steps Washington can take in its diplomacy toward Eastern Europe.[90]

In its relations with Moscow, liberals are widely convinced that the United States has a no-less-vital contribution to make in launching the "new Russia" on a course leading to stable democratic government, a free-market economic system, and a constructive role in regional and global affairs.[91] Liberal voices call on policymakers in Washington to use the power at their disposal to prevent (or at least to limit) civil war and political upheaval within the former Soviet empire.[92] This group was also persuaded that Washington ought to exert influence on Moscow to inaugurate needed internal political reforms—especially the installation and operation of a democratic political system—within Russian society.

Specifically, American policymakers should endeavor to avert two ominous developments within the new Russia: a resurgence of the Communist Party, which quite possibly could take control of the state if the incumbent government failed to solve prevailing problems; and a seizure of power by the Russian military, many of whose members were increasingly disaffected by chaotic conditions at home and by a number of serious challenges and the decline of Russian influence and prestige abroad. Either eventuality of course would constitute a serious setback for the quest for Russian democracy.[93]

A no-less-urgent goal of the United States and its European allies is ensuring that Moscow does not once again embark upon the path of expansionism and intimidation of its weaker neighbors. As one recent study observed, it is imperative that Russia's leaders abandon "visions of grandeur" and come to terms with the reality of the nation's reduced power base, a fact severely limiting Moscow's ability to intervene in the affairs of other nations.[94] (As our earlier discussion emphasized, traditionally liberals have contended that progress toward extending democracy abroad and the quest for international peace and security are inextricably linked. And to their minds, that old principle governs efforts directed toward ensuring that Russia's future diplomatic behavior is peaceful and constructive.) As one observer has expressed the idea, the goal of the USA and its allies after the Cold War should be to transform Russia into a "strategic partner" with the West in seeking to solve common problems.[95]

It might be noted that this issue is one (among many) concerning which officials in Washington have been subject to considerable foreign pressure to pursue an interventionist course abroad.[96] As one study has pointed out, for example, Russia's younger generation "looks to America" for enlightened leadership and guidance in solving many of their country's deep-seated problems.[97]

The long-standing and destructive crisis that accompanied the disintegration of Yugoslavia also elicited pleas by members of the liberal community that Washington "do something" to control conflict in the Balkans and to lay the foundations for lasting political stability in this unstable and violence-prone region. (As we shall see more fully in Chapter 6, when, where, and how the United States ought to intervene to restore peace and security in the Balkans proved to be a highly contentious issue within the Clinton administration and among President Clinton's liberal supporters. As often as not, Clinton's closest advisers were divided over the question of what course the USA ought to follow in responding to the recurrent crises in the Balkans.)

Some liberals complained that "Clintonism" (or what often appeared to be a policy of indecision and procrastination on the issue) "blights everything it touches." The result of such diplomatic uncertainty will be the death of "democrats and humanists" in the former Yugoslavia.[98] Or, as another analysis of the Balkans imbroglio contended, the Clinton White House should make clear to the world that the USA will use its power—not excluding its *military power*—to bring an end to genocide and violence in the region. Officials in Washington should declare plainly that this step is imperative in order to avert a regional war; they should declare unequivocally that America is deeply involved in the Balkans problems because of the need to protect its "values and interests"; they should indicate that an extended period of time may be required before the

USA is able to achieve its objectives; they should inform the American people that if the USA does not exhibit clear and decisive leadership on the Balkans questions, no other nation is likely to do so; and they should leave no doubt that the word of the United States government "is good," when it comes to honoring its commitments abroad. By contrast, instead of the decisive and dynamic action by Washington demanded by the Balkans crisis, more often than not the American people and foreign governments alike have heard "the hum of provincialism and the buzz of indecision" by their leaders in responding to the challenge.[99]

After the Cold War, stated a former diplomatic official, the United States remains "the principal guarantor of security and stability" in the Middle East.[100] Or as another observer has expressed it, in the new era Washington must continue its efforts to "lay the groundwork for a better, more stable Middle East."[101]

As has been the case for some fifty years, America's close ties with the State of Israel remain strong. Along with several of the Arab states, Israeli officials and citizens alike still look to Washington to play a vital mediatory role in removing the remaining obstacles to peace in the Arab-Israeli conflict.[102] As all participants recognize, such progress as has been made on that front owes much to the diplomatic initiatives of successive American presidents. In the new millennium, difficult and complex questions of course remain to be resolved. As in the past, deadlocks and delays continue to characterize negotiations between the two sides, and Washington's good offices are nothing less than essential in providing momentum to the search for peace.[103] Specifically, the USA has a vital contribution to make in convincing the government of Syria that it must abandon or scale down many of its regional ambitions and, at long last, negotiate a peace agreement with the Israeli government.[104]

Other liberals are concerned about nuclear escalation in the Middle East. The government of Iraq, for example, is widely suspected of continuing its effort to acquire a nuclear arsenal, in defiance of American warnings, UN directives, and world opinion. Under these circumstances, one liberal observer contended, the USA must be prepared at some point to take decisive action—not excluding reliance on armed force—to avert a new and ominous Iraqi-instigated threat to regional and global peace.[105] Similarly, another liberal source called on officials in Washington to take the steps required to prevent a dangerous buildup of chemical weapons by the government of Libya.[106]

Along with a number of other industrialized nations, America's own dependence upon the oil supplies from the Middle East remains high, in large part because for many years officials in Washington have neglected to adopt an effective national energy policy. For the foreseeable future, the American society's prosperity, well-being, and high standard of living will depend upon continued access to Middle Eastern oil reserves.[107] Economically and strategically, it would be difficult to think of a region in which the USA has a more compelling national interest.

After the Persian Gulf War, the power of the United States was no less indispensable in countering expansionist tendencies by Iraq and Iran, and in opposing the behavior of Middle Eastern governments and political movements that sponsor terroristic activities directed against the USA and other Western nations.[108] Some commentators believe that, in the years ahead, the USA will still play an important, if reduced, role in preserving the security of the region.[109]

Another liberally approved cause in the foreign policy field—highlighted by anti-American activities and political unrest erupting in Saudi Arabia in 1996—is encouraging the democratization of Middle Eastern political systems. After the Persian Gulf War, Saudi Arabia and Kuwait were high on the list of states in this category. A number of qualified students of Middle Eastern affairs believed that political pressures are steadily building up in these societies, and that a political explosion could erupt in them at any time.[110]

Most observers in the liberal political tradition also believe that after the Cold War, the United States continues to be deeply involved in East Asian affairs. (The classical isolationist stance, it should be recalled, never applied to U.S. foreign policy toward East Asia. Instead, the "Open Door Policy," demanding active American steps to preserve the peace and security of China, and bringing the USA more and more into conflict with an expansive Japan, governed Washington's approach to East Asian questions before World War II).[111] The term "Pacific century" has been widely used to call attention to contemporary East Asia's dynamism and rapid economic progress.[112]

The end of the Cold War has not altered Washington's keen interest and involvement in East Asian developments. Several specific problems and tendencies within the region will demand constructive responses by American policymakers. One of these is encouraging the emergence of Asian regional mechanisms and institutions, permitting these in time to assume greater responsibility for peacekeeping ventures and other collaborative undertakings.[113]

A different challenge lies in preventing North Korea's acquisition of a powerful nuclear arsenal, which its rigidly Communist regime might be tempted to use.[114] Washington is also called on to direct its efforts toward achieving a reduction of tensions, and eventual peace, between North and South Korea. Meanwhile, the USA must preserve its close military ties with the government of South Korea, which still faces almost daily provocations and overt signs of hostility from the north.[115]

Japanese-American relations are another vital dimension of U.S. foreign policy in East Asia.[116] American influence during the ten-year occupation of

Japan after World War II was of course crucial in democratizing the nation's political system and in restoring Japan to the community of nations.[117] For over a half-century, American military power has made an indispensable contribution to the preservation of Japanese security and to the overall peace and stability of East Asia. This reality was a key factor in enabling the Japanese nation to recover economically from the effects of the war in time to emerge as one of the most financially influential powers on the globe. Economically and commercially, if not politically, modern-day Japan qualifies to be called "a superpower."[118] In time, Japan became the largest source of foreign aid for many of Asia's less-developed societies.

It seems certain that eventually Japan's great economic and financial power will be translated into growing regional and global political influence.[119] As one well-informed commentator has predicted, East Asia, anchored in the power of Japan, "is destined to be a leading center of world power" in the twenty-first century. The emergence of a friendly and vibrant "Pacific community" would be a constructive development for the achievement of U.S. foreign policy goals in East Asia. By contrast, an East Asia that is "alienated" from the USA, and that emerges as a rival economic bloc, would pose "a serious threat to United States security and global stability."[120]

This likelihood presents Washington with another challenge to its diplomacy in East Asia: ensuring that Tokyo does not once again embark on the path of regional expansionism and hegemony. Many informed students of East Asian affairs believe that, in the final analysis, only the superior power of the United States can prevent that ominous development.[121] Conversely, preserving close Japanese-American relations (despite disagreements at times over trade policy questions) remains a key to peace and stability in East Asia.[122]

Similarly, in the years ahead, with more than two billion people a resurgent China will almost certainly become more powerful and diplomatically independent.[123] After almost a generation of estrangement, by the early 1970s the United States and the People's Republic of China had begun the process of rapprochement—a process initiated by the Nixon White House and completed by the Carter administration.[124] As Napoleon anticipated (and feared), the Chinese "sleeping giant" has awakened—with momentous consequences for international relations.

As far-reaching political, economic, and social changes occur in contemporary China, liberals are as always especially interested in the prospects for the emergence of a democratic system within the society and in efforts to gain greater respect for human rights by Chinese authorities. Liberal individuals and groups, therefore, have been active in urging officials in Washington to accord these goals high priority on the nation's diplomatic agenda.

Within the liberal community, two schools of thought with regard to Sino-American relations after the Cold War may be identified. One group—what might be called the "hard-liners"—views a resurgent China as posing a serious actual or potential threat to regional security and to the diplomatic interests and economic well-being of the USA. As one analysis concluded, China's leaders routinely violate international law and the rules of comity among nations; it is charged that Beijing "picks fights" with its weaker neighbors; a large volume of China's exports is produced by "prison labor"; the regime continues to repress internal dissent—and it does so "brazenly"; and China has now surpassed Japan as the largest contributor to America's trade deficit. Therefore, this study vocally condemns the "failure" of the Clinton administration's diplomacy toward China, which has done little or nothing to promote or protect America's diplomatic and security interests in Asia.[125]

Another study in this vein concluded that contemporary China "has the potential to exercise suzerainty over East Asia . . . to force the states in the region to defer to its preferences and wishes"; and Beijing "is in fact doing so." The PRC is exporting nuclear technology to Third World nations (such as North Korea); it is engaging in "sabre rattling" in its effort to impose its authority over Taiwan; and Beijing's ultimate aim is defined as trying to "control the South China Sea"—a vital waterway for oil shipments to Japan. In brief, the PRC "relentlessly builds up its military power and spurns democratization and human rights."[126] In the light of such realities, this school of thought concludes that the United States has no choice but to regard contemporary China as an adversary.[127]

An interesting development in recent years has been the change in the attitude of many American labor leaders and unions toward mainland China. Since the New Deal, unions have usually endorsed a liberal trade policy, calling for tariff reductions and the elimination of other barriers to expanded trade between the USA and other nations. With regard to contemporary Sino-American relations, however, a number of influential American labor unions have taken the lead in opposition to granting trade concessions to China and in supporting Beijing's proposed entry into the World Trade Organization (WTO)—moves that would unquestionably spur a larger volume of trade between the PRC and the USA. By the late 1990s, labor unions played a prominent role in widely publicized demonstrations directed against the Clinton administration's efforts to lower trade barriers with China and to encourage its participation in the WTO. As one analysis explained, some union leaders and members had become convinced—despite the steadily rising standard of living in the United States, made possible in part by a high volume of foreign trade—that the policy of "free trade is simply a vehicle for moving [American] jobs abroad." On that assumption, some unions want in effect to "slam the door" against the importation of foreign-made goods and services. (It should be noted, however, that other unions—along with farmers, agricultural workers, and those employed in the aircraft, chemical, electronics, and several other industries—were equally outspoken in *opposing* efforts to limit trade with China and other foreign countries.)[128]

The other school of thought—exemplified by the approach of the Clinton White House to mainland China—is what can be labeled "the dialoguists."[129] While not denying many of the realities identified by the "hard-line" school of thought, this latter group emphasizes other ideas that ought to be kept at the forefront in Washington's approach to China. One of these is the contention that, in the future as in the past, China's leaders are likely to be preoccupied with preserving their nation's security from real or imagined external threats. A leading one is the prospect that, if internal conditions deteriorate and the nation's authoritarian political system collapses, China will lapse into anarchy and chaos, as has occurred several times in the past. Being well aware of this prospect, authorities in Beijing will be motivated to co-operate with other nations (such as the USA and Japan) that are in a position to assist China in solving its internal problems.[130]

Another significant reality, as already emphasized, is that in recent years China has made significant progress politically, especially since the death of Mao Tse-tung. While contemporary China in no sense qualifies as a Western-style democracy, it has a considerably less repressive political system than was the case two decades ago.[131] Moreover, to the minds of some liberal observers, China's economic power may well be exaggerated. As one commentator has emphasized, Chinese society faces critical domestic problems in the years ahead—such as a mounting food shortage—caused by its still-high population growth and its stagnant agricultural production.[132] (It might be noted that the failure of the Soviet Union's agricultural policies was a leading factor in the economic demise of its Communist system.)

As this school of thought sees it, the most promising prospect for accelerating democratic tendencies within China is for the USA and other nations to conduct "a dialogue" with Beijing, thereby exposing the regime continually to political concepts, ideas, and criticisms from abroad.[133] To employ a term frequently used in an earlier period with regard to developments in Africa, Chinese society needs to be exposed to "the winds of change" if it is to advance economically and politically.

For these reasons, the "dialoguists" believe that little is to be gained by adopting a confrontational approach to Beijing. In the first place, there is no real evidence that an adversarial posture in dealing with the Chinese Commu-

nist regime achieves any useful diplomatic purpose. In the second place, no evidence can be adduced to show that such a policy actually influences the
behavior of China's leaders—except to make them more defensive and obdu-
rate in defending the government's actions at home and abroad. Based on the
evidence to date, the more Chinese authorities are placed "on trial" before the
world and are embarrassed by foreign criticisms of their behavior, the more resistant they appear to become to external pressures.

In the third place, a confrontational policy toward the PRC would almost
certainly find the USA lacking the support of its friends and allies abroad. As
has been true for many years in Washington's approach toward Castro's Cuba,
other nations would have no hesitation about defying American-instigated
trade boycotts and other sanctions directed against the PRC. And in the end,
that reality alone would virtually guarantee the failure of a hard-line policy.
Therefore, as one study of Sino-American relations concluded, the USA
should do everything possible to encourage the "peaceful evolution" of the
Chinese political system.[134]

Elsewhere in Asia, liberals believe that the United States should use its
power to promote democracy, often in the face of powerful adverse tendencies. Thus, one liberal source called on officials in Washington to support civilian officials in Pakistan against military-led attempts to defy their authority.[135]
Similarly, other liberal voices urged policymakers to lend their support to the
civilian-led government of Myanmar (formerly Burma) in its efforts to make
its authority effective within a society that has long been subject to military
rule.[136] By the same token, other liberal observers urged officials in Washington
to support the cause of democracy in South Korea, in the face of efforts by
authorities to suppress political dissent.[137]

After the Cold War, liberal individuals and organizations have also advocated a decisive American role in African affairs. The intensification of a long-
standing political crisis in Sierra Leone early in the new millennium served as
merely one more occasion for many liberals to call on Washington to "do
something" about violence gripping this key West African nation. (As always,
little unanimity existed about just what the USA and other nations were expected to do to resolve this conflict on the African scene.)[138] Afro-American
commentators and groups within the United States have naturally exhibited
great interest in the African dimension of the nation's diplomacy; they have
been outspoken and politically active in attempts to persuade the policymakers
to address a long list of urgent problems existing on the African continent.[139]

Three specific challenges posed by problems and conditions in Africa demand Washington's attention. One of these is engaging in ongoing efforts to
bring an end to tribal and ethnic conflicts in several African countries.[140] Such

conflicts have given rise to attendant and grave problems of malnutrition, conditions of rampant disease and ill health, and refugee relief and rehabilitation.[141] At the same time, a number of liberal observers also acknowledge that effecting long-term and lasting solutions to such problems on the African scene would almost certainly require America's involvement in the continent's political affairs for an indefinite period in the future.[142] And even then, there is of course no guarantee that Washington's intervention will be successful.[143]

Another difficult challenge facing most African societies for the indefinite future is conducting a successful campaign against poverty, disease, ignorance, and overall economic backwardness. To say that Africa's "development" since World War II has disappointed many students of the region's affairs would be to understate the matter.[144] Projections are that, for many African societies, these problems are becoming increasingly critical. According to most liberal observers, African societies have little chance of overcoming such adverse conditions without the generous assistance of the USA and other industrialized nations; and even then, the economic prospects for most African societies remain highly uncertain.[145]

President John F. Kennedy once declared that "Democracy is the destiny of humanity." As he defined it, America's unique mission in foreign affairs was to demonstrate that "economic growth and political democracy can develop hand-in-hand."[146] A test case of Kennedy's theory was provided by developments in Zimbabwe (formerly British-ruled Southern Rhodesia). Led by the African nationalist Robert Mugabe, independent Zimbabwe was enthusiastically welcomed to the community of free nations by most Western observers; it received generous financial support from the USA and other advanced nations; and it was widely cited as an leading example of an evolving "African democracy."

Then with the passage of time, as happened in certain other African societies, Mugabe and his followers seriously abused their power. Vast quantities of foreign aid were wasted; the country's resources were squandered; corruption became pervasive; and Zimbabwe was saddled with an increasingly oppressive political regime that tolerated no real opposition. What had once been almost unanimous praise by liberal observers in the United States turned into a chorus of condemnation of the Mugabe regime. The turn of events in East Africa put liberals in a real quandary regarding U.S. policy toward this key African society. They appeared to have no clear answers about how the United States ought to respond to what was by no means an isolated phenomenon on the African scene.[147]

As many liberals see it, a third and paramount goal of U.S. policy toward Africa remains promoting democracy and respect for human rights, in a political environment where the practice is frequently to the contrary. As a number of observers cautioned for many years, Washington must make a concerted effort to avoid "consorting with dictators" on the African scene (as well as elsewhere), as often occurred during the height of the Cold War. American officials must leave no doubt that a firm commitment to democracy by African governments and political movements is a prerequisite for co-operative relations with the United States; and some liberal commentators propose that Washington's assistance to African societies be explicitly conditioned upon clear evidence of such a commitment, as often prescribed as a precondition for assistance by the International Monetary Fund (IMF).[148] As we have seen, following this course would mean in practice that the USA would have no (or minimal) relations with most governments on the contemporary African scene. And such a situation would open officials in Washington the charge that, as in the past, they are "neglecting" the African continent! The end of the Cold War has not fundamentally altered the reality that, in most respects, the continent of Africa ranks at or near the bottom of America's regional concerns.

Late in 1993, an official of the Clinton administration declared that 1994 was going to be "the year of Latin America" in U.S. foreign policy. In the months that followed, at a hemispheric "summit meeting," President Clinton and other heads of government within the hemisphere pledged to create a regional free-trade area, to renew their efforts to promote democracy, to protect the environment within the hemisphere, and to improve social conditions throughout the New World. The White House believed that with the end of the Cold War, a new era had opened for Latin America. As one observer has expressed it, the other American republics no longer served as "pawns" of rival superpowers; they had become free to concentrate on internal and hemispheric problems.[149] Yet informed commentators are no less aware that—despite such promising developments—social, economic, and political problems existing within the region often threaten to outstrip progress made in addressing them.[150]

In its approach to Latin America, according to a number of liberal observers, Washington was required to demonstrate leadership in solving a number of critical hemispheric problems. For example, in one Latin American state after another—Guatemala, Mexico, Brazil, Venezuela, to name only the more prominent cases—the societies were in the grip of economic crises; and these in turn contributed to high levels of social tension and political unrest and instability.[151] The initiative exhibited by the Clinton White House in "rescuing" Mexico from an acute financial crisis was hailed as a promising step, benefiting not only the nation's nearest southern neighbor, but with positive economic results for other Latin American nations as well. Nevertheless, the economic future of Mexico remains precarious.[152]

Despite the Mexican case, for the most part in recent years officials in Washington appeared to be largely indifferent to problems existing south of the border.[153] A pervasive problem is endemic poverty in a number of Latin American societies. While some segments of Latin America's population have unquestionably "developed" and improved their standard of living significantly since World War II, other groups toward the bottom of the income scale have made little or no progress. For those in the latter category, "national development" remains little more than a slogan, conferring few tangible benefits on millions of underprivileged people.[154]

Another adverse tendency in most Latin American societies is runaway population growth. From Mexico to Chile, the "population explosion" threatens to nullify economic gains for many Latin American states (it is a primary cause of ongoing and perhaps increasing political unrest, for example, in Mexico).[155] If not reversed, in one Latin American society after another, runaway population growth could doom national development programs and efforts to improve living standards to failure.

Still another persistent challenge is the removal of barriers to trade by Latin American nations, including those impeding the sale of their products in foreign markets (not excluding markets in the USA). The Clinton administration's initiative in obtaining congressional approval for the North American Free Trade Agreement (NAFTA) was a highly significant step in this direction.[156]

Moreover, while a number of regional institutions and mechanisms have been established within the Western Hemisphere, for the most part, these remain feeble and only partially effective. This is especially true insofar as peacekeeping operations within the hemisphere are concerned. To date, much as they might resent interventionist behavior by "the North American Colossus," Latin American governments have been unable to agree upon a substitute for unilateral intervention by the USA in efforts to preserve regional peace and stability.[157]

Finally, as in external policy toward other regions, political liberals are keenly interested in the future of democracy within the Western Hemisphere. We have already alluded to President Woodrow Wilson's determination to teach the people of Mexico "to elect good men." Wilson acknowledged that achieving this goal might require repeated interventions in the affairs of its southern neighbor until its people "learn to vote and rule themselves."[158] Liberals since Wilson's time have not lost their zeal for democratizing Latin America, as well as other regions, as illustrated by U.S. intervention in Haiti during the Clinton administration.[159] One contemporary observer, for example, has asserted that promoting democracy abroad ought to become the "centerpiece" of American foreign policy in the post–Cold War period.[160] Another analysis contends that the foremost diplomatic mission of the USA is to "extend democracy" around the globe—an objective which, in this view, enjoys overwhelming public support.[161]

As our earlier discussion emphasized, time and again in modern history liberals have expressed the conviction that a direct correlation exists between the "march of democracy" throughout the world and the prospects for international peace and security.[162] Within the Western Hemisphere, at intervals since World War II officials in Washington have been euphoric about the progress toward democracy witnessed south of the border. (All too often, however, nascent democratic systems in Central and South America have in time succumbed to militarism or other forms of authoritarian governance.) Since the early nineteenth century, the people of Latin America have embraced the democratic ideal; and progress in creating democratic institutions and processes has unquestionably been made within most Latin American societies.[163]

Yet even today, as a generalization, democracy within the other American republics remains fragile. To employ a term from physics, in most cases Latin American democratic systems exist in a state of "unstable equilibrium": they exhibit a limited capacity to maintain their balance in the face of a number of adverse tendencies threatening their existence. Throughout the Caribbean and South America, civilian leaders confront formidable domestic problems, rendering their ability to govern effectively, and to retain popular support, highly questionable. To the liberal mind, protecting and strengthening democratic institutions and practices within the hemisphere—not excluding at times *by relying upon military force*—is a challenge that has not disappeared with the end of the Cold War.[164]

Although today, as in the past, they advocate interventionist behavior by the United States in approaching certain global issues, liberal voices are heard calling upon national leaders to concentrate upon America's domestic agenda. One analysis of public attitudes toward external affairs found broad public support for an "internationalist" foreign policy. However, citizens were also committed to the idea that the nation's efforts abroad must support American society's domestic needs.[165] A study of the Clinton administration's diplomacy concluded that the president "is at his best when there is a domestic economic dimension to an international problem."[166]

Throughout the nation's diplomatic history, one liberal spokesman after another has emphasized that American society future will be determined by its ability to respond constructively to crucial domestic problems and concerns.

By contrast, a "strong" or active foreign policy has frequently been regarded by those in the liberal tradition as a serious distraction from this dominant quest (a viewpoint identified especially with groups like the Populist Party and the "Bryan Democrats" before World War I).[167] Indeed, some segments of liberal opinion have denounced an activist foreign policy as a deliberate tactic relied upon by the Eastern-dominated political establishment to avoid facing and solving pressing domestic problems, especially those involving disadvantaged groups. At any rate, traditionally and in the contemporary era, few informed students of the nation's diplomacy doubt that an indissoluble relationship exists between domestic issues and forces and the nation's activities abroad.[168]

Liberal commentators call attention to several important aspects of this vital relationship. In the first place, there ought always to be a clear and evident connection between what the United States government does abroad and the well-being of American society. As in all aspects of national policy, developments in foreign affairs should promote "the general welfare."[169]

In the second place, a prerequisite for diplomatic success—underscored by the Vietnam War experience—is the need for legitimacy regarding the nation's conduct abroad. In the final analysis, no foreign policy can succeed without a firm basis of public support. Whatever the elusive phrase "the national interest" may mean precisely, in the liberal view it clearly demands that the nation's diplomatic efforts contribute in some way to the benefit of American society.[170]

In the third place, the connection between domestic and foreign affairs is important because internal political stability and tranquillity are essential for a successful policy abroad. As the Vietnam War conclusively demonstrated, diplomatic objectives are unlikely to be achieved when a high degree of public disunity and uncertainty exist about the nation's conduct overseas. For example, whether the president's actions and statements actually represent the will of the American people is a fundamental question that foreign governments and political movements will ask concerning the nation's diplomatic activities. In the well-known phrase from the Declaration of Independence, the activities of the nation's leaders must have "the consent of the governed," or in the end they will also certainly fail.

CHAPTER 6

THE PRAGMATIC FOREIGN POLICY OF
PRESIDENT WILLIAM CLINTON

W HEN HE ADDRESSED THE PARLIAMENT OF SOUTH AFRICA EARLY in 1998, President Bill Clinton declared that the United States had "a profound and pragmatic stake" in the nation's democratic development. He called for "genuine partnership" between the two nations in an effort to solve mutual problems.[1] Several years earlier, in a speech to the United Nations, President Clinton informed the world forum that in the future the United States would become deeply involved only in global problems that are "containable, manageable, cheap and close-ended," except in cases posing a direct threat to American security. In effect, President Clinton modified President John F. Kennedy's widely quoted statement of American goals abroad. Under Clinton's direction, as one commentator expressed the idea, the USA would "pay only some prices, fight only some foes, and bear only some burdens in the defense of freedom."[2]

Referring to the attempt by the NATO allies to bring peace and security to Kosovo, Secretary of State Madeleine Albright cautioned against attempts to extract a universal principle of American foreign policy from that effort. According to this official, any future decision about whether the United States would engage in what was called "humanitarian interventionism" would be "made on a case-by-case basis after weighing a host of factors." In other words, Madeleine Albright was convinced that the concept of "do-ability" ought to guide the administration's approach to specific foreign policy issues. In every case, the question ought to be whether the USA "can do good in the world," that is, whether, on the basis of existing facts and conditions, the outcome of the application of American power abroad is likely to be positive and constructive. If not, presumably the USA should refrain from such intervention. Her view was that all "circumstances are unique."[3]

President Clinton's National Security Adviser, Sandy Berger, concurred. Before engaging in interventionism abroad, he declared, "the United States needed to weigh its national interest in a country before deciding to employ military power."[4] A member of the U.S. Senate observed that, with the end of the Cold War, the nation's foreign policy had to be "of necessity ad hoc." In his judgment, in an increasingly complex global environment, it was simply not possible to formulate and adhere to "a totally coherent foreign policy" that was applied worldwide.[5]

From a different perspective, an analysis of public attitudes on foreign policy questions found that citizens favored an approach to global problems that could accurately be described by the term "pragmatic internationalism." By the 1990s, citizens quite clearly wanted to avoid "another Vietnam" or "overinvolvement" in the affairs of other countries; and they believed that domestic problems must be given high priority by officials in Washington.[6] Yet the people were also convinced that the United States remains a superpower, and at times the nation has no choice except to use its vast power for the purpose of influencing the course of events abroad—in other words, public opinion was *opposed* to particular forms of interventionism overseas, while it also *favored* interventionist behavior by the USA in responding to certain kinds of challenges beyond its own borders. The term "pragmatic" accurately described overall public attitudes in the foreign policy field.[7]

Critics, no less than supporters, of the Clinton administration's foreign policy used terms like "pragmatism," "incrementalism," and "ad-hocism" to describe Washington's approach to global problems. As one right-wing observer assessed it, in the post–Cold War period the United States "shouldn't be anti-interventionist all the time, or pro-interventionist all the time." Instead, the USA ought to become involved in crises overseas only when its vital diplomatic and security interests are clearly at stake. And he added an important proviso, which many other conservative critics also endorsed: once policymakers have decided to commit the nation's power overseas, then "we must prevail." To his mind, this approach was "synonymous with a strategic view of the world."[8]

Another observer has lamented that the Clinton White House lacked any kind of "farsighted plan that would give the country a clear sense of direction" in the foreign policy field.[9] In the same vein, a different commentator complained that the Clinton administration appeared to be without a "geopolitical compass" by which to chart a steady and predictable diplomatic course.[10] In his administration's response to the ongoing crisis in the Balkans, another observer deplored the fact that the Clinton White House "provided no steady leadership." President Clinton was "like a cork bobbing about on the waves"; his policy "was all over the place."[11] According to another commentator, what was sometimes referred to as "the Clinton Doctrine" was in reality no doctrine at all. Clinton's guiding principle in external affairs appeared to be nothing more than "expediency and an ingrained aversion to conflict." In effect, his diplomatic "doctrine" was "whatever you have to do right now to get by."[12] Another observer complained that, in order to discover what the administration's "foreign policy" actually was, it had "to be checked hourly."[13] And an experienced Democratic legislator was unable to discern any kind of "organizing principle" that integrated the separate and disconnected moves of the Clinton White House abroad. Clinton and his advisers appeared incapable of providing clear answers to such questions as, "What threatens the United States?" and the corollary question of what the nation ought to do about it.[14] Similarly, an experienced military officer found Bill Clinton to be a "vacillating commander in chief," who would be remembered for his "piecemeal deployment of U.S. armed forces abroad in behalf of unclear diplomatic objectives."[15] Another student of national security policy indicted the Clinton administration for exhibiting "strategic aimlessness" in responding to a series of international crises. When it was examined closely, the administration's "foreign policy" was found to consist of a "piecemeal, ad hoc, reactive pastiche of opportunistic rhetoric, and expedient motion."[16]

PRAGMATIC TENETS AND MAJOR DIMENSIONS

In their different ways, these judgments underscore the central idea of this chapter: the essentially pragmatic nature of President Clinton's approach to foreign policy questions. For many students of American affairs, the designation "pragmatic" is admittedly often mystifying and difficult to define clearly. A major reason is that the term has two levels of meaning: it possesses a number of vernacular connotations, or one set of meanings in ordinary discourse; and it also has different connotations in the philosophical mode of thought that emerged in the United States in the late nineteenth century. Looking initially at the term's connotations in everyday discourse, pragmatism has both a negative and a positive dimension.

One of Shakespeare's characters alluded disparagingly to another as "that damn'd pragmatist." As the quotation implies, the adjective "pragmatic" may sometimes be used as an epithet. Describing someone as a pragmatist may imply that the individual is opportunistic and manipulative, excessively ambitious, or indifferent toward ethical and moral constraints governing human conduct. This historic connotation of the term, we may add, is infrequently encountered today.

In its vernacular dimension, the term pragmatist also has a number of positive aspects. A leading student of Chinese affairs, for example, has called for an American approach to the PRC that is governed by the principle of "common sense," one that takes full account of the possibilities, realities, and limitations inherent in the equation of Sino-American relations.[17] Other connotations of a pragmatic mentality include such terms as businesslike, practical, factual, involved, realistic, sensible, non-theoretical, and actively engaged in solving concrete problems.

To qualify as a "pragmatic" approach to external problems, the nation's policy must satisfy one or more of the following criteria. First, a pragmatic approach means that policymakers decide each case "on its merits." By definition, a pragmatic orientation to problem-solving is tantamount to the absence of an overall diplomatic strategy or theoretical framework applicable to the nation's diplomatic activities from the Western Hemisphere to East Asia. More than one official or informed student of the American foreign policy process, however, has questioned whether the application of such a diplomatic grand design is either possible or desirable in the complex post–Cold War global environment.[18]

This leads to a second important characteristic of a pragmatic approach to diplomatic questions: its essentially ad hoc or incremental nature. (In the philosophical tradition, some devotees of pragmatism in fact preferred to call this mode of thought "incrementalism.") In popular usage, pragmatically motivated decisionmakers endeavor to solve "one problem at a time"; they are preoccupied with the solution of here-and-now, immediate issues, rather than with constructing grand theories or engaging in long-range diplomatic planning.[19]

A third important connotation of a pragmatic orientation to foreign affairs is the avoidance of ideological extremes and polar positions. The pragmatic mentality is often viewed as synonymous with a "centrist" or "balanced" approach to solving internal and external problems.[20] For example, in the debate over America's international role after the Cold War, pragmatists reject both the extreme isolationist and the interventionist positions. They emphatically disagree with the idea that, following its victory in the Cold War, the United States can in effect "withdraw from the world." At the same time, they also part company with those who believe that, after the collapse of the Soviet Union, the USA can impose its own values, and its unique political and economic system, indiscriminately throughout the world.

In other words, a pragmatic policy represents a compromise between these two polar positions. For example, a diplomatic pragmatist may at times take an isolationist or neo-isolationist position (as in wishing to avoid deep involvement in Africa's deep-seated crises and problems, or having the USA play a leading role in certain peacekeeping ventures around the world). Yet in some instances, devotion to a pragmatic foreign policy may also dictate selective interventionism (as in the Balkans, the Persian Gulf region, or the Caribbean area).

Fourth, in popular usage, a pragmatic approach to problem-solving requires decisionmakers to "face facts" realistically; to be responsive to circumstances and events as they exist; to avoid Utopian schemes and expectations; and to adapt the nation's foreign policy flexibly and creatively to what are often rapidly changing and unanticipated events and conditions confronting the United States abroad.[21] The old military maxim—"Expect the unexpected"—comes to mind as an applicable pragmatic guideline for diplomatic action.

This conception of pragmatic diplomacy means that officials must make a concerted effort to be well and accurately informed about conditions and events abroad. In turn, this requirement necessarily demands the existence and effective operation of a well-informed and experienced diplomatic corps.

Another essential element is the existence and effective operation of an intelligence system designed to provide policymakers with pertinent, current, and accurate information about conditions and problems beyond America's borders, and to present officials with a range of policy options for responding to them. For their part, in arriving at decisions, the president and the members of his advisory circle must avoid ideological rigidity and fixed *a priori* positions when they formulate and implement external policy. Policymakers must be receptive to the information and advice provided them by the intelligence community, by area specialists, and by others who are in a position to contribute insights into a particular set of conditions or events overseas.

A fifth connotation of pragmatic decisionmaking is that it requires the formulation and careful weighing of possible alternatives, often referred to as "policy options." In effect, pragmatically based decisionmaking employs the concept of "cost-benefit analysis" so familiar to economists. More often than not, perhaps, the policy that emerges from the process of pragmatic decisionmaking may be the "least of evils," or the course of action that has the fewest defects and negative consequences relative to all other alternatives.[22]

The model from post–World War II diplomatic experience that stands out in this regard is the one employed by the Kennedy administration during the Cuban Missile Crisis of 1962.[23] After the president was given irrefutable evidence by the intelligence community of an ongoing buildup of Soviet missiles in Cuba, he and the members of his foreign policy team formulated and carefully considered several possible responses to what was viewed as an extremely ominous development close to America's own shores. Possible alternatives ranged from doing nothing (in effect, overlooking the escalation of Soviet military power in Cuba), to launching a full-scale air attack designed to wipe out Russian missile bases on the island.

In the end, and after the most careful and objective evaluation of the pros and cons of each possible course of action, the Kennedy White House chose a response that fell between these extremes. Washington imposed a naval blockade against Cuba, and it warned both Moscow and Havana in the strongest possible terms about the possible consequences of a continuing threat to hemispheric peace and security. As all students of American diplomatic history are aware, the strategy worked: the Cuban Missile Crisis resulted in a dramatic diplomatic victory for the Kennedy White House.

A sixth characteristic of pragmatic decisionmaking relates to perhaps the core meaning of "pragmatism" as an influential school of thought in the modern philosophical tradition. Above all, the pragmatist is interested in the results achieved by a particular policy or course of action at home and abroad.[24] A foundationstone of pragmatic thinking has always been the idea that the lessons derived from experience provided the only reliable guide for testing the validity of truth of an idea or proposition. Irrespective of its ideological or logical merits, pragmatists believe that to be accepted as true, an idea must pass the test of experience in the realm of human affairs. That is to say, its value or usefulness or "truth" is ultimately determined by its observable results or effects.

This means, of course, that the pragmatist is interested above all in how a given policy *actually works*. In practice, how does it promote the national interests of the United States? What are the demonstrable effects associated with it? What are its most significant positive and negative consequences? In turn, answering such question requires periodic review and re-evaluation of existing policies, accompanied by a willingness to make changes in those that no longer serve the nation's interests at home and abroad.

Another important tenet of pragmatic thought (one especially prominent in the teachings of William James) is that the members of society must constantly be engaged or involved in efforts to solve human problems.[25] In the pragmatic view, a stance of isolationism or non-involvement or *immobilism* in the face of foreign and domestic challenges and threats to human well-being is not permissible. The diplomatic activism of the Clinton White House—its "engagement" with a long list of global and regional problems—is clearly in keeping with this key pragmatic axiom.

A related pragmatic tenet is the concept of *meliorism*. This means that, in the pragmatic perspective, very few human problems can be "solved" in any definitive sense.[26] If most human problems cannot be eliminated, however, they can and should be ameliorated, lessened, improved, and made endurable.

Pragmatic thought thus stands in clear opposition to two contrary ideological positions. On the one hand, it rejects Utopian schemes for totally remaking human society. By contrast, the pragmatic mind-set also differs from the position of many conservatives who question whether beneficial change in the human condition is either possible or desirable.

Still another pivotal idea in pragmatic thought is the concept of the "pluralistic universe," conspicuously associated with the teachings of William James.[27] As the pragmatic mind conceives it, the universe consists of an infinite variety of dichotomous, contrary, dynamic, and often mystifying phenomena and forces.[28] Some of these are positive and beneficial for human well-being, while others are negative and at times highly inimical to the human condition. (A familiar example of this phenomenon is nuclear energy. On the one hand, it has made possible momentous and often highly beneficial developments in the practice of medicine, saving countless lives. On the other hand, it has presented society with the awesome and continuing problem of controlling nuclear weapons and preventing a global holocaust.) By the same token, the post–Cold War global political environment poses many dangers for American society, while concurrently offering numerous opportunities for creative and positive activities by the United States.

As the case studies that follow will indicate, the Clinton administration's approach to external affairs implicitly accepted the concept of the "pluralistic universe." In one instance after another, the president and his advisory circle believed that after the Cold War, numerous opportunities existed for beneficial American interventionism or "engagement" in efforts to solve global and regional problems. By contrast, as policymakers of the Clinton administration saw it, other aspects of a highly pluralistic global environment quite clearly militated against successful interventionist efforts by the United States. In other words, the essentially pluralistic nature of the post–Cold War political milieu called for discrimination, selectivity, and care in the application of American power abroad.

Finally, the pragmatic approach to truth is what might be called "ideologically omniverous." Pragmatists recognize that nearly all systems of thought have something to offer in the solution of human problems, and they have not been reluctant to draw freely from a wide range of highly diverse sources.[29] The epitome of this state of mind, of course, was Franklin D. Roosevelt's New Deal—a program that was an ideological melange of ideas taken from an extraordinarily diverse range of sources. FDR's approach to existing national problems was ideologically mixed, flexible, experimental, and creative in its continuing efforts to respond to the challenges confronting American society at home and abroad.[30]

Similarly, in this respect, it is possible to say that the Clinton administration's approach to foreign affairs has been a kind of diplomatic New Deal. For instance, President Clinton and his aides more than once expressed admiration for the Wilsonian tradition and other examples of the American society's idealistic legacy.[31] And they have also invoked the thought of other idealists, such as Franklin D. Roosevelt, John F. Kennedy, and Jimmy Carter, in their approach to certain international and regional issues.

At the same time, the diplomacy of the Clinton White House no less reflected certain *Realpolitik* calculations, with its emphasis upon the central importance of national power and national interest. During Clinton's last year in office, for example, the White House recommended the largest increase in national defense spending witnessed since the Reagan era.[32] Under Clinton's direction (and despite the contrary expectation of many liberal groups), the nation's military budget remained at an extremely high level; and some of his supporters (not to mention his right-wing critics) were convinced that defense spending is still *too low* relative to America's global obligations and commitments. In the Balkans, in the Persian Gulf area, in Haiti, in the Taiwan Straits,[33] in counter-terrorist activities—in these and other instances, the Clinton White House did not hesitate to use (or in some cases, threaten to use) military force to protect the national interest and to achieve America's foreign policy objectives.

With this summary of pragmatic tenets in mind, we turn to an examination of four case studies illustrating the application of a pragmatic approach to diplomatic problem-solving by the Clinton White House.

IRAQ AND PERSIAN GULF SECURITY

The Clinton administration's responses to a continuing challenge posed by Saddam Hussein's government in Iraq illustrated a number of pragmatic ideas and tenets. On August 2, 1990, Iraqi troops invaded the oil-rich Emirate of Kuwait, thereby triggering what came to be called the Persian Gulf War.[34] In overrunning his weaker neighbor, Iraqi dictator Saddam Hussein sought to gain control over some 20 percent of the world's known oil reserves; and Baghdad's move posed an ominous threat to the world's largest oil producer, the government of Saudi Arabia. Iraqi aggression, therefore, constituted an extremely grave threat to the security and diplomatic interests of the United States and its allies, along with a number of Third World nations.[35]

During the fall of 1990, Washington implemented a wide range of measures—diplomatic negotiations, UN resolutions, and an economic embargo—

aimed at securing the withdrawal of Iraqi troops from Kuwait. The Bush administration sought and got permission to deploy American armed force in several Persian Gulf states. Deterrence, however, soon turned to preparations for more active steps to compel withdrawal of Iraqi forces from Kuwaiti soil, as Baghdad remained contemptuous of world opinion.

In justifying the need for a military buildup in the Persian Gulf area, President Bush articulated several policy goals, including (1) the immediate and unconditional withdrawal of all Iraqi troops from Kuwait; (2) the restoration to power of the legitimate Kuwaiti government (immediately after Iraq's aggression, most Kuwaiti officials went into exile); (3) the protection of American lives in the region; and (4) the preservation of regional security and stability. Bush would later add another goal: (5) dismantling Iraq's growing arsenal of nuclear, chemical, and biological weapons and preventing its acquisition of new weapons of mass destruction. This last objective would become the focus of Washington's policy toward Iraq during the 1990s.[36]

When peaceful means of securing Baghdad's compliance with UN resolutions mandating withdrawal of its forces from Kuwait failed to produce the desired result, only one option was left: the application of military force. With the approval of both the United Nations and the American Congress, on January 15, 1991, President George Bush ordered the armed forces to launch military strikes against Iraq.[37]

An intense six-week bombing campaign by the United States and its allies served as a prelude for a massive ground offensive ("Operation Desert Storm"). In only one hundred hours, the military forces of the allied coalition scored a massive victory over Iraqi troops and liberated Kuwait from Baghdad's control.

Although the Persian Gulf War represented one of the most lopsided victories in the nation's military history, the period following a ceasefire agreement left several issues—principally, Baghdad's development and possession of weapons of mass destruction—unresolved. Moreover, although his regime sustained an overwhelming defeat, Saddam Hussein continued to hold the reins of political power in Iraq. Efforts by both the Bush and Clinton administrations to change this reality invariably failed.[38]

Despite the change of administration that occurred after the election of 1992, American policy toward Iraq exhibited considerable continuity. The Clinton administration's main goals in dealing with Baghdad were to contain Iraq and to prevent it once again from jeopardizing regional security and stability; and to make the Iraqi government adhere to the terms of the 1991 ceasefire agreement, especially with regard to prohibitions against the development and possession of modern weapons of mass destruction.[39]

In assessing the Clinton administration's diplomatic and security moves toward Iraq, it is reasonable to conclude that they were characterized not so much by a theory of action or preconceived strategy as by *reactions* to developments in the Persian Gulf area with which Washington was confronted. Saddam Hussein's intransigence and repeated provocations caused the United States to be continuously involved in the region. For nearly a decade, UN-imposed sanctions against Iraq have remained in place (although they were violated on all sides). Despite the crippling effects of these sanctions upon the Iraqi economy (and the hardships were endured mainly by the Iraqi people), Saddam Hussein's regime survived and managed to evade most external constraints on its ambitions.[40]

Only three months after Bill Clinton entered the Oval Office, Saddam Hussein put the new president to the test, in order to take the measure of his opponent. In April 1993, during a visit to Kuwait by ex-president George Bush, evidence was discovered of an attempt by Iraqi intelligence operatives to kill the former president.[41] In response, President Clinton ordered the U.S. Navy to launch a cruise missile attack against the headquarters of the Iraqi intelligence service. Baghdad's plot, Clinton declared, was "an attack against our country and against all Americans. We could not, and have not, let such actions against our nation go unanswered."[42]

The second major episode occurred in October 1994, when Baghdad once again massed some 80,000 troops on the border with Kuwait. The UN Security Council immediately responded by adopting Resolution 949 mandating the withdrawal of Iraqi forces and admonishing Baghdad from acting in a "hostile or provocative manner" toward its neighbors.

In order to deter Iraq from further aggressive conduct, on October 7, 1994, President Clinton ordered a major buildup of American military power in the Persian Gulf area. An additional 2,000 troops were sent to Kuwait to shore up its defenses. Within weeks, the USA had deployed some 40,000 soldiers, 600 warplanes, and a naval task group within the region.[43] The American military presence was supplemented by 1,000 British Royal Marines. After several tense weeks, the crisis ended with the unilateral withdrawal of Iraqi troops from the contested border zone.

Perhaps the most enduring challenge to United States policy in the Persian Gulf area, however, was Saddam Hussein's episodic defiance of the terms of the 1991 armistice accord. The Clinton administration was determined to compel the Iraqi dictator's compliance with the agreement by any means necessary, including the application of military force. The Iraqi president continually tested the resolve of the allies by challenging both the UN-established "no-fly zone" and the northern Kurdish sanctuaries. His repeated unwillingness to honor these UN-imposed constraints on his actions led Washington unilaterally to extend the southern "no-fly zone" northward, up to the suburbs of Baghdad (another constraint which Saddam Hussein's regime time and again flouted with impunity).[44]

Although UN-supervised weapons inspection had been ongoing since the end of the Persian Gulf War, the appointment of Australian Richard Butler as the new head of the UN Special Commission on Iraq (UNSCOM) on May 1, 1997, represented a critical turning point in relations between Iraq and the allied coalition. Under Butler's direction, UNSCOM became more assertive in enforcing the weapons-inspection program and related disarmament provisions.[45] In response, the Iraqi government forbade UNSCOM inspection of so-called "presidential" or "sovereign" sites and placed other obstacles in the way of the agency's successful operations. In January 1998, Baghdad accused American Scott Ritter of engaging in "espionage" and refused to co-operate any further with UNSCOM's activities.

In response, Washington attempted to rally international support for a long-range attack against Iraqi military targets. While Great Britain, Germany, and Kuwait supported the idea, it encountered widespread opposition from other members of the international community. The crisis was defused, when UN Secretary General Kofi Annan was able to broker another agreement with Baghdad. While President Clinton accepted the resulting "Memorandum of Understanding," the White House made it clear that the USA would continue to pressure Saddam Hussein until his government was in full compliance with its terms. Predictably, perhaps, such compliance was not forthcoming.[46] Baghdad was not deterred by this agreement from its efforts to develop or acquire an arsenal of dangerous chemical and biological weapons.

By December 1998, a new crisis impended. UN inspection teams were denied access to what Baghdad called "sensitive sites," including the Ba'ath Party's headquarters in the center of Baghdad. (It was long believed that this was the locale of a covert arsenal.) In addition, the Iraqi government obstructed the removal of missile components and refused to provide information to UN inspectors on its biological weapons program.[47]

To punish Baghdad for its continuing intransigence, the United States and Great Britain launched a joint attack against Iraq ("Operation Desert Fox"), carried out on December 16–20, 1998. Primary targets were Ba'ath Party buildings, military installations, and facilities believed to be crucial in the nation's ongoing military buildup. The allied strike so enraged Saddam Hussein that he ordered the execution of several of his military commanders in the southern region.[48]

As the foregoing account indicates, the Clinton administration's policies toward Iraq were decisively influenced by pragmatic concepts and calculations.

In nearly all instances, its military and diplomatic moves in the Persian Gulf area were responses to changing conditions and circumstances within the region. Moreover, the behavior of the Clinton White House toward Iraq was the product of the resolution of several highly diverse forces operating upon the American foreign policy process. These included preserving the continuity of U.S. policy, as established by the Bush administration; the Clinton administration's determination to maintain unimpeded access to vital Persian Gulf oil supplies; concern in Washington about impending threats to the security of Kuwait, Saudi Arabia, and other Persian Gulf states; continuing apprehensions by the State of Israel and its supporters in the United States about Saddam Hussein's aggressive intentions; the necessity to demonstrate and maintain the "credibility" of the United States and of the United Nations; the administration's sincere desire to protect Iraq's Kurdish population and other groups that had been subjected to Saddam Hussein's oppression; an underlying desire in time to withdraw most American forces from the crisis-prone Persian Gulf region; the necessity to maintain unity within the allied coalition and to take into account the views of other nations in responding to Baghdad's provocations;[49] and not least, critics of the administration charged, efforts to divert the attention of the media and public opinion from Bill Clinton's sexual escapades.

What had the Clinton administration's pragmatically based policies and behavior toward Iraq actually accomplished? Critics used such terms as "betrayal" of American interests and "a disaster" to describe its results. To their minds, the positive results of the Clinton White House's military and diplomatic activities were heavily outweighed by their liabilities and failures. Saddam Hussein's regime remained in power. It continued to oppress the Kurds, the Shiite element, and other actual or suspected dissidents within Iraq. Repeatedly, Baghdad had successfully defied United Nations directives and impeded its inspection activities. From the available evidence, the regime's determination to acquire an arsenal of highly destructive modern weapons remained undiminished (and was being aided by certain foreign countries). Clinton's policies toward Iraq had weakened the cohesion of the allied coalition; and they served as a serious obstacle to more constructive American-Russian relations. In brief, as a result of President Clinton's policies, the USA appeared to be "locked into" a costly and frustrating state of affairs in the Persian Gulf area that admitted of no easy or really satisfactory resolution.

By contrast, defenders of President Clinton's pragmatic diplomacy believed that it had several achievements to its credit. During Clinton's tenure in office, no new regional war had engulfed the Persian Gulf area. The United States and other industrialized nations still had access to the vital oil supplies of the region. Because of quick and decisive action by the Clinton White House, the security and independence of Kuwait, Saudi Arabia, and other Persian Gulf states had been successfully preserved. Although violations and evasions of it occurred, the economic boycott of Iraq continued and unquestionably caused genuine hardships for Saddam Hussein's regime. (How long the boycott could be maintained, in the face of mounting criticisms of it, was of course questionable.)

The advantages of a pragmatic approach to Iraqi-American relations can perhaps be summarized by saying that, despite its undoubted flaws, a pragmatic response to the Iraqi challenge was superior to two other possible outcomes. One was the eruption of a new, devastating, and costly war in the Persian Gulf area. That possibility would have entailed a long list of serious liabilities, massive costs, and unforeseen consequences. The other conceivable approach was America's withdrawal from the crucial Persian Gulf region, leaving its density to the interplay of several destabilizing and often violent forces at large within it. That outcome also—which could in time deny the United States and its allies (along with several Third World nations) access to Middle East oil and result in area-wide political upheavals—would almost certainly have entailed deleterious consequences for the security and diplomatic interests of the United States.

"HUMANITARIAN INTERVENTION" IN THE FORMER YUGOSLAVIA

Our next case study focuses upon what Secretary of State Warren Christopher once described as "a problem from Hell": the latest conflict to grip the historically turbulent Balkans. The Clinton administration's reliance upon pragmatic diplomatic guidelines is clearly illustrated by its policy of "humanitarian interventionism" as applied to the crisis in the province of Serbia called Kosovo.

In accordance with President Woodrow Wilson's concept of "self-determination," several new nations were created in Europe after World War I. The union of Serbia, Croatia, Slovenia, Macedonia, Montenegro, and Bosnia-Herzegovina was called Yugoslavia. The nation was invaded by Nazi Germany in 1941, and for four years the Yugoslav "Partisans," led by Josip Broz (whose popular name was "Tito") and others, fiercely resisted Nazi rule.

After the Axis defeat and an ensuing struggle for political power within Yugoslavia, Tito ultimately emerged as its acknowledged leader. By force of his personality, and the authoritarian nature of his unique Marxist regime, President Tito somehow managed to preserve national cohesion (although in retrospect it is clear that Yugoslav unity was always extremely fragile). As the first national leader within the international Communist movement to defy Moscow's domination, Tito's regime was applauded by successive American administrations and received substantial military and economic assistance from Washington. Following Tito's death on May 4, 1980, the fabric of the Yugoslav nation began to disintegrate.[50]

Croatia, Slovenia, and Macedonia withdrew from the Yugoslav union in 1991, and a new "Federal Republic of Yugoslavia," dominated by Serbia, emerged early in 1992. Support for national autonomy was also strong, however, among the Muslims and Croats of Bosnia-Herzegovina, whose independence was asserted following a referendum in 1992. Its independence was widely recognized by the USA and other nations.

Over the next three years, fierce fighting engulfed Bosnia, among the Serbian, Croatian, and Muslim communities. The Bosnian Serbs' ruthless policy of "ethnic cleansing"—abetted by Serbia and directed especially against the Muslims—was designed to leave the Bosnian Serbs in decisive control of the region.

Ethnic cleansing and the accompanying atrocities resulted in untold thousands of casualties, the dislocation of thousands of people, and the devastation of much of Bosnia. Efforts by the United Nations to end the violence and restore some semblance of stability to the region proved fruitless. Finally, early in 1994, the members of the North Atlantic Treaty Organization (NATO) delivered an ultimatum to Bosnian Serb forces and Serbia to desist from further aggression. When these warnings were ignored, NATO resorted to air strikes against Bosnian Serb positions. In the face of NATO's air offensive, the Bosnian Serbs finally agreed to enter into cease-fire negotiations, whose terms were subsequently broadened into what came to called the "Dayton peace agreement," signed by the parties to the conflict on December 14, 1995.[51] A few days later, a NATO peacekeeping force (subsequently known as the "Stabilization Force," or SFOR) assumed responsibility for enforcing the terms of the Dayton accord. SFOR was assisted by some 1,500 United Nations advisers.

Besides enforcing the Dayton agreement, SFOR was assigned another responsibility, in which, as events proved, it encountered great difficulty in carrying out successfully: apprehending "war criminals" and bringing them to justice before an international tribunal. And in the months that followed, SFOR's troops often found themselves in a deadly cross-fire between Serbian and Muslim elements, neither of whom was really enthusiastic about the Dayton peace pact.

Meanwhile, tensions were rising in another part of Yugoslavia, the Serbian province of Kosovo.[52] In a move to consolidate nationalist Serbian support, Serbian president Slobodan Milosevic had, several years before, revoked the province's autonomy, effectively disenfranchising the province's ethnic Albanian majority in favor of the minority Serbian population. Resistance to Serb authority among the ethnic Albanians grew and included a declaration of independence by Kosovar secessionists and the formation of the Kosovo Liberation Army (KLA). In 1997, in response to certain KLA attacks, Serbia instituted a brutal crackdown in Kosovo, killing hundreds of non-combatant ethnic Albanians and displacing thousands more. A truce brokered by American diplomat Richard Holbrooke in October 1998 resulted in the temporary withdrawal of Serb military forces, but further intransigence on the part of the Milosevic government left NATO with little choice but to use military action. The subsequent air war against Serbia from March to June 1999 largely destroyed Serbia's industry and left its economy debilitated.

From the inception of these crises in the Balkans, fundamental divisions had existed among the Western governments concerning the best courses to take. During most of his first term in office, for example, President Clinton's mindset exemplified the old Populist belief that foreign affairs were a worrisome distraction from the nation's principal business: the solution of domestic problems.

Insofar as he appeared to be interested in NATO, the president was mainly preoccupied with the "expansion" of the alliance eastward by the addition of new members. Clinton and his advisers tended to view the accelerating crisis in the Balkans primarily as "a European problem." One commentator has stated that during the early 1990s, Washington's policy toward the region could be described by the word "drift."[53] Clinton was convinced that most Americans, along with a majority in Congress, firmly opposed the commitment of American ground forces in the Balkans.[54] NATO's strategy of what was called "aggressive air power" represented a compromise approach among the Western allies.

Although it made a positive contribution, it is too early to conclude that external intervention by the United Nations and NATO has succeeded in defusing the "powder keg of Europe." As the only national-religious group in Yugoslavia that did not have their own autonomous nation, most ethnic Albanian Kosovars saw the NATO intervention as a crucial step toward achieving their ultimate objective: total independence from Serbia. For their part, Serbians tended to be unenthusiastic about the situation, fearing that sooner or later it would lead to the partition of their country. Serbians have not abandoned their belief that the soil of Kosovo is sacred: in their tradition, the Serbian nation emerged after a crucial battle in the region in 1389. (And by the new millennium, some well-informed commentators on the Balkans question had become convinced that these fears were justified: to their minds, formal "partition" into separate Serbian and Albanian states appeared to offer the only hope of ending the continuing violence—if, in fact, even this step would stabilize the Balkans.)[55]

Almost daily, the headlines remind us that, despite the Dayton agreement and NATO intervention over Kosovo, peace and stability in the Balkans remain highly elusive. By the new millennium, news commentator referred to the "murderous inter-ethnic violence still going on" in Kosovo. It was clear— even if American officials refused to admit it—that the goal of a peaceful and pluralistic society in Kosovo was unattainable.[56] Other news reports referred to "a deteriorating situation in the [Kosovo]" that was "spinning out of . . . control." The presence of NATO forces and UN administrative personnel has thus far "failed to prevent de facto partitioning of Kosovo or continued ethnic bloodshed." The available evidence indicated that, while it was still in power, President Slobodan Milosevic's regime in Serbia was attempting to determine the future of Kosovo. Concurrently, elements of the Kosovo Liberation Army (KLA) were seeking to create an autonomous state, free of Serbian influence.[57] Vocal dissatisfaction was being expressed in the U.S. Congress with the continued presence of American forces in the Balkans;[58] and fundamental questions about the future of peacekeeping in the region were being raised in European capitals. Meanwhile, UN officials expressed the view that inadequate funds were available to them to carry out their responsibilities satisfactorily. And in spite of hopes in America for their early withdrawal, NATO peacekeeping forces were still stationed in the crisis zone; in fact, NATO's military commander called for additional American forces which, in his view, were essential for enforcing the peace in Kosovo.[59]

The Clinton administration's diplomatic behavior toward the crises in the Balkans can accurately be described as "pragmatic" in several senses. As many critics complained, throughout the crises the White House appeared to lack any kind of overall diplomatic strategy or long-range plan capable of relating Washington's moves in the Balkans to its diplomatic activities regionally and globally. Typically, President Clinton's approach to the Balkans problems was ad hoc and reactive. In nearly every instance, Washington's policy was a response to rapidly unfolding events that demanded some kind of reaction by the United States.[60]

Likewise, the approach of the Clinton White House to the Balkans issues avoided extremes and endeavored to be "balanced." Specifically, one extreme position it avoided was non-involvement or isolationism. President Clinton and his aides were basically agreed that a leadership role by the USA was essential if any kind of solution for the Balkans conundrum could ultimately be found.

Conversely, the Clinton White House also avoided the extreme of overinvolvement in the Bosnian and Kosovo conflicts. The "lessons of Vietnam," along with other lessons derived from more recent instances of unsuccessful American intervention in the affairs of foreign countries, unquestionably played some part in shaping the views of President Clinton and the members of his advisory circle.

In addition, the diplomatic behavior of the Clinton White House illustrated the pragmatic concept of a "pluralistic universe." The policymaking context during the 1990s was extremely "pluralistic": a long list of factors and forces arising out of both the domestic and foreign environments influenced the diplomatic behavior of the Clinton White House. These included the Wilsonian tradition and America's customary identification with the concepts of democracy and self-determination abroad; the necessity to demonstrate NATO's "relevance" in the post–Cold War era, especially when the Clinton administration was seeking to expand its membership;[61] Washington's desire to maintain cooperative relations with its European allies (who experienced great difficulty arriving at a unified course of action in the Balkans); the concurrent necessity to provide a demonstration of America's role as a global leader vis-à-vis the rising power of the European Union;[62] the administration's desire to cultivate and preserve constructive relations with "the new Russia" and to motivate Moscow to behave peacefully after the Cold War; and an evident reluctance by policymakers—reflecting what they were convinced was overwhelming American public opinion—to become heavily involved from a military viewpoint in a prolonged and inconclusive crisis overseas.[63]

Although it would be difficult to prove, it seems reasonable to conclude also that the Clinton administration's approach to the conflict in Kosovo in some measure exemplified a "wag the dog" strategy.[64] President Clinton would not be the first national leader to use a foreign crisis for the purpose of diverting public attention from domestic problems and concerns—in this instance, the sexual scandals growing out of his own conduct. By the same token, the conflicts in the Balkans were undoubtedly useful in reinforcing the administration's case for higher defense spending and for the purpose of enhancing America's status as a global leader.[65]

Finally, there was what many commentators regard as perhaps the key to Washington's diplomatic improvisations and military moves in the Balkans: the overt absence of a clear understanding by President Clinton and his aides of precisely how the national interests of the United States were affected by the course of events in the Balkans.[66]

Viewed from the perspective of its results, President Clinton's policy toward the Balkans can also be described as pragmatic. The policy quite clearly had both positive and negative consequences. On the one hand, without question, the Dayton formula reduced the scale of "ethnic cleansing" in the region and offered hope that, sooner or later, the practice would be terminated. Moreover, the agreement provided a forceful demonstration of American diplomatic leadership. It supplied a new rationale for the existence of an "enlarged" NATO and demonstrated that the alliance was capable of dealing with "out of area" crises. Moreover, despite the existence of serious obstacles, officials in Washington were successful in achieving a multinational approach to peacekeeping in the Balkans and gaining acceptance of the principle (repeatedly emphasized by members of Congress) of more equitable "burden-sharing" among the allies. President Clinton's actions were also successful in ultimately compelling President Milosevic to accept the idea of a resolution of the crisis in Kosovo that accorded the ethnic Albanians substantial autonomy.[67] It could be contended as well that Western intervention in Kosovo "sent a message" to other governments and political groups throughout the world, that oppression and atrocities committed against internal minorities were matters of global concern, and such behavior might provoke intervention by the United States and its allies.[68]

Yet President Clinton's policy of "humanitarian interventionism" in the Balkans was also quite clearly a failure in several key respects. One detailed indictment of his diplomacy, for example, describes its results as "marked by military success and political failure." Its liabilities included creating tensions in relations with the governments of mainland China and Russia; generally accepting the de facto partitioning of Bosnia; largely reducing Serbia "to rubble," thereby creating a massive future problem, involving billions of dollars needed for regional reconstruction and recovery; and generally contributing to the *instability* of surrounding countries.[69]

External intervention finally led in the year 2000 to the ouster of Serbian president Milosevic's regime and his replacement by a new, democratically elected government. This government has pledged to end the conflict that has gripped the country for many years. This crucial transition, of course, augured well for the peace and stability of the Balkans and of Europe generally, although it left a number of underlying and difficult problems—such as the political future of Kosovo—unsolved. American and other external military forces would likely be required to remain in the region for a prolonged period ahead.

The most formidable obstacle to a durable peace in the region may well be the expectations of each side concerning Kosovo. All parties to the conflict view it as a compromise. For most ethnic Albanians, it is a transitional step toward ultimate political independence. For the Serbs, it is an infringement upon what is viewed as their sovereignty within Kosovo. For the NATO allies it has become an agreement that is increasingly difficult to enforce.[70]

As nearly every informed student of contemporary American foreign policy is aware, the last word on President Clinton's policy toward the Balkans crises has yet to be written. The prospects for lasting peace and security, in what can only be called this "volcanic region" of the political universe, remain highly uncertain.

"DEMOCRATIZING" HAITI

United States involvement in the Caribbean basin has a history almost as long as the republic itself. The invasion of Haiti in 1994 by the Clinton administration, however, was a watershed event in recent American foreign relations.[71]

The USA first became directly involved in Haiti's future in 1915, when President Woodrow Wilson ordered U.S. Marines to land in the country and take over the operation of its government because of a record of chronic political and financial mismanagement. The Marines remained in Haiti until 1934, when they were withdrawn as evidence of a totally new direction in Washington's Latin American policy ("the Good Neighbor Policy") by the administration of President Franklin D. Roosevelt.[72]

For Haitians and other Latin Americans, this interventionist episode left deep-seated suspicions and resentments toward the North American Colossus. In the main, after 1934 Washington largely ignored Haiti, with successive administrations allowing the country to wallow in its own poverty, misgovernment, and despair.[73] During his first term in the Oval Office, President Bill Clinton devoted his attention almost exclusively to domestic affairs, largely ignoring developments in Haiti, along with most other foreign countries.[74]

In 1991, Haiti experienced its initial taste of democracy when Jean-Bertrand Aristide became its first popularly elected president.[75] Aristide attempted certain reforms, but his efforts to streamline the economy, revitalize agriculture, and revamp the tax collection system were blocked by members of the parliament who supported the old order. Although Aristide reached out to Haiti's elites, he may have overplayed his hand politically by appeals to the country's poor, who were urged "to resort to harsher measures if the popular will were thwarted."[76] In the light of such appeals, the president's days as Haiti's leader soon appeared to be numbered.

On September 30, 1991, the Haitian military staged a coup d'etat which overthrew the Aristide regime. Although the coup was universally condemned within the hemispheric and global communities, reversion to military rule in Haiti went relatively unchallenged.[77] The army and police were quick to move against Aristide's supporters (actual or suspected). Homes were looted, political opponents kidnapped, and pro-democracy groups suppressed. Within weeks following the coup, some 200,000 people fled into the countryside for safety.[78]

In Washington, the Bush administration imposed an economic embargo in an effort to bring an end to widespread violations of human rights in Haiti. For its part, the junta, led by General Raul Cedras, responded by intensifying its crackdown on opposition groups, including students and foreign journalists.

As the repression in Haiti intensified, thousands of refugees tried to escape. Besides flight to the countryside and to the neighboring Dominican Republic, some chose a much riskier course. Boarding unseaworthy boats and leaky rafts, a virtual tidal wave of refugees attempted to find sanctuary in the United States.[79]

This problem acquired unusual urgency in 1992 when it became embroiled in the American presidential election. The Bush administration followed a policy of returning these "boat people" to Haiti, without allowing them to make the case for political asylum in the USA. (The Bush White House took the position that the refugees were fleeing adverse economic, rather than oppressive political, conditions.) By contrast, presidential candidate Bill Clinton denounced the Bush policy as "cruel"; and he pledged to "grant fleeing Haitians refuge and consideration for political asylum" until the restoration of democracy in their country.[80] The policy of his administration, President Clinton declared, was "to support the advance of democracy everywhere."[81]

Yet once in office, Clinton continued the policy of returning the Haitian refugees to their troubled homeland. This approach alienated many of Clinton's supporters at home, including influential interest groups like the Black Caucus and Trans-Africa, which vocally called for direct intervention by the USA to restore democratic rule to Haiti.[82]

In 1993, President Clinton's strategy toward Haiti was to put additional pressure on the Cedras regime by imposing economic sanctions, to be accomplished mainly by an international embargo and the freezing of Haitian assets abroad. External pressure on the junta was dramatically increased when, on June 23, 1993, the United Nations Security Council imposed an embargo on the sale of oil and arms to Haiti.[83]

This strategy had its desired effect. Within days, General Cedras and his delegation arrived in New York to enter into negotiations designed to resolve the crisis. Under intense pressure from the Clinton White House, Aristide and Cedras signed what came to be called the "Governor's Island Agreement."[84] According to its terms, Aristide was to reassume the presidency; he would appoint a new prime minister; General Cedras would be allowed to relinquish office quietly; and an amnesty would be granted to those individuals involved in the coup. "In return, the Parliament would enact a reform of the army and the police under supervision of a UN mission." The United Nations would also lift the existing economic sanctions on Haiti.[85]

Despite the Clinton administration's expectations that democracy would soon be restored in Haiti, within three weeks these high hopes would be dashed. As a prelude to the restoration of Aristide to the presidential office, in October 1993, the White House dispatched the vessel USS *Harlan County* to Haiti in order to discharge a shipload of military advisers, trainers, and engineers (the "Seabees"). Taking its cue from events concurrently going in East Africa, the Cedras regime sent armed thugs to the landing area in Port-au-Prince where the ship was supposed to dock.[86] Violent, angry mobs greeted the *Harlan County,* taunting its crew with shouts of "Somalia! Somalia!"—a clear reference to the slaughter of U.S. Marines by tribal forces in an encounter that had recently taken place in Mogadishu, Somalia. After officials in Washington determined that it was not safe to disembark the American and Canadian military personnel abroad, the *Harlan County* was ordered to withdraw and to return to the naval base at Guantanamo Bay.[87] This episode marked the demise of the Governor's Island Agreement.

As conditions in Haiti continued to deteriorate, "the UN Security Council imposed wide-ranging trade and financial sanctions on Haiti, later reinforced by a ban on commercial flights. The only trade still permitted was in essential foods, cooking gas, and printed material."[88]

Diplomatic overtures by the Clinton administration to the Cedras regime proved fruitless. Finally, acknowledging the failure of diplomacy, on June 30, 1994, the UN Security Council passed Resolution 940. This measure authorized member states to use "all necessary means" to restore the legal government of Jean Bertrand Aristide to power. Direct military intervention in Haiti now became inevitable.

As the Pentagon drew up plans for a military operation, the Clinton White House made one final attempt to negotiate a solution to the crisis. President Clinton dispatched a three-man team of dignitaries—consisting of former President Jimmy Carter, Senator Sam Nunn (D–Ga.), and the chairman of the Joint Chiefs of Staff, General Colin Powell—which arrived in Haiti on September 17.[89] And in a clear warning that this would be its last chance to step down under favorable conditions, President Clinton admonished General Cedras that "Your time is up. Leave now or we will force you from power." Even as discussions between the negotiating team and the junta were in progress, an American invasion fleet was steaming toward the island. Realizing that its position had become untenable, the junta finally agreed to relinquish power and to allow President Aristide to return to office.

On September 19, 1994, a U.S. military contingent of some 21,000 troops once again landed on Haitian soil, but not as an occupier, rather as a welcome force whose mission was to restore democracy to the troubled country. On October 15, 1994, President Aristide returned to his homeland in triumph.[90]

Ostensibly, in Haiti President Bill Clinton had gotten the victory that had eluded the USA in Somalia. In this Caribbean nation, for a time human rights abuses were ended (or, at least, curtailed), a brutal military dictatorship was removed, and the legitimate civilian government was returned to power. With a few exceptions, these things had been accomplished without bloodshed.

Perhaps out of fear of becoming involved in another unsuccessful Somalia-style "nation-building" exercise, President Clinton pledged that the deployment of the nation's armed forces in Haiti would not be open-ended.[91] True to his word, in March 1995, Clinton saw to it that most of the duties associated with the maintenance of law and order in Haiti were handed over to a United Nations mission, comprising some 5,700 soldiers and supplemented by 900 police officers.[92] The final withdrawal of U.S. forces was accomplished in April 1996.[93] Moreover, the Haitian intervention was carried out with relatively little political opposition in the United States.[94]

In the short term, the policy of the Clinton White House was overtly successful, but the long-term prognosis for democracy and stability in Haiti was far less promising.[95] A functioning democratic system was installed, with national elections held in 1995. As a result, the swearing-in of the new President Preval marked the first time in Haiti's history that one democratically elected president had succeeded another.

Economic improvement in Haiti, however, essential for the survival of democracy, has thus far largely been lacking. Despite U.S. aid, coupled with reforms undertaken by the government, Haiti remains the poorest society in the Western Hemisphere, and its prospects for significant economic progress in the years ahead remain bleak.[96]

Much also remains to be done in Haiti with regard to respect for human rights, since political dissidents are still sometimes treated harshly by the authorities. In an effort to prevent future military-instigated coups, and to reduce political repression by military elements, the old Haitian army was disbanded and replaced by a new police force. Even though the new constabulary has been trained by international advisers, evidence to date indicates that the level of professionalism and respect for the rights of citizens by the Haitian police under the new government are at times little better than the record of the old regime.[97]

Regarding Clinton's diplomatic behavior toward Haiti, three important observations can be made. The first is that, reflecting the pattern established in Somalia, and later repeated in the Balkans, the latest instance of U.S. military intervention in the Caribbean might conceivably have been avoided had President Clinton been more assertive at an earlier stage.[98] Without question, the abortive *Harlan County* episode made the United States appear impotent, and it most likely prolonged the crisis by stiffening the Haitian junta's resolve to resist external influence. Quite possibly also, this policy setback served to encourage what are now called "rogue states" (such as Iraq and North Korea) to threaten American diplomatic and security interests with impunity.

Second, as William Hyland has pointed out, the motivation supporting Clinton's interventionism in Haiti appears to have been driven less by a concern for human rights than by a "traditional geopolitical framework" based on the Monroe Doctrine.[99] (For example, in a letter to Congress justifying his policy, Clinton asserted that, "The United States has a particular interest in responding to gross abuses of human rights when they occur so close to our shores." Earlier, the president had declared that, "When brutality occurs close to our shore, it affects our national interest, and we have a responsibility to act."[100])

In the third place, the relatively low cost of the Haitian operation, in terms of any loss of life and of domestic opposition within the USA, may well have encouraged future interventions in places where the national interest of the USA is dubious, at best.[101] At any rate, flushed with his overt success in Haiti, President Clinton lost no time in again committing American forces abroad. As explained in an earlier case study, in 1995, the USA intervened directly in the conflict in Bosnia-Herzegovina. Then in 1999 the USA led the way in launching an air offensive because of human rights violations by the Serbian government in Kosovo. Moreover, the air campaign, inaugurated during the Persian Gulf War, continues against the government of Iraq.

According to several criteria, the foreign policy of the Clinton administration toward Haiti can be accurately described as pragmatic.[102] Initially, it reflected the impact of a number of domestic factors upon diplomatic behavior. As the foregoing discussion indicated, at almost every stage Washington's response to the ongoing crisis in Haiti represented a compromise among the diverse viewpoints and policy options advocated by members of President Clinton's foreign policy team.[103] As often as not, the specific action taken by the United States represented a choice among several possible policy alternatives—most of them in varying degrees unappealing!

Washington's behavior during the Haitian crisis also provides a poignant example of the often decisive role played by special interests in the foreign policy process—in this case, such African American pressure groups as Trans-Africa and the congressional Black Caucus. These and other organizations were at the forefront in calling for an interventionist approach by the Clinton White House in dealing with the Haitian junta.

A key influence in shaping Washington's response to events in Haiti also was America's own ideological heritage, leading it in this and other cases to champion the cause of democracy abroad. Domestic political calculations—such as a desire to demonstrate President Clinton's resolve and ability to manage foreign affairs successfully—also doubtless played some part in determining Washington's behavior toward Haiti.

External factors, of course, also influenced the diplomatic activities of the Clinton White House. As already emphasized, there seems little room for doubt that the nation's historic attachment to the Monroe Doctrine entered into policy calculations in this case. Some commentators are convinced that other *Realpolitik* calculations, involving the perceptions of American power and its position of global leadership, influenced the diplomatic conduct of the Clinton administration toward Haiti, as well.

Moreover, ample awareness existed in Washington that if the Haitian crisis was going to be resolved, the USA would have to take the lead in doing so. As events demonstrated, in this and other instances, the United Nations was prepared to act only in response to American initiatives.[104] There was also the impact of recent diplomatic experience in shaping Washington's approach to Haiti, especially the damage done to the nation's credibility by the abortive intervention in Somalia. One can say that "No More Somalias!" was an implicit principle at the forefront of official American concern in the Haitian case.

In brief, the policy of the Clinton White House toward Haiti emerged as the resolution of a number of diverse forces. It was a "compromise solution" to an extremely complex and difficult problem, and as such it left observers along the entire range of the political spectrum dissatisfied.

"PRAGMATIC ENGAGEMENT" WITH CHINA

On the eve of his trip to mainland China in 1998, President Bill Clinton defined his approach to Beijing as a "moderate policy"—one that was "principled and pragmatic." In another context, his administration's approach to the People's Republic of China was described by the term "pragmatic engagement."[105] As we shall see, no chapter in his administration's diplomatic record perhaps proved as controversial as Clinton's approach to Beijing.

Relatively few Americans are aware that the ties between the United States and China extend back to the late eighteenth century, when the sailing ship *Empress of China* inaugurated trade between the two nations.[106] For over two centuries, the lure of the "China market" has attracted American business interests.[107] Informed citizens are cognizant that one of the most important chapters in the diplomatic history of the United States was the issuance of the "Open Door Policy" at the end of the nineteenth century. As this policy was interpreted during the years that followed, the USA assumed an obligation to protect the "territorial integrity" (or, in a word, independence) of the Chinese nation. That commitment in time brought the United States more and more into conflict with an expansive Japanese Empire, whose warlords were determined to extend Tokyo's imperial hegemony from the Chinese mainland to Australia.[108] The United States and other nations were unwilling to act in opposition to Japanese aggression. America's largely verbal response to it, therefore, was described as one of "sticking pins in tigers" (an allusion to the Japanese Empire's symbol of a menacing tiger)![109]

From this period until the end of World War II, the United States supported the Nationalist government of China, headed by Chiang Kai-shek, against two enemies: the Japanese imperialists and the Communist Party of China, led by Mao Tse-tung. At the end of the war, the long-standing conflict between the Nationalist government and the Communist insurgents erupted with new intensity, with the former steadily losing ground against the latter. Finally, at the end of 1949, after losing the support of the Chinese people, Chiang Kai-shek and his followers in the Kuomintang Party fled to the island of Formosa, where they largely dominated the political and economic affairs of what came to be called "The Republic of China" (Taiwan).[110]

Until the "normalization" of relations between the United States and the People's Republic of China by the Carter administration in 1978, relations between the two countries were marked by tensions, deep suspicions, and (during the Korean War) actual military hostilities.[111] To the Chinese mind, the USA epitomized one of the "foreign devils" that throughout history have attempted to control their nation's destiny. On the American side, the Sino-Soviet Axis was viewed as an extremely dangerous alliance between the world's two most powerful Marxist nations.[112] Mainland China was regarded by officials in Washington as a major instigator of insurrection, political upheaval, and insecurity around the globe.[113]

In common with other aspects of U.S. foreign policy, the end of the Cold War witnessed significant changes in the pattern of Sino-American relations—involving a transition from overt confrontation to "pragmatic engagement." Officials on both sides of the Pacific in time concluded that at least a limited degree of collaboration between the two governments served their interests. Accordingly, after 1979, Beijing and Washington endeavored to collaborate in seeking mutually acceptable solutions for Asian and global problems. At the same time, recognition also existed on both sides that several significant problems—and for Americans, the leading ones were the Chinese government's poor record in the sphere of human rights and its suppression of overt political opposition, along with Beijing's ongoing threat to bring Taiwan under its hegemony—continued to be contentious issues between the two nations.

The Clinton administration's approach to the PRC may justifiably be called pragmatic for several reasons. Initially, it was a result of a highly diverse "mix" of internal and external factors. For example, it quite clearly reflected the ambivalent nature of public opinion on the question of Sino-American relations. As always, the American people favor progress toward democracy in China and other foreign societies. They advocate respect for human rights and other freedoms in China, as well as in other countries. Yet by the period of the Clinton administration, Americans also exhibited little enthusiasm for an overtly interventionist policy toward mainland China. Studies of public attitudes found that citizens basically approved attempts to reduce tensions between the USA and the PRC; to seek opportunities for expanding trade with, and investment in, China; and to enlist Chinese co-operation in efforts to preserve peace and stability in Asia. In brief, a foundation of public support underlay President Clinton's policy of "pragmatic engagement."[114]

Yet geopolitical factors and *Realpolitik* calculations also entered into the foreign policy of the Clinton White House.[115] Again, several dimensions of this idea were noteworthy. After the dissolution of the Sino-Soviet alliance, the Chinese government played a key role in the containment of Russian power and influence within Asia, and even globally. Many American officials believed that, to the degree that Moscow was "preoccupied" with Beijing's activities and ambitions, it would be inhibited from engaging in expansive and interventionist moves in other regions. China also had a significant role to play in solving such problems as curtailing North Korean expansionism and its determination to acquire nuclear weapons. Moreover, China's assistance could well be needed in an effective attempt to prevent open warfare between India and Pakistan.

Preventing an overt military clash between the PRC and the Republic of China on Taiwan was, of course, another long-standing American objective, vigorously advocated by several organizations constituting "the China lobby."[116] After the Vietnam War, Beijing's efforts were also essential in endeavoring to limit expansionism throughout Southeast Asia by a victorious North Vietnam. In the view of American officials, Chinese co-operation was no less indispensable in preventing nuclear weapons and advanced missile technology from falling into the hands of "rogue governments."[117]

For their part, Chinese officials left little doubt that, although the USA had lost the Vietnam War, they regarded a strong American position in Asia as essential for the preservation of regional peace and security. A leading Chinese goal, for example, was to prevent the resurgence of a financially and economically powerful Japan, whose leaders might once again embark upon the path of expansionism. Only the power of the United States was available to prevent that prospect from becoming a reality.[118]

Economic incentives also played a role in President Clinton's policy of pragmatic engagement with mainland China. With the largest population on the globe—by the new millennium, estimated at over two billion people—China offered what many business corporations and interest groups in the USA regarded as an almost unlimited market for American-made goods and a favorable environment for foreign investments. (Historically, Americans have always been captivated by the idea of a vast "China market" for their products. Throughout most of modern history, however, a potent constraining factor meant that this vision was never more than a dream: where would one of the most poverty-stricken societies on the globe get the purchasing power needed to acquire expensive American-made goods and services?)[119]

As emphasized earlier, Americans also naturally favored the emergence of a free enterprise system within Chinese society, in the belief that such a system was indispensable for future Chinese economic growth and higher standards of living. In addition, it has long been an article of faith with Western liberal opinion that economic growth in the Chinese and other societies would provide momentum for more rapid movement toward political democracy and respect for human rights.[120]

On the Chinese side, in time officials in Beijing were increasingly receptive to the idea that a rising level of trade with the USA served the nation's interests. By the period of the Clinton administration, mainland China was one of the largest exporters of products to the American market. And Chinese purchases of American-made commercial aircraft, chemicals, computer technology, and other goods contributed significantly to the prosperity of certain segments of the American economy.[121]

By the late 1990s, Chinese officials accorded high priority to two other goals: being chosen for membership in the World Trade Organization (WTO) and gaining "most favored nation" status, qualifying Chinese exports for preferential treatment under American trade laws. Under the Constitution, the latter issue involved the U.S. Congress centrally in shaping American policy toward China. Ever since the late 1940s, legislators have been extremely sensitive about possible efforts by the PRC to threaten the independence of Tai-wan.[122] At times, members of the House and Senate denounced Beijing's record in the sphere of human rights, ill-concealed Chinese efforts to influence the outcome of American elections, and what appeared to be evident attempts by the Chinese government to acquire sensitive information about American industrial and military technology.[123]

It has been said that President Abraham Lincoln once told one of his gener-als who was attempting to govern a key "border state" that the time for him to worry about the correctness of his policies was when he was no longer criti-cized *by both sides!* By that standard, President Clinton's policy of "pragmatic engagement" with China would have to be judged an outstanding success. It was found wanting by critics of every political hue and orientation.

For example, environmentalists objected to Chinese society's poor record of environmental pollution, which they believed Washington was ignoring—a problem that would most likely get worse as China forged ahead with rapid industrial growth. Several American labor unions (although by no means all) vocally protested against the growing importation of Chinese-made goods, which in their view threatened jobs and prosperity at home. From a different perspective, interest groups that championed the cause of human rights abroad and expanding freedom—and by the late 1990s, that included several churches and religious organizations in the USA—denounced the PRC's continued suppression of political dissent and its discrimination against certain religious organizations and practices.

From a military-strategic point of view, another group of critics was appre-hensive about growing Chinese military power, which was viewed as endan-gering the peace and security of Asia and, quite possibly in time, that of the world.[124] To their minds, China's emergence as a formidable military power was the key factor in the equation of Sino-American relations; and it was a phenomenon to which the Clinton White House appeared to be totally indif-ferent. Predictably, the still-active "China lobby" continued to demand that the USA protect Taiwan against attempts by the PRC to "liberate" it forc-ibly—a threat that authorities in Beijing renew periodically.[125]

At the same time, other informed commentators were convinced that most of the doubts and anxieties about a policy of "pragmatic engagement" with China were unfounded. One of the nation's most experienced diplomats and commentators, for example, was convinced that there was always a tendency in America to exaggerate China's power and importance in global affairs.[126] As another observer has expressed it, China is "overrated as a market, a [military] power, and a source of ideas." At worst, the PRC is "a theoretical power"; repeated promises by its leaders "to deliver" or achieve ambitious goals have been consistently disappointing; and the Chinese nation's military power today and for many years to come tends to be highly exaggerated by most Western observers.[127]

Another observer is convinced that the Chinese political system is characterized by fundamental weaknesses. Unless radical "reforms" designed to democratize the system are undertaken—a remote possibility—it will most likely collapse in the not-too-distant future. Thus far, China's leaders have failed to comprehend the inseparable connection between successful economic and political reform.[128]

President Clinton and his advisers were attracted to a pragmatic approach to the People's Republic of China for perhaps one paramount reason: it served America's interests better than any other conceivable policy alternative. For example, as an administration in the Wilsonian tradition, President Clinton reiterated America's historic interest in the progress of democracy and the condition of human rights abroad. Toward the PRC, as toward most other foreign governments, the United States would not be true to its own history and cherished traditions if it ignored such issues beyond its own borders. Most recently, as American officials reminded authorities in Beijing, Russian leaders had finally discovered that sooner or later the people's demands for better political and economic conditions will prove to be decisive.

In contrast to many of its critics, the Clinton administration rejected a hardline or confrontational approach to the People's Republic of China. Time and again, the Clinton White House insisted that a return to the Cold War stance of tension and hostility toward mainland China would pay few dividends in terms of achieving American goals in Asia and globally. Throughout history, the Chinese have resisted attempts by "foreign devils" to impose their will on their society; and by the new millennium, no credible evidence existed to indicate that this condition had fundamentally changed. In fact, to the degree to which authorities in Beijing felt threatened, their rule could well become even more repressive than ever.

Basically, therefore, the Clinton White House advocated the same approach to the PRC that Washington took toward Moscow during the Cold War: maintaining relations (sometimes called "a dialogue") between the two governments; endeavoring in every feasible way to *modify* the government's viewpoints and behavior; assisting Beijing in solving a multitude of internal problems; and awaiting more favorable circumstances in order to induce farreaching changes in the domestic and foreign policies of mainland China. On balance, the Clinton White House believed that this approach best served the nation's interests in responding to a complex and difficult challenge abroad.[129]

NOTES

CHAPTER 1

1. More-detailed analyses of America's historic isolationist policy may be found in Paul A. Varg, *Foreign Policies of the Founding Fathers* (East Lansing: Michigan State University Press, 1963); Selig Adler, *The Isolationist Impulse: Its Twentieth Century Reaction* (New York: Abelard-Schuman, 1957); Manfred Jonas, *Isolationism in America: 1935–1941* (Ithaca: Cornell University Press, 1966); and Leroy N. Rieselbach, "The Basis of Isolationist Behavior," *Public Opinion Quarterly* 24 (winter 1962): 645–57.

2. See ex-president Richard Nixon's views in his analysis of post–Cold War American foreign policy in *Beyond Peace* (New York: Random House, 1994), 21.

3. See Bill Kaufman in *America First! Its History, Culture and Politics* (Amherst, N.Y.: Prometheus Books, 1995), 27.

4. See the views of Stephen S. Rosenfeld in the *Washington Post,* November 8, 1996.

5. As merely one indication of the low priority assigned to foreign affairs by Americans, by the late 1990s spending for foreign aid was only some 0.15 percent of the nation's gross national product; the USA ranked *last* among the industrialized nations in the level of its global assistance programs. See Arthur Schlesinger, Jr., "Back to the Womb: Isolationism's Renewed Threat," *Foreign Affairs* 74 (July–August 1995): 6–7; and Walter Laqueur, "Save Public Diplomacy: Broadcasting America's Message Matters," *Foreign Affairs* 73 (September–October 1994): 19–25.

6. See, for example, the discussion of President Johnson's mind-set in dealing with foreign policy questions in Cecil V. Crabb, Jr., and Kevin V. Mulcahy, *Presidents and Foreign Policy Making: From FDR to Reagan* (Baton Rouge: Louisiana State University Press, 1986), 198–237.

7. The divergent views among prominent individuals and groups calling for continued adherence to the nation's traditional isolationist policy on the eve of World War II are highlighted in Jonas, *Isolationism in America;* in Adler, *The Isolationist Impulse;* in Wayne S. Cole, *America First: The Battle against Intervention, 1940–1941* (Madison: University of Wisconsin Press, 1953); and in Raymond L. Buell, *Isolated America* (New York: Alfred A. Knopf, 1940).

8. Arthur H. Vandenberg, Jr., ed., *The Private Papers of Senator Vandenberg* (Boston: Houghton Mifflin, 1952), 1–21; and see the discussion of the isolationist credo in Cecil V. Crabb, Jr., *Policy-Makers and Critics: Conflicting Theories of American Foreign Policy* (New York: Praeger Publishers, 1976), 3–5.

9. See this legislator's views in Wayne S. Cole, *Senator Gerald P. Nye and American Foreign Relations* (Minneapolis: University of Minnesota Press); and the discussion of pre–World War II isolationism in Crabb, *Policy-Makers and Critics,* 5.

10. For the results of this poll, see the *New York Times,* January 20, 1997.

11. For a poignant expression of this position, see the views of James P. Hoffa in the *New York Times,* May 11, 2000. The leader of the International Brotherhood of Teamsters expressed a major tenet of Buchananism by asserting that "thousands of our members have lost jobs" because of the nation's trade policy. Many other American workers have suffered a serious erosion of their wages because of "unfair" foreign competition. Yet as other commentators have pointed out, the livelihood of a substantial number of Teamsters, along with members of other labor unions, depends upon maintaining a high volume of American sales abroad.

12. Our analysis of Buchananism draws upon the more detailed treatments of Pat Buchanan's views in the *New York Times,* March 21, 1995, dispatch by Richard Berke; March 27, 1995, dispatch by Steven Greenhouse; May 31, 1995, dispatch by Richard Berke; *Newsweek,* March 4, 1996, pp. 21–27; and *Time,* November 6, 1995, pp. 22–30.

13. See the analysis of Pat Buchanan's views on various foreign policy issues in Kaufman, *America First!* 212–19; and in David Frum, *What's Right: The New Conservative Majority and the Remaking of America* (New York: Harper/Collins, 1996), 61–64.

14. For more-detailed analysis of this influential isolationist movement, see Cole, *America First.* Several recent commentators on U.S. foreign policy have noted the similarity between Pat Buchanan's views on external policy questions and those of leading isolationists during the 1930s, such as Father Charles Coughlin and the America First movement, which opposed the diplomatic moves of the Roosevelt administration on the eve of World War II. See Kaufman, *America First!* 218–19. Other commentators trace Buchanan's approach to an even earlier era—the period of the Populists and the Bryan Democrats, around 1900. Like Buchanan, these political movements advocated an isolationist course abroad; exhibited deep suspicion of both the domestic and foreign policies of what was called the "Eastern Establishment"; were convinced that all too often the nation's internal and external policies were dictated by powerful business and commercial interests; and called on policymakers to devote their attention almost exclusively to domestic issues. To the minds of spokesmen for these movements, foreign affairs were a major and costly distraction from the nation's primary business—the solution of internal problems. See the analysis of Buchananism in Steven Stark, "Politics: Right-Wing Populist," *Atlantic Monthly,* February 1996, pp. 19–30.

15. See *Time* magazine's detailed analysis of Pat Buchanan's viewpoints in the issue of November 6, 1995, pp. 22–29.

16. See the views of Adolph Reed, Jr., in "Ebony and Ivory Fascists," *The Progressive,* April 1996, p. 20.

17. See Buchanan's views, as reported in *Time* magazine, November 6, 1995, p. 30.

18. One political analyst pointed out that several years earlier, when the Cold War was being waged intensely, Pat Buchanan had been equally outspoken *in favor* of "promoting democracy and free market economies" throughout the world. He had himself become personally wealthy in the market conditions existing within the American society. See the *New York Times,* December 3, 1995, dispatch by Ernest Tollerson.

19. See Jeremy D. Rosner, "The Know-Nothings Must Know Something," *Foreign Policy* 101 (winter 1995–96): 117–18; Norman J. Ornstein, "Foreign Policy and the 1992 Election," *Foreign Affairs* 71 (spring 1992): 9–10; and Daniel Yankelovich, "Foreign Policy after the Election," *Foreign Affairs* 71 (fall 1992): 6–7.

20. These and other conservative assessments of Buchananism may be found in Kaufman, *America First!* 211–12.

21. Frum, *What's Right,* 59.

22. See "Rabid Run," *The Progressive,* April 1996, p. 4.

23. Stark, "Politics: Right-Wing Populist," 29.

24. See Stark, "Politics: Right-Wing Populist," 28–29; and John Nichols, "Buchanan Fodder," *The Progressive* 60 (April 1996): 23–25.

CHAPTER 2

1. See the *New York Times,* November 18, 1995, dispatch by Tim Weiner. President Bill Clinton took the position that the action of the House had no binding force on his powers; and in fact he contended that, even if the Senate joined in supporting the measure, such congressional actions could not restrain the president's conduct of foreign affairs.

2. Secretary of State Baker's views are quoted in the *New York Times,* May 14, 2000, dispatch by Blaine Harden.

3. George Bush's comments on America's proper foreign policy role after the Cold War are quoted in the editorial in the *New Republic,* March 6, 2000, p. 12.

4. One study calls attention to a number of specific steps initiated by conservative groups on Capitol Hill in an effort to restrain America's activities abroad. These include significant reductions in the foreign aid programs; attempts in the House and Senate to abolish the United States Information Agency, the Agency for International Development, and the Arms Control and Disarmament Agency; reductions in exchange-of-persons programs with other nations; significant cuts in America's financial support of the United Nations and other multilateral agencies; the closing of several embassies and other American posts abroad; and attempted restraints imposed by Congress on the president's powers in the foreign policy field. According to the author, these moves reflect a prevailing view in Congress that the size and scope of government generally—in foreign, no less than domestic, affairs—must be drastically reduced. Preoccupied with domestic problems, the "new majority" in Congress exhibited little or no concern about America's place in the world and its international responsibilities. See Robert S. Greenberger, "Dateline Capitol Hill: The New Majority's Foreign Policy," *Foreign Policy,* no. 101 (winter 1995–96): 159–69. Or as another study of the matter emphasizes, the United States needs a new set of norms for guiding its interventionist moves abroad in the post–Cold War era. See Laura Reed and Carl Kaysen, eds., *Emerging Norms of Justified Intervention* (Cambridge, Mass.: American Academy of Arts and Sciences, 1994).

5. See the views of Cal Thomas in the *Baton Rouge Morning Advocate,* December 1, 1995. Another commentator has said that America's military forces must not be regarded as "firefighters to be used whenever an alarm bell rings; nor robocops to be used as international policemen; nor paid Foreign Legionnaires to be flung into hotspots" around the world. The central purpose of the armed forces is to "defend our Constitution and our country"; and they "must be employed judiciously." See the views of David Hackworth in the *Baton Rouge Morning Advocate,* November 30, 1995. Similarly, one of America's military leaders has cautioned that the military establishment cannot serve as "the rapid-reaction force for the global village." He cautions against a tendency to rely upon the armed forces to achieve a long list of questionable objectives that make little positive contribution to the well-being of the American society. See the views of former army chief of staff General Dennis Reimer, as quoted in John Hillen, "General Chaos," *National Review,* December 31, 1996, p. 22.

6. See the views of Ted G. Carpenter in *A Search for Enemies: America's Alliances after the Cold War* (Washington, D.C.: CATO Institute, 1992).

7. According to one experienced commentator, the Vietnam War—which involved stag-

gering casualties and billions of dollars in expenditures for the USA—"should stand as an endur-ing testament to the pitfalls of interventionism" and to the "limits of power" for Americans. See George C. Herring, "America and Vietnam: The Unending War," *Foreign Affairs* 70 (winter 1991–92): 119. In the same vein, another commentator has offered a highly critical analysis of what is called "the Clinton Doctrine" governing America's global role. In effect, the doctrine states: "Something must be done [about a particular global or regional problem], this is some-thing, therefore we must do it"! In this view, it is a recurring error by some policymakers to base diplomatic decisions on "intentions" rather than on the actual or likely "results" of a particular course of action. Hillen, "General Chaos," 21. In William Pfaff's view, after the Cold War, offi-cials in Washington must abandon the kind of "universalist pretensions" that too often motivated American diplomatic behavior in the past. See his analysis in the *Chicago Tribune*, November 12, 1996.

8. As one conservative commentary on recent American policy toward Africa expressed it, officials in Washington need a set of "ground rules" providing guidance for the nation's involve-ment in problems beyond its own borders. Experience has made clear, for example, that in far too many instances, "humanitarian intervention" by the USA has failed to achieve its purposes and more often than not has resulted in serious diplomatic reverses for the United States. In the future, policymakers should avoid interventionist moves abroad that lack "foresight, understand-ing, or strategic purpose." See the editorial entitled "Into Africa," *National Review*, December 9, 1996. Another prominent conservative observer and a member of President Ronald Reagan's foreign policy team has cautioned against the belief that the USA can "democratize" foreign soci-eties. This idea is "belied by an enormous body of evidence based on the experience of dozens of countries." In her view, the nation's leaders have consistently overestimated their ability to influence foreign political movements and tendencies. See the views of Jeanne Kirkpatrick, as cited in Mark Gerson, ed., *The Essential Neo-Conservative Reader* (Reading, Mass.: Addison-Wesley, 1996), 169–71.

9. For a number of examples of such differences of opinion among conservative observers, see the more detailed discussion in John Ehrman, *The Rise of Neoconservatism: Intellectuals and For-eign Affairs, 1945–1994* (New Haven: Yale University Press, 1995). The author also calls atten-tion to the evolution in conservative thought about America's global role since World War II. Another analysis of attitudes toward foreign policy issues among the Republican majority in Con-gress found substantial confusion among legislators concerning Washington's approach to global problems. Almost never was there a sense of unanimity among conservative legislators concerning a clear and consistent course of diplomatic action by the USA. See Greenberger, "Dateline Capi-tol Hill," 165–66. On a specific international issue—U.S. policy toward an increasingly assertive China—another study found considerable disagreement among conservative legislators on the question. See the dispatch by Tom Plate to the *Los Angeles Times,* January 21, 1997.

10. More-detailed discussions of the major tenets of conservative thought are available in George H. Nash, *The Conservative Intellectual Movement in America* (New York: Basic Books, 1979); Peter Steinfels, *The Neoconservatives* (New York: Simon and Schuster, 1979); Irving Kristol, *Reflections of a Neoconservative* (New York: Basic Books, 1983); Russell Kirk, *The Conservative Mind,* rev. ed. (Chicago: Regnery, 1987); William F. Buckley, Jr., *Did You Ever See a Dream Walk-ing? American Conservative Thought in the Twentieth Century* (Indianapolis: Bobbs-Merrill, 1970); Thomas Fleming, *The Conservative Movement* (Boston: Twayne Publishers, 1988); Clinton Ros-siter, *Conservatism in America* (New York: Random House, 1962); and Barry Goldwater, *The Con-science of a Conservative* (New York: Macfadden, 1970).

11. See the views of Abraham Lincoln as quoted in Russell Kirk, *The Politics of Prudence* (Bryn

Mawr, Pa.: Intercollegiate Studies Institute, 1993), 145; and Russell Kirk's own views in *ibid.*, 18–20.

12. The skepticism of conservatives about the possibility of achieving rapid progress in human affairs is especially relevant for America's efforts to promote democracy beyond its own borders. Among conservatives, former president Richard Nixon was prominent in raising serious questions about this goal of U.S. foreign policy. In Nixon's view, there were actually *fewer* people living under democratic governments in the mid-1990s than around 1900! In other words, from a democratic perspective, most of the world's societies *have retrogressed* in the twentieth century. (Obviously, in assessing the validity of such conclusions, much depends upon how "democracy" is defined. As we shall see in Chapter 5, using a different definition of the concept, liberals have arrived at a totally different conclusion about the feasibility of American interventionist moves in behalf of democracy abroad.) See Nixon's study *1999: Victory without War* (New York: Simon and Schuster, 1995), 17. Former secretary of state Henry Kissinger is equally skeptical that democracy is expanding throughout the world; and he is dubious that it lies within the power of the USA to change that reality. See his views as quoted in Tony Smith, *America's Mission: The United States and the Worldwide Struggle for Democracy in the Twentieth Century* (Princeton: Princeton University Press, 1994), 210–11. Another conservative analysis concludes that President Jimmy Carter's efforts to promote democracy overseas were, in the vast majority of cases, failures. Despite its deep devotion to the goal, the Carter White House was never able to produce an effective diplomatic strategy for accomplishing the objective. In general terms, this observer is skeptical that the power of the United States has been a decisive factor in progress toward democracy beyond America's own borders. See Smith, *America's Mission*, 265, 306, 344–45.

13. See the views of Irving Kristol as quoted in J. David Hoeveler, *Watch on the Right: Conservative Intellectuals in Post-Modern America* (Madison, Wis.: University of Wisconsin Press, 1990), 93.

14. Conservative commentators quote with approval the views of Senator Daniel Moynihan (D–N.Y.), who observed that it was time liberals learned from conservatives the lesson of "a healthy skepticism" about "the power of government agencies to do good." His views are quoted in E. J. Dionne, Jr., *Why Americans Hate Politics* (New York: Simon and Schuster, 1991), 69. See also Kirk, *The Politics of Prudence*, 21–23.

15. As one example of this phenomenon, one observer cites the Alliance for Progress, formulated by the Kennedy administration, as a case in point. As a multibillion-dollar venture designed to promote democracy throughout Latin America, the program not only failed to achieve its goals, but in some respects may actually have *impeded* the emergence of democracy south of the border. The author concludes that whether stable democracy does or does not emerge in Latin American societies is basically a decision that will ultimately be made by the citizens of the societies involved. See Smith, *America's Mission*, 234–235. Another recent British study concluded that, with rare exceptions, foreign assistance programs by the United States and other nations had accomplished little in promoting progress and national development throughout the Third World. See the *New York Times,* April 7, 1996, dispatch by Howard W. French. Yet another study of U.S. intervention to establish stable democratic institutions in the Philippines is also quite negative concerning the results achieved by Washington's efforts. See Sheila S. Coronel, "Dateline Philippines: The Lost Revolution," *Foreign Policy,* no. 84 (fall 1991): 166–86.

16. A forceful expression of this view is the analysis by Eisuke Sakakibara, "The End of Progressivism: The Search for New Goals," *Foreign Affairs* 74 (September–October 1995): 8–14. Basically the same conclusion is arrived at by several of the contributors to the symposium by Rex Brynen, Bahgat Korany, and Paul Noble, eds., *Political Liberalization and Democratization in the Arab World: Theoretical Perspectives* (Boulder, Colo.: Lynne Rienner, 1995). Comparable conclu-

sions about the results of Washington's intervention to promote freedom and democracy in Latin America are reached by several of the contributors to Joseph Tulchin, ed., *The Consolidation of Democracy in Latin America* (Boulder, Colo.: Lynne Rienner, 1995); and in Tina Rosenberg, "Beyond Elections," *Foreign Policy*, no. 84 (fall 1991): 72–93. Still another study concludes that relatively few Third World societies are destined to have democratic political systems, at least not in the foreseeable future. As the author assesses it, Western-style political democracy "travels a course of declining relevance" for most societies throughout the world. Instead, the twenty-first century is likely to witness "many more Beiruts" (or conditions of internal anarchy) around the globe. See Patrick E. Kennon, *The Twilight of Democracy* (New York: Doubleday, 1995), 253–55.

17. As one student of U.S. foreign policy has expressed it, Americans may expect "continued suffering and carnage" throughout the world in the years ahead. Life outside the zone of industrialized nations will most likely become "nastier, more brutish and shorter . . . but it will also be televised"! See Michael Mandelbaum, "The Reluctance to Intervene," *Foreign Policy*, no. 95 (summer 1995): 18. Another commentator arrives at basically the same conclusion about the external political environment. To his mind, the last decade of the twentieth century had conditions remarkably like those in Europe during the Thirty Years' War! Instead of a benign "New World Order" that many Americans expected, the global system remained Hobbesian; and for the most part, it was unreceptive to the achievement of Washington's foreign policy goals. In his judgment, Americans are much too prone to attribute "rationality" to political developments abroad. They mistakenly believe that officials in other states will exhibit the same kind of restraint and rationality in the policymaking process, for example, that Washington and Moscow displayed to avoid a nuclear conflagration during the Cuban Missile Crisis of 1962. See the views of Stanley Kober in "Revolutions Gone Bad," *Foreign Policy*, no. 91 (summer 1993): 63–85. See also the assessment of the nature of the global system in Gerson, *The Essential Neo-Conservative Reader*, 161–62. Another conservative analysis concludes that the post–Cold War international system will almost certainly be an increasingly dangerous and unstable milieu, as local and regional conflicts *increase*. Nevertheless, in this view, relatively few of these conflicts will threaten the American nation's vital diplomatic and security interests directly. See Ted G. Carpenter, "The New World Disorder," *Foreign Policy*, no. 84 (fall 1991): 24–25. Yet another observer has called attention to the fact that the emerging international system is likely to be "less predictable" and in some respects more dangerous for the United States than was true under conditions of bipolarity. See Thomas H. Henriksen, "The Coming Great Power Competition," *World Affairs* 158 (fall 1995): 66–68. To the mind of another commentator, in responding to developments abroad Americans have too often ignored the "fragility of reason and the ubiquity of evil" characteristic of the international system. See John Gray's review of the study by Conor Cruise O'Brien, *On the Eve of the Millennium* (New York: Free Press, 1996), in the *National Review*, April 8, 1996, pp. 53–54.

18. See the views of Peter F. Drucker in *The New Realities* (New York: Harper/Collins, 1989), 37–40. Reflecting on the end of the Cold War, another observer has concluded that with regard to international conflicts and disorders, "Incredible as it may seem, the worst part of the worst century in history might still be ahead of us"! Kober, "Revolutions Gone Bad," 83. Joseph Nye makes the point that in the existing global political environment, the ability of *all* "powerful" nations to influence the course of events outside their own borders has *declined*, primarily because of developments like growing economic interdependence, the emergence of transnational actors, the eruption of strong nationalistic tendencies in weak states, and the spread of advanced technological changes. Policymakers in the USA must somehow come to terms with the paradox that weak and poor countries can, nevertheless, exercise considerable influence upon the course of international relations—as in the cases of Peru, Bolivia, Mexico, and Thailand in per-

petuating the "drug problem" for the United States and other advanced societies, or the power that economically weak states possess in their ability to disrupt the international financial and monetary system. See his analysis of the changing nature of national power in "Soft Power," *Foreign Policy* no. 80 (fall 1990): 153–72.

19. As William Clinton prepared to take the presidential oath of office for the second time, a prominent student of American diplomacy warned about "impending or actual international disorders with potentially severe consequences" for the USA. He enumerated a long list of serious global problems, many of which would likely become even more critical and difficult to solve with the passage of time. The overall conclusion was that the new Clinton administration should abandon "universalist" pretensions in its foreign policy and concentrate on solving crucial domestic problems. See the views of William Pfaff in the *Chicago Tribune,* November 12, 1996. In the same vein, after reflecting on the experience of the Persian Gulf War, another commentator concluded that the episode showed that the post–Cold War world "could be far more disorderly," and in some respects more dangerous, than the period of overt Russian-American confrontation. He admonished Americans to keep in mind that, despite the military victory achieved in the Persian Gulf conflict, "military tactics, even when dazzling, do not make a foreign policy"! See the views of Dionne, *Why Americans Hate Politics,* 350.

20. See the summary of the study by Freedom House on the prospects for freedom and democracy abroad in Alan Tonelson, "Jettison the Policy," *Foreign Policy,* no. 97 (winter 1994–95): 125–26.

21. See Nicholas Eberstadt, "Population Changes and National Security," *Foreign Affairs* 70 (summer 1991): 128–29. As this observer sees it, present tendencies could in time produce an international system that is even more dangerous for the security of the United States than the period of the Cold War. The emerging global political environment is becoming increasingly "fractious, contentious and inhumane," posing formidable obstacles for the realization of Western political values. He emphasizes the reality that these values *are not shared* by the vast majority of the world's people. Another study is equally skeptical about efforts by the USA to encourage the spread of democracy throughout the Middle East. See Brynen, Korany, and Noble, eds., *Political Liberalization.*

22. See Senator Moynihan's views as quoted in Gerson, *The Essential Neo-Conservative Reader,* 161–62.

23. See the views of Jeanne Kirkpatrick, as contained in the excerpt from her writing in Gerson, *The Essential Neo-Conservative Reader,* 163–89. Another conservative observer believes that there is no convincing evidence showing that the American people, in contrast to many of their leaders, really support a vigorous campaign to promote human rights overseas. In his view, most citizens understand the deleterious consequences that often result from such a policy better than officials in Washington. Tonelson, "Jettison the Policy," 128.

24. See the views of Herring, "America and Vietnam," 117–19.

25. Richard M. Nixon, *The Real War* (New York: Warner, 1980), 105–106.

26. See, for example, the views of Jeanne Kirkpatrick in Gerson, *The Essential Neo-Conservative Reader,* 169–72; and Kober, "Revolutions Gone Bad," 63–85. Another observer concludes that what he calls "progressivism" (a synonym for Western-style democracy) has become less and less influential on a worldwide basis. See Sakakibara, "The End of Progressivism," 8–14. A different study is dubious about American efforts to "democratize" the world. It also calls into question the long-standing assumption of liberals, that a democratized world is equivalent to a more peaceful and stable world. See Edward Mansfield and Jack Snyder, "Democratization and War," *Foreign Affairs* 74 (May–June 1995): 79–98.

27. According to a leading conservative commentator, it has been a "fundamental fallacy of American foreign policy to believe, in the face of the evidence, that all peoples everywhere are immediately entitled to a liberal government." In his view, such thinking derives from a liberal state of mind in America that seeks to "universalize entitlement programs and the welfare state." See Hoeveler, *Watch on the Right,* 169.

28. See the views of Peter W. Rodman, in "Points of Order," *National Review,* May 1, 1995, p. 36.

29. Referring to abortive efforts by the USA to bring about peace in settings like Zaire, Somalia, and Bosnia, one conservative assessment cautioned against "misguided efforts at nation-building" which resulted in little more than "death and humiliation" for America's armed forces and in dramatic diplomatic setbacks for Washington. The challenge of achieving peace and lasting political stability in these and other cases "is too big a task even for the sole remaining superpower." See the editorial in the *Chicago Tribune,* November 15, 1996. Similarly, a conservative analysis of Washington's efforts to create a durable democratic system in Haiti views those efforts as a conspicuous failure. By its intervention, the USA acquired "a certain responsibility" for Haiti's future and well-being. Moreover, in this view, Haiti's internal problems are becoming more and more critical with the passage of time and are beyond America's capacity to solve. See Nina Shea, "Voodoo Diplomacy," *National Review,* June 17, 1996, pp. 26–27. According to yet another analysis, at some point American policymakers must accept the reality that Haiti's problems—and, by extension, those of many other Third World societies—cannot be solved by other nations, not even by a superpower. See the views of Senator Mike DeWine (R–Ohio) in the *Wall Street Journal,* January 24, 1997. Still another conservative source has admonished policymakers to "remember Somalia" in formulating America's response to crises erupting abroad. National officials must avoid assuming "endless" international commitments, often involving "confused" diplomatic and military missions by the USA. See the editorial in the *Los Angeles Times,* November 15, 1996.

30. Responding to those Americans who called for a campaign in behalf of freedom in other countries (specifically, the Greek effort to win independence from oppressive Turkish rule), Secretary of State John Quincy Adams stated on July 4, 1821, that America's "heart, her benedictions, and her prayers" were always with those people seeking to acquire greater freedom; the American republic was the "well-wisher to the freedom and independence" of people everywhere. At the same time, the United States "goes not abroad in search of monsters to destroy"; it is the "champion and vindicator" only of its own freedom. See the long excerpt from Adams's address in Norman A. Graebner, ed., *Ideas and Diplomacy: Readings in the Intellectual Tradition of American Foreign Policy* (New York: Oxford University Press, 1964), 87–90.

31. Thus, one observer emphasizes that, while the United States is currently the only superpower in the international system, this condition must not be regarded as permanent. In his view, it will almost certainly change, as other increasingly powerful entities—such as the European Community, Germany, Japan, and China—acquire the power to play a more assertive role in international affairs. The idea—fashionable among some recent commentators on U.S. foreign policy—of a stable, U.S.-controlled "unipolar" global system is, in this assessment, "a mirage." See Carpenter, "The New World Disorder," 28–29. Comparable conclusions are reached in the study by Jeffrey T. Bergner, *The New Superpowers: Germany, Japan, and the U.S. and the New World Order* (New York: St. Martin's Press, 1991).

32. See Gerson, *The Essential Neo-Conservative Reader,* 161.

33. Walter Lippmann was the author of numerous books and articles on American foreign policy. A convenient listing of his principal works may be found in Joel H. Rosenthal, *Righteous*

Realists: Political Realism, Responsible Power, and American Culture in the Nuclear Age (Baton Rouge: Louisiana State University Press, 1991), 179–80. Basically the same conclusion about the nation's diplomatic behavior was reached by the architect of the containment policy, George F. Kennan, in his *American Diplomacy: 1900–1950* (New York: New American Library, 1951).

34. A notable example of such commitments is provided by what has come to be called "humanitarian interventionism" by the United States, undertaken to relieve crisis conditions providing a serious threat to human life in societies overseas. According to a number of conservative observers, while the temptation for the USA to intervene on humanitarian grounds often seems compelling, Washington is seldom able to achieve the proclaimed goals—and in the end the venture is abandoned by national officials. A fundamental reason why such intervention fails is that sooner or later, in order to improve existing conditions within the society concerned, the United States must engage in *political* intervention; and in time the American people and their leaders are unwilling to pay the price that prolonged political intervention entails. See Mandelbaum, "The Reluctance to Intervene," 11–13.

35. See Christopher Layne and Benjamin Schwarz, "American Hegemony—Without an Enemy," *Foreign Policy*, no. 92 (fall 1993): 23. Other terms used by conservative spokesmen to describe the desired policy of the United States after the Cold War are a position of "strategic independence" and of "benign detachment" in dealing with international issues. See Doug Bandow, "Avoiding War," *Foreign Policy*, no. 89 (winter 1993–93): 173.

36. The principal tenets of realist political thought, especially as they might apply to the foreign policy of the United States, are identified and analyzed in Hans J. Morgenthau, "The Mainspring of American Foreign Policy," *American Political Science Review* 44 (December 1950): 833–49; and his *In Defense of the National Interest* (New York: Knopf, 1951). See also Kennan, *American Diplomacy*. Another useful study is Ernst B. Haas, "The Balance of Power as a Guide to Policy-Making," *Journal of Politics* 15 (August 1953): 370–99. Other helpful analyses of the realist approach to U.S. foreign policy are Greg Russell, *Hans J. Morgenthau and the Ethics of American Statecraft* (Baton Rouge: Louisiana State University Press, 1990); Norman A. Graebner, ed., *America as a World Power: A Realist Appraisal from Wilson to Reagan* (Wilmington, Del.: Scholarly Resources, 1984); Joseph Frankel, *National Interest* (New York: Praeger Publishers, 1970); and W. David Clinton, *The Two Faces of National Interest* (Baton Rouge: Louisiana State University Press, 1994). For a collection of essays evaluating the utility of *Realpolitik* for the contemporary and future international system, see Michael E. Brown, Sean M. Lynn-Jones, and Steven E. Miller, eds., *The Perils of Anarchy: Contemporary Realism and International Security* (Cambridge, Mass.: MIT Press, 1995).

37. William G. Hyland is but one among a number of informed commentators who account for America's victory in the Cold War mainly in *Realpolitik* terms. In brief, Moscow lost the contest with Washington primarily because, by the decade of the 1990s, the "correlation of forces" throughout the world became highly unfavorable for Russia. See his "Foreign Affairs at 70," *Foreign Affairs* 71 (fall 1992): 171–93. Another observer believes in the post–Cold War era, the dominant goal of U.S. foreign policy should not be "global hegemony"; instead, Washington should seek to promote global peace and security by relying upon "interlocking balances of power" in the major regions of the world. See Ramesh Thakur, "India after Nonalignment," *Foreign Affairs* 71 (spring 1992): 181–82. In the same vein, another study calls upon officials in Washington to create and maintain what is called a "loose balance of power" among Russia, China, Japan, and the USA to preserve peace and stability in Asia. See Michael Mandelbaum, *The Strategic Quadrangle: Russia, China, Japan, and the United States* (New York: Council on Foreign Relations, 1995). This is also the view of Henriksen, as the United States confronts the growing power of Japan

and China in global affairs. See Henriksen, "The Coming Great Power Competition," 68. Similarly, a longtime observer of Russian affairs believes that in its relations with Moscow after the Cold War, Washington must base its policy upon *Realpolitik* principles. See Dimitri Simes, "America and the Post-Soviet Republics," *Foreign Affairs* 71 (spring 1992): 73–89.

38. Alternatively, one observer has used the term "benign *Realpolitik*" to describe what he believes ought to be America's approach to foreign affairs after the Cold War. See the letter by John B. Kotch to *Foreign Policy,* no. 94 (spring 1994): 172–73.

39. Daniel Deudney and G. John Ikenberry, "After the Long War," *Foreign Policy,* no. 94 (spring 1994): 29–30. See also the views of Robert D. Hormats in "The Roots of American Power," *Foreign Affairs* 70 (summer 1991): 132–50. In this assessment, the American society's *economic* strength has become the key to its influence abroad. Or as another student of U.S. foreign policy concludes, there is a prevailing mind-set among the American people that the nation is "in decline," owing primarily to the existence of certain serious economic conditions within the society. See Jagdish Bhagwati, "The Diminished Giant Syndrome: How Declinism Drives Trade Policy," *Foreign Affairs* 72 (spring 1993): 22–26. A variation on this idea is the conclusion arrived at in another study, that the deterioration in the value of the dollar vis-à-vis other currencies will have a "shattering effect" upon America's overall power abroad. See Diane B. Kunz, "The Fall of the Dollar Order: The World the United States Is Losing," *Foreign Affairs* 74 (July–August 1995): 26.

40. Stanley Hoffmann, "The Case for Leadership," *Foreign Policy,* no. 81 (winter 1990–91): 20–39.

41. More-detailed discussion of the approach to foreign affairs known as the "new realism" may be found in Nye, "Soft Power," 153–72, and the same author's "What New World Order?" *Foreign Affairs* 71 (spring 1992): 83–97; Martin Van Creveld, *The Transformation of War* (New York: Free Press, 1991); Hormats, "The Roots of American Power," 130–49; James Chace, *The Consequences of the Peace* (New York: Twentieth Century Fund, 1992); Richard N. Haass, "Paradigm Lost," *Foreign Affairs* 74 (January–February 1995): 43–59; and Earl C. Ravenal, "The Case for Adjustment," *Foreign Policy,* no. 81 (winter 1990–91): 3–20. Ravenal, for example, is convinced that the old *Realpolitik* concept of balance of power will no longer be relevant globally, although it *will* in some instances still be a useful concept in preserving *regional* peace and stability. In an analysis of future U.S. relations with Asia, another observer believes that Washington's approach must increasingly take into account the fact that economic factors have now become the key element in a nation's power. See Robert A. Scalapino, "The United States and Asia: Future Prospects," *Foreign Affairs* 70 (winter 1991–92): 19–40. Still another observer is convinced that in recent years the security of the United States has been jeopardized, primarily because of a number of adverse economic tendencies weakening the nation's power and influence abroad. See Theodore H. Moran, "International Economics and National Security," *Foreign Affairs* 69 (winter 1990–91): 74–90. A former director of the CIA believes that sweeping changes are needed in the process of collecting and analyzing intelligence data. In the past, officials engaged in this aspect of foreign affairs devoted undue attention to collecting and analyzing the *military* aspects of national power. In the future, they must operate upon the basis of a "neo-realistic" assessment of developments abroad, recognizing that *economic* factors have become the most decisive element in national power. See Stansfield Turner, "Intelligence for a New World Order," *Foreign Affairs* 70 (fall 1991): 148–66.

42. A specific example of such thinking is provided by one analysis of American diplomacy in dealing with the crisis in the Balkans. To the mind of this commentator, Washington's primary responsibility lay in achieving a "consensus" among its European partners with regard to external

intervention to restore peace and stability to this volatile region. America's proper approach in responding to the challenge in the Balkans, in other words, was to play a "supportive role" in Western efforts to deal with the crisis. See Martin van Heuven, "Rehabilitating Serbia," *Foreign Policy*, no. 96 (fall 1994): 38–48.

43. Martin Walker, "The Establishment Reports," *Foreign Policy*, no. 89 (winter 1992–93): 90. For an analysis of post–Cold War U.S. foreign policy from a neo-realistic perspective, see Edward N. Luttwak, "Toward Post-Heroic Warfare," *Foreign Affairs* 74 (May–June 1995): 109–22.

44. For a forceful statement of this view, see Henriksen, "The Coming Great Power Competition," 63–71. According to this observer, the period following the Cold War will witness a return to nineteenth-century-era "power politics," in which the pursuit of national interest and the maintenance of the balance of power were high-priority diplomatic goals. More than ever, officials in Washington must stand ready to protect America's interests in global affairs. This requires them to be prepared militarily and to use armed force when necessary to protect the nation's diplomatic and security interests. It is worth noting that, even among devotees of the "new realism," it is acknowledged that military power is still sometimes a decisive factor in determining political outcomes. Nye emphasizes, for example, that for many years Japan's vast economic and financial power has been built up and made possible by America's guarantee of Japanese military security. Yet as advocates of this approach to international affairs assess it, the *relative* importance of military power has declined. As Nye views it, in the new era a nation's influence abroad is more likely to be determined by what he calls "soft power." A synonym for this idea is "cooperative power," or the ability of a nation to gain the support of other nations for its foreign policy goals. See Nye, "Soft Power," 166–67.

45. Rodman, "Points of Order," 38.

46. According to Henriksen, the emergence of the "new Russia" signifies no necessary change in the nation's foreign policy behavior. Russia remains "imperial and expansionist" in dealing with the outside world; if and when its internal economic problems are solved, these tendencies may well become *more* pronounced in Moscow's external behavior. See Henriksen, "The Coming Great Power Competition," 69–70.

47. For example, Zbigniew Brzezinski emphasizes that, in the post–Cold War period, U.S. foreign policy must take fully into account "geo-strategic" factors affecting its relations with other nations, such as the new Russia. Despite the collapse of its Communist regime, this observer does *not* believe that Russia's relations with other countries will be free of crises; the nations of Eastern Europe, for example, remain suspicious of Moscow's intentions toward them. See Zbigniew Brzezinski, "Selective Global Containment," *Foreign Affairs* 70 (fall 1991): 1–20. Another observer points out that within the orbit of Russia's former empire, Moscow's influence and power will always be greater than Washington's. In its diplomacy toward the former Soviet republics, Washington must avoid arousing fears of Russian "encirclement" by outside nations, since this might well engender a revival of Russian hostility and aggressiveness abroad. See the letter from Philip H. Gordon to *Foreign Affairs* 73 (May–June 1994): 177–78. Similarly, another authority warns that in dealing with the former members of the Soviet Union, the USA must avoid the temptation to form new security systems in the region linked with the West. Moscow would almost certainly view such a development as a threat to its own security. See Simes, "America and the Post-Soviet Republics," 88–89.

48. See, for example, the views of Adam Yarmolinsky, in his review of several books dealing with the Cold War, in *Foreign Policy*, no. 97 (winter 1994–95): 168–69. Similar conclusions are reached by Carpenter in "The New World Disorder," 38–39, who urges policymakers to take preventive action to deter aggression or other serious dangers to the security of the United States.

49. See, for example, the views of former secretary of state Henry Kissinger, who proposes that Washington give highest priority to promoting the democratic ideal "by fostering close co-operation where it already exists, especially among the nations bordering the Atlantic and within the Western Hemisphere." Outside that zone, in Kissinger's view, the USA has little prospect for imposing and protecting democratic principles and American values. His views are quite comparable to advocates of the Hoover-Taft approach to U.S. foreign policy. *Newsweek,* January 27, 1997, p. 80.

50. The concept of "Fortress America" is explained more fully in Crabb, *Policy-Makers and Critics,* 227–30. Senator Robert A. Taft's views on America's proper global role are spelled out in his *A Foreign Policy for Americans* (Garden City, N.Y.: Doubleday, 1951); those of Barry Goldwater are in his *Conscience of a Conservative.*

51. The guiding principle of U.S. foreign policy, according to one observer, is to protect the nation's security. While this is the foremost objective, policymakers must also understand that most conflicts and crises abroad do not impinge directly upon the security interests of the United States. Washington's intervention in such developments has often in the end merely aggravated the problem of safeguarding national security. See Bandow, "Avoiding War," 164–65. This same basic viewpoint is expressed by Elliott Abrams in *Security and Sacrifice: Isolation, Intervention and American Foreign Policy* (Indianapolis: Hudson Institute, 1995).

52. A specific example of such thinking is provided in the analysis of the challenge of continuing nuclear proliferation on the global scene. In this view, multinational efforts to restrain such proliferation have quite clearly failed. Under these conditions, the United States must scale down its global security commitments to avoid becoming involved in possible regional conflicts in which nuclear weapons might eventually be used. See Ted G. Carpenter, "Closing the Nuclear Umbrella," *Foreign Affairs* 73 (March–April 1994): 8–13. See also several of the essays in Lori F. Damrosch, ed., *Enforcing Restraint: Collective Intervention in Internal Conflicts* (New York: Council on Foreign Relations, 1993).

53. One study of U.S. foreign policy contends that in recent years, Washington has tended to exaggerate, and has overreacted to, global developments threatening national security. In the post–Cold War era, policymakers must restrain this impulse. See Robert H. Johnson, *Improbable Dangers: U.S. Conceptions of Threats in the Cold War and After* (New York: St. Martin's, 1994). As another commentator has expressed the idea, most foreign crisis and conflicts do *not* pose a direct or imminent threat to the security and well-being of the American society. See Bandow, "Avoiding War," 167. Another observer believes that several diplomatic setbacks by the United States in recent years can be attributed to the fact that policymakers did not define the national interest clearly and unambiguously before they intervened in crises abroad. See Kotch, letter to *Foreign Policy,* 173. To cite a specific case in point, a study of U.S. policy toward the Middle East is convinced that in most respects, the movement known as "Islamic Fundamentalism"—widely condemned in the Western news media—as a rule poses no direct or imminent threat to America's security and diplomatic interests. See Graham E. Fuller and Ian O. Lesser, *A Sense of Siege: Geopolitics of Islam and the West* (Boulder, Colo.: Westview Press, 1995).

54. In the words of another leading conservative observer, too often in the past, officials in Washington have made unduly optimistic assessments of developments and tendencies abroad, such as the receptivity of other nations to Western democratic ideas and ideals. In a number of instances policymakers have mistaken "evidence of popular discontent" abroad with a "will to democracy" in foreign societies; and this error in turn prepared the way for a diplomatic "disaster" for the United States. See the views of Jeanne Kirkpatrick in Gerson, *The Essential Neo-Conservative Reader,* 163–89.

55. Carpenter, "The New World Disorder," 37.

56. See Jennone Walker, "Keeping America in Europe," *Foreign Policy,* no. 83 (summer 1991): 128–29. See also Owen Harris, ed., *America's Purpose: Visions of U.S. Foreign Policy* (San Francisco: ICS Press, 1991). Most of the contributors to this symposium call for a reordering of national priorities, with greater attention being devoted to domestic problems.

57. According to one prominent conservative, who represented the United States at the United Nations, the organization was not a "place of rational discourse" about global problems. Despite the expectations of its founders, the UN does not "express some transcendent world interest to which individual nations would subordinate their narrow pursuits." She was convinced that, to the contrary, in too many cases the organization's deliberations and actions were at variance with America's diplomatic interests; with the passage of time, "anti-American fever" became pervasive among the members of the organization. See the views of Jeanne Kirkpatrick in Hoeveler, *Watch on the Right,* 161–62. To the mind of another commentator, not only have peacekeeping efforts under the aegis of the United Nations failed in most cases, but even worse, in certain respects they have *aggravated* the task of achieving peace and stability in a number of societies abroad. See Saadia Touval "Why the U.N. Fails," *Foreign Affairs* 73 (September–October 1994): 45. Another conservative source denounced the concept of "assertive multilateralism" and criticized the Clinton administration's foreign policy team for relying upon the United Nations and the mythical "world community" to provide guidance and legitimacy for America's diplomatic moves. See the editorial in the *National Review,* December 31, 1996, p. 6.

58. See Donald J. Feith, "Chemical Reaction," *National Review,* July 15, 1996, pp. 40–41; the views of Saadia Touval in "Why the U.N. Fails," 44–45; and the conclusions reached by Bandow in "Avoiding War," 156–58. Another commentator is convinced that in many cases, unsuccessful multinational peacekeeping efforts do more harm than good, since they tend to discourage efforts by the society concerned to solve its own problems. See the examination of several case studies in Damrosch, ed., *Enforcing Restraint.*

59. See, for example, the views of a number of right-wing critics of U.S. foreign economic policy, as reported in Bhagwati, "The Diminished Giant Syndrome," 24–26.

60. Bandow, "Avoiding War," 57.

61. As one commentator has phrased it, Americans value the concept of "muscular unilateralism" in dealing with global issues. Greenberger, "Dateline Capitol Hill," 169. Another observer has concluded that in the new era, the United States must follow an interventionist course abroad only when its own diplomatic and security interests are threatened by developments overseas—a decision to be arrived at by officials in Washington. See Elliott Abrams, *Security and Sacrifice: Isolation, Intervention, and American Foreign Policy* (Indianapolis: Hudson Institute, 1995).

62. The concept of the diplomatic "free hand" was an integral feature of classical isolationist thought down to World War II. The basic idea was that the United States government must at all times preserve the right to determine its own position in international affairs unilaterally. Correctly or not, this was widely interpreted as an essential element in the nation's sovereignty. During the 1930s, for example, on a number of occasions Washington collaborated independently (or offered to collaborate) with the League of Nations in its efforts to respond to developments threatening global peace (such as Japan's aggression in Manchuria). But as required by the concept of the "free hand," such diplomatic decisions by the USA were made by policymakers *in Washington,* not by majority vote in international agencies like the League of Nations or the allied coalition. The concept of the free hand is explained more fully in Cecil V. Crabb, Jr., *The Doctrines of American Foreign Policy: Their Meaning, Role, and Future* (Baton Rouge: Louisiana State University Press, 1982), 384–86.

63. Thus, a leading conservative spokesman has concluded that with the end of the Cold War, America's position as a superpower is rapidly eroding. Russia of course is no longer a superpower, but with the passage of time the very concept of the superpower becomes increasingly questionable. In the new global system, no superpowers will exist. There will be no such thing as a "center'" in world politics. Therefore, it will be "increasingly difficult for the United States to have a foreign policy at all." Drucker, *The New Realities,* 37–38. See also Bergner, *The New Superpowers.* And for a detailed analysis of factors undermining America's position as a military superpower, see Earl C. Ravenal, *Designing Defense for a New World Order: The Military Budget in 1992 and Beyond* (Washington, D.C.: CATO Institute, 1991).

64. Prominent among the exceptions are Taiwan, South Korea, Singapore, Brazil, and Turkey. Many commentators put Iran on the list before the overthrow of the monarchy in 1979. After that event, the country entered a prolonged period of economic decline.

65. One conservative source, for example, criticized the Clinton White House for being enamored of the mythical "world community" and of engaging in "assertive unilateralism" in efforts to solve global problems. See the editorial "No Dream Team," in the *National Review,* December 31, 1996, p. 8. Other criticisms of U.S. policy in this vein may be found in Robert Strausz-Hupé, *Democracy and American Foreign Policy: Reflections on the Legacy of Alexis de Tocqueville* (New Brunswick, N.J.: Transaction Press, 1995); Samuel M. Makinda, *Seeking Peace from Chaos: Humanitarian Intervention in Somalia* (Boulder, Colo.: Lynne Rienner, for the International Peace Academy, 1993); Thomas Carothers, *In the Name of Democracy: U.S. Policy toward Latin America in the Reagan Years* (Berkeley: University of California Press, 1993); and several of the essays in the symposium Harris, ed., *America's Purpose.*

66. See the analysis of multilateral peacekeeping efforts in Touval, "Why the U.N. Fails," 44–57. A more detailed analysis of the problem is Paul F. Diehl, *International Peacekeeping* (Baltimore: Johns Hopkins University Press, 1993).

67. For example, one commentator is extremely doubtful that democracy is emerging on a global basis or that it will become the prevalent form of government in the foreseeable future. It has little prospect of being established in what the author calls "stagnant societies" throughout the Third World. See Jacques Delors, "Europe's Ambitions," *Foreign Policy,* no. 80 (fall 1990): 14–27. Another commentator anticipates that "progressivism" (a synonym for democracy) will in fact become *less* widespread throughout the international system with the passage of time; Washington must accommodate itself to this reality. See Sakakibara, "The End of Progressivism," 8–14.

68. A leading French advocate of European unification once stated that a dominant purpose of the movement was to "obtain independence from America." See the views of François Mitterrand as quoted in the *National Review,* May 20, 1996, p. 10. See also Jonathan Clarke, "Replacing NATO," *Foreign Policy,* no. 93 (winter 1993–94): 22–41; Adrian Hyde-Price, *European Security beyond the Cold War* (London: Sage, 1991); and Carpenter, *A Search for Enemies.* As another commentator assesses the matter, the concept of Western "security" must be redefined after the Cold War. Today and in the future, threats to the peace and stability of the West will arise mainly from conflicts *within* nations, and from the inability of governments to make their authority effective within their own borders—problems that NATO is poorly equipped to solve. See Daniel N. Nelson, "Europe's Unstable East," *Foreign Policy,* no. 82 (spring 1991): 137–59.

69. A number of specific examples illustrating the point are provided in Layne and Schwarz, "American Hegemony—Without an Enemy," 5–24; Carpenter, "The New World Disorder," 24–26; and Ravenal, *Designing Defense for a New World Order.*

70. For a detailed examination of a specific case illustrating this danger, see Nancy B. Tucker,

Uncertain Friendships: Taiwan, Hong Kong, and the United States, 1945–1992 (New York: Twayne Publishers, 1994).

71. This is the view of several of the contributors to the symposium on U.S. policy after the Cold War in Harris, *America's Purpose*. See, for example, C. Michael Armstrong, "Up to the Challenge?" *Foreign Affairs* 74 (July–August 1995): 21. Other pressing economic and social problems facing American society are identified and examined in detail in Drucker, *The New Realities*. From a different perspective, another commentator is convinced that with very rare exceptions, interventionist efforts by the USA to promote human rights abroad have failed and are likely to continue to be unsuccessful. Therefore, as many pre–World War II isolationists contended, the most effective contribution Americans can make in achieving this goal overseas is to concentrate upon promoting human rights at home. See Tonelson, "Jettison the Policy," 121–33.

72. Steven F. Goldman, "Revitalizing the Special Relationship," *World Affairs* 158 (fall 1995): 80–81.

73. Goldman, "Revitalizing the Special Relationship," 82–83.

74. See Clarke, "Replacing NATO," 22–23.

75. In the view of a leading British official, from the beginning NATO had three major purposes: to keep Russia out of Europe; to keep America in Europe; and to keep Germany down. With the end of the Cold War, the first and third of these goals were no longer applicable. See Goldman, "Revitalizing the Special Relationship," 82. Some U.S. commentators call for the outright dismantling of NATO, in the belief that the alliance has outlived its original purpose and no longer contributes to the achievement of U.S. foreign policy goals. See, for example, Ted G. Carpenter, *Beyond NATO: Staying Out of Europe's Wars* (Washington, D.C.: CATO Institute, 1994). Other conservative U.S. commentators take a less drastic approach, holding that in time, NATO will need to be replaced with a new security system that is better adapted to meet the kinds of challenges likely to confront the West in the future. See Nelson, "Europe's Unstable East," 156–58. Another analysis basically concurs with this view, concluding that NATO no longer serves the interests of its members. The alliance needs to be replaced with a "continent-wide security structure" designed to respond to those specific challenges likely to arise in the post–Cold War era. See Clarke, "Replacing NATO," 22–23. Still other views concerning NATO's value and future are expressed in several of the essays in Charles Kupchan, ed., *Nationalism and Nationalistic Conflicts in the New Europe* (Ithaca: Cornell University Press, 1995).

76. Jenonne Walker, "Keeping America in Europe," 129. Another commentator is convinced that as time passes, a unified Europe will take positions opposed to those of the USA. In this view, the move toward greater regional unity in Europe is basically an "illiberal and anti-American" development. See John Laughland, "Fortress Europe," *National Review*, April 8, 1996, pp. 44–46.

77. For these and other criticisms of NATO from a conservative perspective, see Nixon, *1999*, 206–207.

78. A strong case against the augmentation of NATO is made, for example, by Karl-Heinz Kemp in "The Folly of Rapid NATO Expansion," *Foreign Policy*, no. 98 (spring 1995): 116–29. Regarding an "expanded" NATO, this commentator raises the question Would the USA be prepared to protect Poland against a possible attack by an independent Ukraine? See also the view of Clarke, "Replacing NATO," 22–41. As this observer assesses it, in the new era the Conference on Security and Cooperation in Europe (CSCE) is a better mechanism for preserving European security than NATO. He therefore urged officials in Washington to "look beyond" NATO in dealing with regional security questions. Another observer is convinced that, with the decline of NATO as a security mechanism, the USA must revive the historic Anglo-American "special

relationship" as a replacement for the alliance. See Goldman, "Revitalizing the Special Relationship," 80–81. Henry Kissinger also identified a number of problems that are likely to result from an "enlarged" NATO. See his views in *Newsweek,* January 27, 1997, p. 81.

79. In the view of one observer, policymakers in Washington must guard against any tendency to view the level of allied co-operation achieved during the Persian Gulf War as normative. On the contrary, it was the result of certain unique factors and special circumstances and, for that reason, is unlikely to be witnessed in future crises. See Carpenter, "The New World Disorder," 27–28. This is also the view of Bandow in "Avoiding War," 166–167. Another experienced observer of European affairs believes that as time passes, there is the real likelihood that a united Europe will become more and more "inward-looking," exhibiting little interest in problems outside its immediate orbit. See Hoffmann, "The Case for Leadership," 34–37.

80. A number of conservative commentators believe, for example, that, as European political and economic unification movements proceed, basic policy differences between the USA and its Western allies will become increasingly pronounced. See "This Week," in the *National Review,* May 20, 1996, p. 10; and Laughland, "Fortress Europe," 44–46.

81. See Laughland, "Fortress Europe," 46.

82. See Kemp, "The Folly of Rapid NATO Expansion," 118–119. American involvement in the ongoing crisis in the Balkans is analyzed more fully in Chapter 6. For a forceful assertion of the view that in the new post–Cold War era the United States should refrain from intervening in Europe's regional conflicts and disputes, such as the Balkans crisis, see Carpenter, *Beyond NATO.*

83. As merely one example, one commentator has noted that efforts by the European nations to form a new "standby peacekeeping brigade" for use in dealing with regional and local conflicts ought to be welcomed by officials in Washington, since it would relieve the USA of the obligation to become involved in "every humanitarian emergency" abroad. See "This Week," in the *National Review,* December 31, 1996, p. 8. In time, as another commentator sees it, America's military forces on the Continent will be withdrawn, with the European allies shouldering the principal burden for regional stability and peacekeeping. See Walker, "Keeping America in Europe," 132–34.

84. See Ravenal, *Designing Defense for a New World Order.* Referring to the crisis in the Balkans, one commentator contended that the American people were opposed to any large-scale military involvement by the United States. Instead, they expected the European allies to assume primary responsibility for peacekeeping in the region. See van Heuven, "Rehabilitating Serbia," 38–48. Former President Richard Nixon was but one among many conservative spokesmen who deplored the fact that the allies had long enjoyed a "free ride" in paying the costs of the Western defense effort. See Nixon, *1999,* 219–20.

85. See Ehrman, *The Rise of Neoconservatism,* 127–28; and Ravenal, *Designing Defense for a New World Order.*

86. See Kissinger's views on U.S. policy toward the "new Russia" in *Newsweek,* January 27, 1997, p. 81.

87. This is the description of conditions in Russia for other formerly Communist countries, as seen by a high official in Czechoslovakia. See Kober, "Revolutions Gone Bad," 77; and Dimitri Simes, "Reform Reaffirmed," *Foreign Policy,* no. 90 (spring 1993): 54–56.

88. Simes, "Reform Reaffirmed," 55–56.

89. Ibid., 55. As this observer sees it, Americans must come to terms with the fact that the Russian version of "democracy" will, in the end, be very different from the American, and more generally Western, conception of it. Stanley Hoffmann is also skeptical about the ability of the United States and other foreign nations to influence developments in Russia and its former empire decisively. See Hoffmann, "The Case for Leadership," 34–37.

90. Mansfield and Snyder, "Democratization and War," 79–98. With regard to Washington's policy toward the new Russia and other regions, this analysis raises serious questions about interventionist moves by the USA to promote democracy abroad. In the view of another commentator, a "slavish" insistence upon the democratic principle of majority rule in Russia and other settings can reinforce centrifugal forces that are "tearing apart" the fabric of the society. See Viktor Alksnis, "Suffering from Self-Determination," *Foreign Policy,* no. 84 (fall 1991): 69–70.

91. See Kennon, *The Twilight of Democracy,* ix, 244.

92. As many members of the Republican-controlled Congress viewed the matter, foreign aid programs must be "budget driven," or determined in the light of the American society's own problems and needs. See Greenberger, "Dateline Capitol Hill," 159–63.

93. According to one commentator, American-led efforts to implant democracy in foreign societies has almost always failed; and in some instances, these efforts have been *antithetical* to the emergence of democratic institutions within the society. See Smith, *America's Mission,* 311–45. This overall verdict is concurred in by Kennon in *The Twilight of Democracy.* In the view of Jeanne Kirkpatrick, Americans must, in dealing with Russia and other societies, abandon the idea that "it is possible to democratize governments, any time, anywhere, and under any circumstances." See her views as quoted in Gerson, *The Essential Neo-Conservative Reader,* 170–72.

94. See the views of Henry Kissinger on U.S. policy toward the Middle East in *Newsweek,* January 27, 1997, pp. 79–80.

95. An experienced observer of Middle Eastern affairs is dubious that rapid progress will be made in resolving the Arab-Israeli conflict. Arabs generally (and in recent years, the government of Egypt is a leading example) have become disillusioned about the prospects for a durable and equitable peace with Israel. Arab opinion is also highly critical of America's diplomatic activities in the region, especially Washington's support of states like Kuwait and Saudi Arabia. See James E. Akins, "The New Arabia," *Foreign Affairs* 70 (summer 1991): 34–49.

96. A leading authority on U.S. policy toward the Middle East has cautioned, however, that the region is becoming increasingly unstable and unreceptive to American influence. In his view, sooner or later the Arabs will demand that America's military forces be withdrawn from the region. In turn, this development will confront the United States and other industrialized nations with "insecure energy sources." See Akins, "The New Arabia," 44–49.

97. See, for example, the analysis of the continuing challenge terrorism presents to the USA and its allies in Conor Cruise O'Brien, "Liberalism and Terror," *National Review,* April 22, 1996, pp. 29–32.

98. See, for example, the analysis by Muhammad Muslih and Augustus R. Norton, "The Need for Arab Democracy," *Foreign Policy,* no. 83 (summer 1991): 3–5; and the editorial in the *Wall Street Journal,* February 3, 1997. Commenting on the failure of America's efforts to bring about fundamental changes in Iraq's political system, one right-wing commentary concluded facetiously that there appeared to be nothing Washington could do to achieve the goals, except send President Saddam Hussein "an exploding cigar every now and then." See "This Week," *National Review,* December 31, 1996.

99. See Smith, *America's Mission,* 339.

100. According to ex-president Richard Nixon, since World War II, Japan has served as "the indispensable linchpin of any strategy for peace in Asia." Nixon, *1999,* 231.

101. See several of the essays in Gerald L. Curtis, ed., *The United States, Japan, and Asia* (New York: W. W. Norton, 1994); and see Nixon, *1999,* 226–30.

102. See Richard Holbrooke, "Japan and the United States: Ending the Unequal Partnership," *Foreign Affairs* 70 (winter 1991–92): 52–53; and the views of Henry Kissinger, in *Newsweek,*

January 27, 1997, pp. 77–78. Another study has concluded that in the postwar period, U.S. policy toward Asia and other regions has often been dictated by the interests and anxieties of small states, a conspicuous example being Taiwan. See Tucker, *Uncertain Friendships*.

103. See Holbrooke, "Japan and the United States," 47–48.

104. Yet as one observer points out, in their demand for greater "burden-sharing" by the Japanese, few Americans are aware that in fact Tokyo already pays a very high percentage of the overall costs of stationing U.S. armed forces within its territory—a greater proportionate share than any other ally. See Holbrooke, "Japan and the United States," 49.

105. The subject of Sino-American relations during the Clinton administration is discussed at greater length in Chapter 6.

106. See the views of George F. Will in the *Baton Rouge Morning Advocate,* April 17, 1997. Although he describes China as a "superpower," Will acknowledges that economically it is internally weak; its leaders are severely challenged to solve such problems as pervasive poverty and runaway population growth.

107. See Kissinger's views in *Newsweek,* January 27, 1997, pp. 74–76. See also the analyses of the factors influencing China's external behavior by Harry Harding in *A Fragile Relationship: The United States and China since 1972* (Washington, D.C.: Brookings Institution, 1992), 313–15; and by William Pfaff in the *Chicago Tribune,* November 12, 1996.

108. See, for example, the analysis by Harding, *A Fragile Relationship.* This observer concludes that America's diplomatic leverage with China is extremely limited, and that Washington will be able to influence Beijing's internal and external behavior most effectively by preserving a reasonably co-operative relationship with the PRC.

109. See the report by Tom Plate in the *Los Angeles Times,* January 21, 1997. One group of legislators believed that, in Washington's relations with Beijing, human rights issues ought to be uppermost in U.S. diplomacy; another group, however, believed that American officials ought to keep economic and commercial dimensions of external policy at the forefront of U.S.-Chinese relations.

110. To the mind of one observer, America's "overreaction" to political developments in China might well "inflame the situation" in Beijing, quite possibly leading authorities to promulgate even more politically repressive measures, thereby creating new obstacles in the path of political reform. See Harding, *A Fragile Relationship,* 225. Henry Kissinger is also concerned that a "confrontational" American approach to the PRC will achieve little more than foster a resurgence of Chinese nationalism; it will also "isolate" America from other Asian nations. See *Newsweek,* January 27, 1997, p. 77.

111. See Harding, *A Fragile Relationship,* 314, 329.

112. According to one right-wing analysis of Sino-American relations, in the years ahead officials in Washington should encourage Chinese economic growth, keep in mind the mutual security interests of the two nations, and make "long-term engagement" with the PRC a leading objective of U.S. policy. Americans must be guided by the thought, however, that in China as in many other societies, "the road to openness and democracy is long and tedious." See the editorial in the *Chicago Tribune,* November 1, 1996.

113. One conservative commentator, for example, believes that the continuing threat of North Korea's quest to become a nuclear power can only be countered by a policy of collaboration between the USA and China, also involving of course co-operation with South Korea. See Harding, *A Fragile Relationship,* 329. Another study finds North Korea's "high-risk" behavior to be "frustrating" for officials in Washington, who appear uncertain concerning the best course of action to take in response to it. Strong congressional opposition to a conciliatory approach to

North Korea has substantially narrowed the freedom of action of American policymakers. See Manwoo Lee, "North Korea: The Cold War Continues," *Current History* 95 (December 1996): 438–42.

114. An editorial in a leading conservative journal, for example, contended that, based on experience in Africa and other regions, before Washington engages in "humanitarian interventionism," policymakers must possess a clear "exit strategy"; such intervention must also reflect "foresight, understanding, or strategic purpose"—qualities that have too often been lacking in the past. See "Into Africa," *National Review*, December 9, 1996, p. 20. Another conservative commentary cautions policymakers that, when they consider intervening abroad for humanitarian reasons, they must "remember Somalia"—a reference to ill-fated American intervention in East Africa that resulted in a dramatic diplomatic setback for the USA. See the editorial in the *Los Angeles Times*, November 15, 1996; and the more-detailed treatment of U.S. intervention in that country in Makinda, *Seeking Peace from Chaos*. Still another prominent conservative source believes that in the past, humanitarian interventionism by the USA has resulted in little more than "death and humiliation for U.S. forces." Achieving lasting peace and stability in Africa, for example, is judged to be "too big a task even for the sole remaining superpower." See the editorial in the *Chicago Tribune*, November 15, 1996.

115. One observer cautions against a tendency by American officials to believe that interventionist moves per se by the United States will eliminate the underlying causes of political upheaval and conflict in foreign societies. The results of such efforts by the USA in a number of recent settings call this assumption into serious question. See Hillen, "General Chaos," 21.

116. The place of the Monroe Doctrine in U.S. foreign policy is examined in greater detail in Crabb, *The Doctrines of American Foreign Policy*, 9–56.

117. The Cuban Missile Crisis of 1962 is examined more fully in Arthur M. Schlesinger, Jr., *A Thousand Days: John F. Kennedy in the White House* (Boston: Houghton Mifflin, 1965), 795–830; and in Theodore C. Sorensen, *Kennedy* (New York: Harper and Row, 1965), 667–719.

118. Speaking of American policy toward Castro's Cuba, for example, a leading conservative source concludes that Washington's interventionist efforts have failed to change the character of the regime or alter the course of its internal political affairs. See the editorial in the *Chicago Tribune*, November 11, 1996. Another commentator has reached basically the same conclusion about American interventionism in Haiti. See Pamela Constable, "Dateline Haiti: Caribbean Stalemate," *Foreign Policy*, no. 89 (winter 1992–93): 175–91. A study of U.S. interventionist moves in efforts to implant democracy in Chile arrived at basically the same conclusion. See Rosenberg, "Beyond Elections," 72–93.

119. The multibillion-dollar program to promote the economic and social development of Latin America launched by the Kennedy administration is described in Arthur Schlesinger, Jr., in *A Thousand Days*, 185–205. Among the program's chief goals was the promotion of democracy within the hemisphere. Ex-president Richard Nixon is merely one among a number of conservative commentators who found the Alliance for Progress a failure. See his *Real War*, 35–36.

120. Commenting on interventionist efforts by the USA to achieve democracy and political stability in Haiti, more than one analysis concluded that the efforts quite clearly failed to achieve the objective. By openly intervening in Haiti's political affairs, Washington has now "acquired a certain responsibility" for the country's problems and well-being; and these are viewed as becoming increasingly critical with the passage of time. See Shea, "Voodoo Diplomacy," 26–27. Similarly, another observer concluded that the task of "turning Haiti around" cannot be successfully undertaken by other countries. See the views of Senator Mike DeWine (R–Ohio) in the *Wall Street Journal*, January 24, 1997.

121. Speaking of attitudes toward foreign policy questions among Republicans in Congress,

one observer believes that the term "muscular unilateralism" describes the approach of many legislators on challenges confronting the USA abroad. See Greenberger, "Dateline Capitol Hill," 169.

CHAPTER 3

1. See James F. Hoge, Jr., "Editor's Note," *Foreign Affairs* 73 (September–October 1994): v.

2. See, for example, Hoge, "Editor's Note," v; Leon T. Hadar, "What Green Peril?" *Foreign Affairs* 72 (spring 1993): 41–42; Stanley Kober, "Idealpolitik," *Foreign Policy*, no. 79 (summer 1990): 8–9; Immanuel Wallerstein, "Foes as Friends" *Foreign Policy*, no. 90 (spring 1993): 145–58.

3. George F. Kennan, *Around the Cragged Hill* (New York: W. W. Norton, 1993), 255.

4. Ibid., 183.

5. Benjamin Schwarz, "Why America Thinks It Has to Run the World," *Atlantic Monthly*, June 1996, 92–104.

6. See Christopher Layne and Benjamin Schwarz, "American Hegemony—Without an Enemy," *Foreign Policy*, no. 92 (fall 1993): 709.

7. See the views of McGeorge Bundy, as quoted in William G. Hyland, "Foreign Affairs at 70," *Foreign Affairs* 71 (fall 1992): 183.

8. Hadar, "What Green Peril?" 41.

9. See the views of Charles W. Maynes, "Relearning Intervention," *Foreign Policy*, no. 98 (spring 1995): 96–113. Among the global problems the author identifies as possibly eliciting an interventionist response by the USA are meeting obligations arising out of America's military alliances; using armed force to counter nuclear proliferation; protecting states that are threatened with internal disorders and conflicts; and supporting democracy in foreign societies. The author sees very little prospect that an interventionist American policy is capable of solving such problems.

10. See the contributions in Sanford J. Ungar, ed., *America and the World* (New York: Oxford University Press, 1985); and Wallerstein, "Foes as Friends," 157.

11. See Morton Halperin, "Guaranteeing Democracy," *Foreign Policy*, no. 91 (summer 1993): 120–24.

12. See Bernard Lewis, "Rethinking the Middle East," *Foreign Affairs* 71 (fall 1992): 99–119.

13. David Callahan, "Saving Defense Dollars," *Foreign Policy*, no. 96 (fall 1994): 95–96.

14. See Dana H. Allin, *Cold War Illusions—America, Europe, and Soviet Power: 1969–1989* (New York: St. Martin's Press, 1995).

15. See a number of the essays in Kevin J. Cassidy and Gregory A. Bischak, eds., *Real Security: Converting the Defense Economy and Building Peace* (Albany: State University of New York Press, 1994).

16. See Morton H. Halperin and Jeanne M. Woods, "Ending the Cold War at Home," *Foreign Policy*, no. 81 (winter 1990–91): 128–41. The authors fear that, in the post–Cold War era, new enemies and threats to national security are being invented by policymakers in order to justify continuing limitations upon domestic freedoms. These include so-called rogue states, foreign guerrilla and terroristic organizations, drug dealers, and those accused of "economic espionage" against the USA.

17. See the summary of the report on U.S. intelligence operations by the Twentieth Century Fund, in the *New York Times,* June 28, 1996, dispatch by Tim Weiner.

18. See Layne and Schwarz, "American Hegemony—Without an Enemy," 5–24.

19. George F. Kennan is but one among a number of liberal spokesmen who in time became

highly skeptical about the value of America's foreign aid program to developing societies. His specific criticisms are that the administration of such programs is often lax; that their goals and purposes are frequently unclear or questionable; and that their results are seldom objectively assessed. Overall, they do little to address the "real problems" existing within most Third World societies. See Kennan, *Around the Cragged Hill*, 201–202.

20. Robin Broad, John Cavanaugh, and Walden Bello, "Development: The Market Is Not Enough," *Foreign Policy*, no. 81 (winter 1990–91): 144–63.

21. See Sherle R. Schwenninger, "The Debate That Wasn't," *The Nation*, November 18, 1996, pp. 22–24.

22. See the views of Ronald Steel in "The Domestic Core of Foreign Policy," *Atlantic Monthly*, June 1995, pp. 85–86.

23. The growth in presidential power throughout American history is analyzed in detail in Arthur M. Schlesinger, Jr., *The Imperial Presidency* (Boston: Little, Brown, 1973). See also Barbara Kellerman and Ryan J. Barilleaux, *The President as World Leader* (New York: St. Martin's Press, 1990); and Amaury de Riencourt, *The Coming Caesars* (New York: Capricorn Books, 1957).

24. For an enlightening study of an interventionist chapter in American diplomatic history—emphasizing the negative consequences of such activity—see John S. D. Eisenhower, *Intervention! The United States and the Mexican Revolution, 1913–1917* (New York: W. W. Norton, 1993). Washington's ill-fated efforts to determine Mexico's political future, it is fair to say, have had a negative impact upon the course of Mexican-American relations down to the present day.

25. For a detailed examination of an instance of U.S. intervention in a key African state, see Sean Kelly, *America's Tyrant: The CIA and Mobutu of Zaire* (Washington, D.C.: American University Press, 1993). According to this observer, the effect of U.S. intervention in this country was to strengthen anti-democratic tendencies within the society. Another study concludes that if interventionist moves by the USA do not have broad international support, this fact alone raises genuine doubts about their wisdom. See David Callahan, "Saving Defense Dollars," *Foreign Policy*, no. 96 (fall 1994): 110.

26. See Michael Mandelbaum, "The Reluctance to Intervene," *Foreign Policy*, no. 95 (summer 1994): 3–19.

27. See, for example, Graham White and John Maze, *Henry A. Wallace: His Search for a New World Order* (Chapel Hill: University of North Carolina Press, 1995).

28. Representative works presenting the "revisionist" viewpoint are William A. Williams, *Empire as a Way of Life* (New York: Oxford University Press, 1982), and the same author's *The Tragedy of American Diplomacy* (Cleveland: World Publishing, 1959); D. F. Fleming, *The Cold War and Its Origins*, 2 vols. (Garden City, N.Y.: Doubleday, 1961); Richard J. Barnet, *Intervention and Revolution: America's Encounter with Insurgent Movements around the World* (New York: World Publishing, 1968); David Horowitz, *The Free World Colossus: A Critique of American Foreign Policy in the Cold War* (London: McGibbon Kee, 1965); Michael Parenti, *The Anti-Communist Impulse* (New York: Random House, 1970); John G. Stoessinger, *Nations in Darkness: China, Russia, and America* (New York: Random House, 1971); and Michael Parenti, ed., *Trends and Tragedies in American Foreign Policy* (Boston: Little, Brown, 1971).

29. See Allin, *Cold War Illusions*. A comparable conclusion has been drawn by the author of a study of U.S. policy toward Castro's Cuba. See Andrew Zimbalist, "Dateline Cuba: Hanging on in Havana," *Foreign Policy*, no. 92 (fall 1995): 151–68. In this view, Washington's unsuccessful efforts to topple Castro's regime have in fact *strengthened* its hold on political power.

30. A clear echo of Senator Fulbright's assessment of the effects of an interventionist American policy is offered by Susan L. Woodward in *Balkan Tragedy: Chaos and Dissolution after the Cold*

War (Washington, D.C.: Brookings Institution, 1995). The author's overall conclusion is that interventionist moves by the USA and other nations in responding to recurrent political crises in this region not only failed, but *intensified* existing conflicts, making them more difficult than ever to resolve.

31. One recent analysis of American diplomacy is convinced that U.S. policy of what is called "deep engagement" in Asian affairs has been an obstacle to the solution of several major problems within the region. See Chalmers Johnson and E. B. Kechin, "The Pentagon's Ossified Strategy," *Foreign Affairs* 74 (July–August 1995): 103–14. Similarly, a former U.S. ambassador to Indonesia contends that the United States should follow a policy of "low profile" throughout the Third World. In most cases, it should exert its influence in concert with other nations and through international agencies. See Marshall Green, *Indonesia: Crisis and Transformation, 1965–1968* (Washington, D.C.: Compass Press, 1991). A student of African affairs has reached basically the same conclusion with regard to U.S. policy in that region. See Kelly, *America's Tyrant*. Similarly, several of the contributors to a symposium on U.S. policy toward the Middle East are also highly critical of its consequences. See Hooshang Amirahmadi, ed., *The United States and the Middle East: A Search for New Perspectives* (Albany: State University of New York Press, 1993).

32. This is another of Fulbright's views that gained wide acceptance among members of the liberal community in dealing with foreign policy issues. As one spokesman for this viewpoint expressed it, the USA was still committed to an interventionist foreign policy primarily because the military-industrial complex and other powerful interest groups "wanted a conservative domestic program and a hawkish foreign policy." According to this interpretation, some groups within the American society "needed" such an external policy in order "to maintain discipline at home or to control unruly allies" abroad. Michael Cox, "Political Theory and the New Cold War," in *From Cold War to Collapse: Theory and World Politics in the 1980s,* ed. Mike Browder and Robin Brown (New York: Cambridge University Press, 1993), 43–44.

33. Senator Fulbright's views on American foreign policy are conveyed in his *Old Myths and New Realities* (New York: Vintage Books, 1963); *The Arrogance of Power* (New York: Vintage Books, 1966); and *The Crippled Giant* (New York: Vintage Books, 1972). An informative commentary is Eugene Brown, *J. William Fulbright: Advice and Dissent* (Iowa City: University of Iowa Press, 1985). For a recent analysis reflecting Fulbright's earlier indictment of American interventionism, see Halperin and Woods, "Ending the Cold War at Home," 128–44.

34. For more detailed discussion of such problems, see Gordon A. Craig and Alexander L. George, *Force and Statecraft: Diplomatic Problems of Our Time,* 2nd ed. (New York: Oxford University Press, 1989). One commentary on the diplomatic activities of the Clinton administration was highly critical of Secretary of State Warren Christopher's frequent trips abroad in an effort to solve the problems of other societies. In this view, Christopher's "frequent flying" stood in "inverse ratio" to the actual diplomatic accomplishments of the Clinton foreign policy team. Such behavior indicated a "manic commitment to process as such" in dealing with international issues. See the editorial in the *New Republic,* November 4, 1996, p. 8.

35. According to Ronald Steel, based on poll results, only one citizen in ten believes that the USA must continue to serve as a "global leader." See "The Domestic Core of Foreign Policy," 85. A recent study of U.S.-Cuban relations expresses this basic idea by saying that in the future, policymakers must distinguish between those developments and problems abroad that are really nothing more than "annoyances" for Americans (such as Castroism) and those that actually threaten the nation's security and diplomatic interests. See Jorge I. Dominguez, "The Secrets of Castro's Staying Power," *Foreign Affairs* 72 (spring 1993): 105. According to another study of U.S. foreign policy in the Middle East, the same basic principle should govern Washington's approach

to that volatile region. For example, according to this assessment, Islamic fundamentalism poses no direct or major threat to the well-being of American society. See Hadar, "What Green Peril?" 26–27.

36. See Callahan, "Saving Defense Dollars," 118; and Mandelbaum, "The Reluctance to Intervene," 3–19.

37. An illuminating study of such problems by a leading liberal spokesman is Daniel P. Moynihan, *Pandaemonium: Ethnicity in International Politics* (New York: Oxford University Press, 1992).

38. According to one observer, today the United States is "just one major power among many in a world of great disorder, a disorder that promises to increase considerably into the next century." Wallerstein, "Foes as Friends" 151. See also the views of Terry L. Diebel, "Bush's Foreign Policy: Mastery and Inaction," *Foreign Policy,* no. 84 (fall 1991): 3–24; and of several of the authors in Cassidy and Bischak, eds., *Real Security.* And for an informative analysis of the growing power of a united Europe and its implications for America's global role, see Axel Krause, *Inside the New Europe* (New York: Harper/Collins, 1991).

39. See, for example, the views of Kober, "Idealpolitik," 9–13; and of Callahan, "Saving Defense Dollars," 96–106.

40. See Edward G. Shirley, "The Iran Policy Trap," *Foreign Policy,* no. 96 (fall 1994): 92.

41. See the findings of the Rockefeller Commission, in Nelson A. Rockefeller, *The Rockefeller Report on the Americas: The Official Report of a United States Presidential Commission for the Western Hemisphere* (Chicago: Quadrangle Books, 1969). See also the detailed treatment of Washington's diplomacy toward Africa, in Jeffrey Herbst, *U.S. Economic Policy toward Africa* (New York: Council on Foreign Relations Press, 1992).

42. This is the viewpoint advocated in a recent analysis by Kennan in *Around the Cragged Hill.* See also the conclusions expressed in Diebel, "Bush's Foreign Policy," 3–24. This commentator attributes the erosion of American power abroad primarily to the critical nature of several domestic conditions and problems.

43. Steel, "The Domestic Core of Foreign Policy," 86.

44. According to one observer, after the Cold War, American diplomacy ought to be based upon the "new idealism," a pivotal concept of which is the idea that a nation's foreign policy is ultimately determined by its domestic institutions and behavior. On that premise, the nation's leaders must give high priority to solving long-neglected domestic problems. The best way for the USA to promote the cause of freedom beyond its own borders is by "setting an example to the world of the benefits of democracy." See Kober, "Idealpolitik," 9–18.

45. As mentioned in note 9 of this chapter, one commentator has identified a range of problems likely to confront the USA.

46. Kennan, *Around the Cragged Hill,* 254–55.

47. One liberal observer believes that Americans must abandon the idea that they have an obligation to "run the world." Once that idea is accepted, substantial reductions in military spending become possible. He was highly critical, for example, of the decision by the Clinton White House to spend $1.3 trillion on national defense during the period 1997–2002 and to keep some 200,000 American forces in Europe and Asia. In his judgment, such steps reflect the unfortunate reality that policymakers have failed to adapt to new conditions existing in the wake of the Cold War. This failure also provided evidence that the USA was opposed to a truly "independent" role by other nations in global affairs. See Schwarz, "Why America Thinks It Has to Run the World," 92–104.

48. As an example of this tendency, one observer cites the case of "rogue states," or those (like Iran, Iraq, and Libya) whose behavior often violates the norms of international law and com-

ity. In this view, as objectionable as such activities might be, very seldom do they actually pose a substantial danger to the security and diplomatic interests of the USA. The idea that they do so is deliberately fostered by the military-industrial complex to justify a high level of defense spending. See Michael Klare, "Itching for a Fight," *The Progressive,* September 1996, pp. 32–33.

49. Kennan, *Around the Cragged Hill,* 185.

50. The role of the United States in sponsoring and supporting the League of Nations, the United Nations, and other multinational agencies is highlighted in Inis L. Claude, Jr., *Swords into Plowshares: The Problems and Progress of International Organization,* 4th ed. (New York: Random House, 1983); James E. Dougherty and Robert L. Pfaltzgraff, Jr., *American Foreign Policy: FDR to Reagan* (New York: Harper and Row, 1986); Gerald J. Mangone, *A Short History of International Organization* (New York: McGraw-Hill, 1954); and Lincoln P. Bloomfield, *The United Nations and U.S. Foreign Policy: A New Look at the National Interest* (Boston: Little, Brown, 1960).

51. See Kennan, *Around the Cragged Hill,* 184–85.

52. See the editorial entitled "Great Satan Is Us" in *The Progressive,* December 1996, p. 6.

53. As merely one example of an effort to establish a scale of regional priorities for the nation's policymakers, one recent study has identified Central America, the Caribbean area, and the Persian Gulf region as zones in which the USA may be required to intervene to counter a threat to national security. By contrast, this observer believes that American military intervention will *not* be required in Africa, South and Southeast Asia, or the South American continent. See Callahan, "Saving Defense Dollars," 106.

54. See, for example, the views of Krause in *Inside the New Europe.*

55. See Alan Tonelson and Robin Gaster, "Our Interests in Europe," *Atlantic Monthly,* August 1995, pp. 28–30.

56. See Elizabeth Pond, "Germany in the New Europe," *Foreign Affairs* 71 (spring 1992): 112, 119.

57. See the editorial entitled "Back to the Balkans," in *The Nation,* December 23, 1996, p. 3.

58. See Dogdan Denitch, "Outdating Dayton," *The Nation,* December 23, 1996, pp. 23–24.

59. See George Kenney, "Basic Democratic Charade," *The Nation,* September 23, 1996, pp. 18–20.

60. See the editorial entitled "No Exit in Bosnia," *The Nation,* December 9, 1996, pp. 4–5.

61. Kennan, *Around the Cragged Hill,* 195–96, 223–24.

62. Tonelson and Gaster, "Our Interests in Europe," 28.

63. For a forceful statement of the case *against* the expansion of NATO, see the views of Michael Mandelbaum, as reported in the *New York Times,* June 9, 1996, dispatch by Thomas L. Friedman. In Mandelbaum's view, the expansion of NATO eastward could be expected to have the following adverse consequences: it would create new obstacles for the emergence of democracy in Russia by undermining the position of the "reformers" within the political system; it would strengthen the position of hard-line nationalists in Russia and elsewhere in Eastern Europe; it would cause officials in Moscow to rethink their position on arms control agreements with the West; it would motivate Russian policymakers to view Central Europe as posing a new threat to Russian security; and it would most likely stimulate a new wave of military spending by Russian authorities.

64. See Ronald Steel, "Mission Creep," *New Republic,* November 25, 1996, p. 29.

65. Schwenninger, "The Debate That Wasn't," 23.

66. Steel, "Mission Creep," 29; and Schwenninger, "The Debate That Wasn't," 23.

67. See Kennan, *Around the Cragged Hill,* 204–205.

68. See Daniel Singer, "The Real Eurobattle," *The Nation,* December 23, 1996, pp. 20–23.

As this commentator sees it, Washington's interest in promoting European unity is nothing more than "a cover for adopting the U.S. model of Reaganomics" on a Continent-wide basis.

69. As merely one example of this American approach to czarist Russia, late in the nineteenth century George Kennan (an observer of Russian affairs, who was a distant cousin of the postwar American diplomatic official and commentator George F. Kennan) lectured widely throughout the USA, where he publicly denounced the czarist regime's "despotism and the persecution of the political opposition" within Russian society. Kennan founded a political society dedicated to the overthrow of the czarist system of government and the achievement of Russian democracy. For these and other examples of American opposition to czarism, see Cecil V. Crabb, Jr., *Policy-Makers and Critics: Conflicting Theories of American Foreign Policy* (New York: Praeger Publishers, 1976), 37–50. Other examples of public and private American efforts to promote democratic government in Russia may be found in Thomas A. Bailey, *America Faces Russia* (Ithaca: Cornell University Press, 1950); and in William A. Williams, *American-Russian Relations, 1781–1947* (New York: Rinehart, 1952).

70. For example, see Edward Mansfield and Jack Snyder, "Democratization and War," *Foreign Affairs* 74 (May–June 1995): 79–98.

71. According to one analysis of the issue, in its relations with Moscow after the Cold War, Washington ought to be guided by a simple principle: "The United States will help only those [regimes abroad] who can demonstrate they are exercising legitimate political authority." Martha A. Olcott, "The Soviet (Dis)Union," *Foreign Policy,* no. 82 (spring 1991): 136.

72. See Martin Malia, "Party Melia," *New Republic,* May 27, 1996, pp. 25–27. According to this commentator, officials in Washington must realize that Russia is now a "poor power" that is seeking to modernize. In this assessment, the new Russia is too weak to pose a threat to the USA or any other nation.

73. See, for example, Zvi Ganin, *Truman, American Jewry, and Israel, 1945–1948* (New York: Holmes and Meier, 1979); Harry S. Allen and Ivan Volgyes, eds., *Israel, the Middle East, and U.S. Interests* (New York: Praeger Publishers, 1983); and Steven L. Spiegel, *The Other Arab-Israeli Conflict: Making America's Middle East Policy, from Truman to Reagan* (Chicago: University of Chicago Press, 1985); and Lee O'Brien, *American Jewish Organizations and Israel* (Washington, D.C.: Institute for Palestine Studies, 1986).

74. America's support of the Zionist cause, leading to the establishment of the State of Israel and to its security and independence afterward, is highlighted in Bernard Gwertzman, *The Lobby: Jewish Political Power and American Foreign Policy* (New York: Simon and Schuster, 1988); and in George Lenczowski, *American Presidents and the Middle East* (Durham, N.C.: Duke University Press, 1989).

75. See Robert Fisk, "Myth of the Pax Americana," *The Nation,* October 14, 1996, pp. 20–24.

76. An especially forceful criticism of Israel's internal and external policies from a liberal perspective is George W. Ball and Douglas B. Ball, *The Passionate Attachment: America's Involvement with Israel, 1947 to the Present* (New York: W. W. Norton, 1992). According to this assessment, Washington's consistent and uncritical support of Israel has seriously weakened American influence throughout the Middle East.

77. According to one commentator, Washington's confrontational approach to the government of Iran has proved to be "in essence a rudderless boat carrying the vital interests of the United States." The result of several years' experience with this policy is that Iran's religiously based regime is stable and shows no sign of disappearing. Relations between Tehran and Washington remain tense and unproductive. And America's policy toward Iran has become a highly

contentious issue in relations with the allies. See Donné Raffat, "Since Cyrus the Great," *The Nation,* November 11, 1996, pp. 33–34. Basically this same conclusion was reached by another study of Washington's diplomacy toward Iran. See Shirley, "The Iran Policy Trap," 75–93. According to this analysis, a major consequence of U.S. policy toward the country since the fall of the shah has been to strengthen the hands of the clerical element governing the country. As this observer sees it, for many years American officials have greatly exaggerated the danger that the internal and external policies of the Iranian regime pose to the USA. A different American approach—encouraging U.S. investments within Iran—is much more likely to produce beneficial changes in the Iranian government's policies at home and abroad.

78. See Mary Anne Weaver, "Blowback," *Atlantic Monthly,* May 1996, p. 26.

79. See Joseph J. Romm and Charles B. Curtis, "Mideast Oil Forever?" *Atlantic Monthly,* April 1996, pp. 57–65.

80. See William D. Hartung, "Mercenaries: How a U.S. Company Props Up the House of Saud," *The Progressive,* April 1996, pp. 26–28; and the editorial entitled "Empire Claptrap" in *The Progressive,* August 1996, pp. 9–10. According to the latter analysis, America's close ties with Saudi Arabia have been dictated by two interrelated factors: preserving access to the country's vast oil supplies and protecting the profits of American oil corporations active in the region.

81. Johnson and Kechin, "The Pentagon's Ossified Strategy," 103–14.

82. See, for example, the views of Andrew W. Mack in "North Korea and the Bomb," *Foreign Policy,* no. 83 (summer 1991): 87–105. For this observer, the presence of America's large and formidable nuclear arsenal in South Korea was a crucial factor in the determination of the North Korean government to build its own nuclear stockpile.

83. A contemporary restatement of Senator Fulbright's objections to extensive U.S. involvement in Asian affairs after the Cold War is Johnson and Kechin, "The Pentagon's Ossified Strategy," 103–14. According to these observers, very few Asian governments want a large American military presence within the region. Some of Asia's political leaders simply do not believe that Washington will use military power to deal with threats to the peace (possibly posed by North Korea or mainland China). Furthermore, in their view the continued U.S. military presence in Japan simply postpones the needed revision of the Japanese constitution and poses an obstacle to a more active role by Tokyo in regional and global affairs, thereby allowing the USA to reduce its commitments in the region. Continued American military involvement in Asia is also viewed as a serious impediment to the growth of democracy in the region.

84. America's military ties with the government of South Korea since World War II are analyzed in detail in Cecil V. Crabb, Jr., and Pat Holt, *Invitation to Struggle: Congress, the President, and Foreign Policy,* 4th ed. (Washington, D.C.: Congressional Quarterly Press, 1992), 134–39.

85. The evolution and role of the Open Door policy in U.S. foreign relations is examined at length in Cecil V. Crabb, Jr., *The Doctrines of American Foreign Policy: Their Meaning, Role, and Future* (Baton Rouge: Louisiana State University Press, 1982), 56–107.

86. The "normalization" in Sino-American relations that took place under the Carter administration is discussed more fully in Jimmy Carter, *Keeping Faith: Memoirs of a President* (New York: Bantam Books, 1982), 186–212.

87. See the *New York Times,* May 11, 1998, dispatch by Anthony Lewis; and *Newsweek,* March 25, 1998, p. 50, and May 11, 1998, p. 45.

88. See Wallerstein, "Foes as Friends" 154–55.

89. This is the view of Marshall Green in his *Indonesia.*

90. This is the position taken by Herbst in *U.S. Economic Policy toward Africa.*

91. See, for example, Chester Bowles, *Africa's Challenge to America* (Berkeley, Ca.: University

of California Press, 1956). And for more recent statements of America's goals in Africa, see Donald P. Kommers and Gilburt D. Loescher, eds., *Human Rights and American Foreign Policy* (Notre Dame: University of Notre Dame Press, 1979), 302–308; Carter, *Keeping Faith,* 141–52.

92. See, for example, the indictment of the Reagan administration's approach to South Africa in Cyrus Vance, "The Human Rights Imperative," *Foreign Policy,* no. 63 (summer 1986): 3–20; and the views of Stephen Weissman, "The Opposition Speaks," *Foreign Policy,* no. 58 (spring 1985): 151–71.

93. The evolution of postwar American foreign policy toward Latin America is emphasized in Harold Molineu, *U.S. Policy toward Latin America: From Regionalism to Globalism* (Boulder, Colo.: Westview Press, 1990).

94. See Eyal Press, "Clinton Pushes Military Aid," *The Progressive,* February 1997, pp. 20–23. According to this observer, U.S. military aid programs to the other American republics have "bolster[ed] security forces responsible for human rights violations throughout much of Latin America." A number of liberal observers have called for closing the "School of the Americas" at Fort Benning, Georgia, established to train Latin American military officers. As critics assessed it, in reality this school taught Latin American military elites torture techniques and other methods facilitating the seizure and maintenance of political power.

95. See, for example, the conclusions reached by several of the contributors to the symposium on U.S. policy toward Latin America in Kenneth M. Coleman and George C. Herring, eds., *Understanding the Central American Crisis: Sources of Conflict, U.S. Policy, and Options for Peace* (Washington, D.C.: Scholarly Resources, 1991). For another study in which contributors are also often skeptical about Washington's efforts to implant democracy within the hemisphere, see the symposium by Abraham F. Lowenthal, ed., *Exporting Democracy: The United States and Latin America* (Baltimore: Johns Hopkins University Press, 1991).

96. See the view of Tad Szulc in the *Washington Post,* November 10, 1996.

97. See the editorial entitled "Cuban Whipping Boy," *The Progressive,* April 1, 1996, p. 8; and Jay Gordon, "Cuba's Entrepreneurial Socialism" *Atlantic Monthly,* January 1997, pp. 18–30.

98. Zimbalist, "Dateline Cuba," 152–54.

99. See the conclusions reached by Dominguez, "The Secrets of Castro's Staying Power," 97–107.

100. See the editorial entitled "Terror Schism," in *The Nation,* September 2, 1996, p. 6.

101. See "Great Satan Is Us," 6.

102. See Kober, "Idealpolitik," 9, 20.

103. See the views of Ronald Steel in "Paradigm Regained," *New Republic,* December 30, 1996, p. 25.

104. See the views of Lucy Komer in the *Los Angeles Times,* January 16, 1997.

105. These are the conclusions reached by America's former ambassador to Indonesia, Marshall Green, in his *Indonesia.*

106. See Amirahmadi, ed., *The United States and the Middle East.*

107. See George F. Kennan's views in *Around the Cragged Hill,* 201–207; and his views as quoted in Tony Smith, *America's Mission: The United States and the Worldwide Struggle for Democracy in the Twentieth Century* (Princeton: Princeton University Press, 1994), 179.

108. See these slogans as quoted in the study by Norman J. Ornstein, "Foreign Policy and the 1992 Election," *Foreign Affairs* 71 (summer 1992): 5–6, 8–9.

109. Kober, "Idealpolitik," 24.

110. Terry L. Diebel, for example is convinced that the inability of the Bush White House to formulate an overall foreign policy strategy was due to the existence of a number of unsolved

domestic problems, such as failure to reduce the federal deficit and the erosion in the nation's competitive position in world trade. See his "Bush's Foreign Policy," 3–24.

111. According to George F. Kennan, "the greatest service" that the United States could render to the world would be "to put its own house in order and to make of American civilization an example of decency, humanity, and societal success." Kennan, *Around the Cragged Hill*, 210. Another forceful expression of this view can be found in Kober, "Idealpolitik," 3–25. And see also Fouad Ajami, "Egyptology," *New Republic*, November 11, 1996, p. 34; the editorial entitled "Why We're for Clinton-Gore," in *New Republic*, November 11, 1996, p. 12; and Layne and Schwarz, "American Hegemony—Without an Enemy," 7–9.

CHAPTER 4

1. See the excerpts from the speech by ex-senator Bob Dole in the *New York Times*, June 26, 1996, dispatch by Adam Nagourney.

2. See the view of Fareed Zakaria in the *New York Times*, August 21, 1996. Edward N. Luttwak believes that in confronting a variety of global challenges and problems, the USA will be required to use its power abroad. See Edward N. Luttwak, "Where Are the Great Powers? At Home with the Kids," *Foreign Affairs* 73 (July-August 1994): 23–28.

3. See James A. Leach, "A Republican Looks at Foreign Policy," *Foreign Affairs* 71 (spring 1992): 19–20. Another study deplored the fact that isolationist sentiments appeared to be growing throughout American society and that they were shared by many of the nation's leaders. See the analysis by Haynes Johnson in *Divided We Fall: Gambling with History in the Nineties* (New York: W. W. Norton, 1994). A number of foreign leaders and observers were clearly apprehensive that American society was reverting to an isolationist approach to foreign affairs. See, for example, the views of several of the contributors to David G. Haglund, ed., *Can America Remain Committed? U.S. Security Horizons in the 1990s* (Boulder, Colo.: Westview Press, 1992).

4. See the summary of the "The Committee of Santa Fe," sponsored by the Republican Party in 1980, in Michael McClintock, *Instruments of Statecraft: U.S. Guerrilla Warfare, Counterinsurgency, and Counter-Terrorism, 1940–1990* (New York: Pantheon Books, 1992), 330–31. Another study focusing on voting patterns in this period found that foreign policy issues ranked very low on the list of most citizens' concerns. Such questions appeared to be getting less and less attention from the voters. See William G. Berman, *America's Right Turn: From Nixon to Reagan* (Baltimore: Johns Hopkins University Press, 1994).

5. Peter W. Rodman, "Points of Order," *National Review*, May 1, 1995, 42.

6. See Richard N. Haass, *The Reluctant Sheriff: The United States after the Cold War* (New York: Council on Foreign Relations, 1997).

7. Richard M. Nixon, *1999: Victory without War* (New York: Simon and Schuster, 1995), 310.

8. Richard M. Nixon, *Beyond Peace* (New York: Random House, 1994), 168.

9. Nixon, *Beyond Peace*, 9–10.

10. This is the contention of Peter W. Rodman in *More Precious than Peace: The Cold War and the Struggle for the Third World* (New York: Charles Scribner's Sons, 1994).

11. Joshua Muravchik, "Carrying a Small Stick," *National Review*, September 2, 1996, 59.

12. For useful background on the subject under discussion here, see John Ehrman, *The Rise of Neoconservatism: Intellectuals and Foreign Affairs, 1945–1994* (New Haven: Yale University Press, 1994).

13. For example, an editorial in a leading conservative publication deplored the existence of

"isolationist undercurrents" in the American society that would "leave the world in a more dangerous place." See the *National Review,* December 31, 1996, p. 10.

14. See, for example, former president Richard Nixon's admonitions that the end of the Cold War will "require just as much determination, vision, and patience" in dealing with difficult and complex international issues as was needed to defeat communism. By his calculation, from World War II down to the mid-1990s there had been some 150 "small wars," in which approximately 8 million people had been killed. (Nixon's tabulation, we may note, took no account of the huge number of casualties sustained in the conflict within the Balkans in recent years.) As he viewed it, the number of such conflicts was increasing within the international system. See his *Beyond Peace,* 8, 35. This overall verdict is confirmed by another study, which concludes that in some respects the post–Cold War global system will be a more dangerous political environment than during the era of bipolarity. This is true, for example, with regard to "the upsurge in violent conflicts among racial, religious, and ethnic groups." See Ernest Evans, "El Salvador's Lessons for Future U.S. Interventions," *World Affairs* 160 (summer 1997): 43.

15. See Loch K. Johnson, "Smart Intelligence," *Foreign Policy,* no. 89 (winter 1992–93): 53–70.

16. McClintock, *Instruments of Statecraft,* 449.

17. According to Robert Kagan, "the natural state of the world," after the Cold War no less than before, is basically Hobbesian. Global stability, for example, is viewed as "a fragile, temporary situation"; its existence depends upon the maintenance of a high level "of American power, influence and engagement" in international developments. See his views as cited in Robert S. Greenberger, "Dateline Capitol Hill: The New Majority's Foreign Policy," *Foreign Policy,* no. 101 (winter 1995–96): 164. See also Luttwak, "Where Are the Great Powers?" 23–28. This commentator is convinced that at some point, the United States may need to recruit a foreign mercenary army or establish its own version of the French Foreign Legion for use when military interventionism is required abroad!

18. See the views of Robert Kagan, as quoted in Greenberger, "Dateline Capitol Hill," 164.

19. See the views of Leslie Gelb on the nature of the global system, as quoted in Rodman, "Points of Order," 36.

20. See the conclusions of Edward Luttwak, in McClintock, *Instruments of Statecraft,* 461.

21. Nixon, *1999,* 28; and *Beyond Peace,* 35.

22. See the views of Charles Krauthammer, as quoted in Rodman, "Points of Order," 40. As one example of the threats facing the USA in the new era, Libya's president Muammar Qaddafi stated that Iraq made a serious mistake in engaging in overt aggression against Kuwait. Instead, Saddam Hussein's regime should have endeavored to achieve its external goals by relying on terrorism and subversion, since America and its allies would have encountered much more difficulty in responding to this strategy successfully. Qaddafi's remarks are quoted in Evans, "El Salvador's Lessons," 43.

23. This is a leading concern identified, for example, by Michael Mandelbaum in "Lessons of the Next Nuclear War," *Foreign Affairs* 74 (March-April 1995): 22–38.

24. See Michael S. Teitelbaum and Myron Weiner, eds., *Threatened Peoples, Threatened Borders: World Migration and U.S. Policy* (New York: W. W. Norton, 1995). Most of the contributors to this study are convinced that the USA must play a leading role in dealing with problems growing out of ongoing world migration.

25. According to a former assistant secretary of state in the Bush administration, the United States and its European allies face "real, direct and growing threats to the lives and security" of their citizens posed by the actions of countries like Iran and Libya which sponsor global terrorism

and appear determined to acquire nuclear arsenals. Accordingly, he believes it is imperative for Western nations to arrive at a common policy in dealing with such "outlaw regimes." See the views of John R. Bolton in the *New York Times*, July 28, 1996.

26. David C. Hendrickson, "The Renovation of American Foreign Policy," *Foreign Affairs* 71 (spring 1992): 59.

27. Thomas Omestead, "Why Bush Lost," *Foreign Policy*, no. 89 (winter 1992–93): 81.

28. See Nixon, *Beyond Peace*, 34, 169. Americans, another observer has declared, must resist "the lure of neo-isolationism" and other approaches to foreign affairs that stem from "nostalgia" for a bygone era. See Leach, "A Republican Looks at Foreign Policy," 19–20. See also Jonathan Clarke, "Leaders and Followers," *Foreign Policy*, no. 101 (winter 1995–96): 116–29; Jeremy D. Rosner, "The Know-Nothings Must Know Something," *Foreign Policy*, no. 101 (winter 1995–96): 116–29; William G. Hyland, "America's Call to Greatness," *Foreign Affairs* 71 (fall 1991): 189; and David C. Hendrickson, "The Recovery of Internationalism," *Foreign Affairs* 73 (September–October 1994): 26–43.

29. See Russell Kirk, *The Politics of Prudence* (Bryn Mawr, Pa.: Intercollegiate Studies Institute, 1993), 212.

30. E. J. Dionne, Jr., *Why Americans Hate Politics* (New York: Simon and Schuster, 1991), 349.

31. According to one observer, officials in the USA will increasingly be required to act in concert with a number of "highly interdependent partners"—especially Germany and Japan—in dealing with international problems. See Hanns W. Maull, "Germany and Japan: The New Civilian Powers," *Foreign Affairs* 69 (winter 1990–91): 91–106. An informative analysis of problems confronting the United States in this regard is Lester Thurow, *Head-to-Head: The Coming Economic Battle among Japan, Europe, and America* (New York: Time Warner Books, 1993).

32. One conservative analysis of American foreign policy after the Cold War contends that unless the USA wants to play the role of the "world's policeman" (an idea most Americans would reject), then it must endeavor to foster the emergence of strong "regional powers." See the view of Fareed Zakaria in the *New York Times*, August 21, 1996. See also Rodman, "Points of Order," 40.

33. In forceful opposition to the position of the "declinists," the views of former senator Bob Dole appear in "Shaping America's Future," *Foreign Policy*, no. 98 (spring 1995): 29–31.

34. Rodman, "Points of Order," 36. Former senator Bob Dole has listed several diplomatic orientations after the Cold War that America must make a conscious effort *to avoid*. These include the views of what he has called the "declinists," the "multilateralists," the "protectionists," the "isolationists," and the proponents of a "new world order." See his "Shaping America's Future," 31–34.

35. Dole, "Shaping America's Future," 36–37.

36. Ibid., 29–32. See also the views of David C. Hendrickson, "The Recovery of Internationalism," *Foreign Affairs* 73 (September–October 1994): 42.

37. For recent analyses of the concept of *Realpolitik* and its applicability to contemporary international relations, see the two works edited by Benjamin Frankel, *Roots of Realism* (Portland, Ore.: Frank Cass, 1997) and *Realism: Restatements and Renewal* (Portland, Ore.: Frank Cass, 1997). The concept of the "new realism" was analyzed in detail in Chapter 3. In brief terms, the basic idea is that by the end of the twentieth century, the classical concept of national power—in which military force played a key role—had become outmoded. As one proponent of this idea expressed it, after the Cold War the lives of most Americans would be affected less by old ideas about national power than by "developments in trade, immigration, or international health pol-

icy." See the views of an unnamed advocate of this approach, in Rodman, "Points of Order," 36. Alternatively, as another advocate of this approach has expressed it, armaments have now become "counterproductive"; large military establishments are a drain on the nation's resources and actually *detract* from its power; today, instead of being an instrument of national policy, reliance on armed force in fact signifies "the defeat of policy"; and costly military aid programs have almost invariably failed to accomplish their objectives. See Peter F. Drucker, *The New Realities* (New York: Harper/Collins, 1989), 43–56.

38. A useful summary of General Clausewitz's theories is Roger A. Leonard, ed., *Clausewitz on War* (New York: Capricorn Books, 1967). Americans, former president Richard M. Nixon was convinced, must "come to grips" with Clausewitzian ideas about the concept of power and its key role in international politics. In his view, it is high time for the American people and their leaders to "accept power, accept its existence, accept its exercise, and accept the ambiguities . . . that are sometimes inherent in its use in a conflict-ridden, imperfect world." Richard M. Nixon, *The Real War* (New York: Warner, 1980), 246.

39. In the presidential campaign of 1996, the GOP candidate, Bob Dole, criticized the Clinton administration because it had "eroded American power and purpose" by unwarranted cuts in the military budget (currently, some $260 billion annually). The conservative Heritage Foundation calculated that *an additional $20 billion annually* was needed to acquire and maintain the kind of armed forces required by America's international role. See the analysis of Republican viewpoints on national defense by Doug Bandow in the *New York Times,* July 6, 1996. And see also Harry G. Summers, Jr., *On Strategy II: A Critical Analysis of the Gulf War* (New York: Dell, 1992). This analyst is convinced that the USA must always possess a potent offensive military capability, which it will be required to use from time to time to protect its security and diplomatic interests.

40. Kirk, *The Politics of Prudence,* 208.

41. This is a basic contention of Peter W. Rodman in *More Precious than Peace.*

42. See the analysis of the Clinton administration's use of force against Iraq in Sherle R. Schwenninger, "The Debate That Wasn't," *The Nation,* November 18, 1996, pp. 22–24.

43. See Dole, "Shaping America's Future," 39–41.

44. See the views of George F. Will in the *Baton Rouge Morning Advocate,* May 22, 1997.

45. See the analysis of conservative viewpoints on the nation's defense budget by Doug Bandow in the *New York Times,* July 6, 1996. See also William E. Odom, "Transforming the Military," *Foreign Affairs* 76 (July–August 1997): 54–64.

46. This is a major theme of the study by Donald Kagan, *On the Origins of War and the Preservation of Peace* (New York: Doubleday, 1995). See also the view of Richard Nixon that the Vietnam War was lost not because the USA lacked the requisite power to achieve its goals, but because policymakers in Washington—under intense pressure from vocal pressure groups—demonstrated a lack of will to use the power available to them for accomplishing the nation's objectives and protecting its interests overseas. Nixon, *The Real War,* 122–23. Another study concludes that, on the basis of experience in recent years, the USA cannot rely on "the international community" to carry out interventions that may be required to maintain peace, order, and security throughout the world. If and when such interventions become necessary, they can best be done by the United States acting unilaterally. See Gene M. Lyons and Michael Mandelbaum, eds., *Beyond Westphalia: State Sovereignty and International Intervention* (Baltimore: Johns Hopkins University Press, 1995).

47. See the views of Irving Kristol, as quoted in Nixon, *The Real War,* 45. Nixon reminds Americans of the old adage about "a stitch in time." Applying the principle to foreign affairs, the

USA must *not* passively acquiesce "in one aggressive move after another." Instead, when necessary it must be prepared to engage in "a timely response" designed to *avert* a major global crisis. Ibid., 45.

48. See the view of Edward Luttwak, as quoted by Doug Bandow in the *New York Times,* July 6, 1996.

49. For a recent study calling attention to the lack of clarity in America's goals when its leaders have used military power abroad, see Richard H. Ullman, *The World and Yugoslavia's Wars* (New York: Council on Foreign Relations, 1996).

50. See Elliott Abrams, "Visiting Contralandia," *National Review,* March 25, 1996, pp. 34– 35. The author draws a general lesson from the Nicaraguan experience: although intervention by the USA was a crucial element in the outcome, ultimately "it was the peasants who saved the country" from Communist domination.

51. This is the contention of Robert Kagan in *A Twilight Struggle: American Power and Nicaragua, 1977–1990* (New York: Free Press, 1996).

52. See Summers, *On Strategy II,* 248–68; and the views of Charles Krauthammer, as quoted in McClintock, *Instruments of Statecraft,* 456.

53. See the *New York Times,* December 1, 1995, dispatch by Elaine Sciolino.

54. See Mandelbaum, "Lessons of the Next Nuclear War," 22–38. According to this observer, preventing nuclear proliferation must be considered one of the highest-ranking objectives of U.S. foreign policy. Another student of the subject is convinced that the president and his advisers must be prepared to use conventional military force against any government that has acquired, and might be tempted to use, nuclear weapons to promote its foreign policy goals. See Seth Cropsey, "The Only Credible Deterrent," *Foreign Affairs* 73 (March-April 1994): 14–20. A recent study of developments in the Persian Gulf area after the war emphasizes that the United States still has a crucial role to play in preserving regional peace and stability. See Steve A. Yetiv, *America and the Persian Gulf: The Third Party Dimension in World Politics* (Westport, Conn.: Praeger Publishers, 1995).

55. A number of conservatives call attention to a prominent "lesson of the Persian Gulf War": the idea that this destructive episode would not have occurred if the USA had been prepared to use its power earlier to deter overt Iraqi expansionism. See Bruce W. Jentleson, *With Friends Like These: Reagan, Bush, and Saddam, 1982–1994* (New York: W. W. Norton, 1994), and Hendrickson, "The Renovation of American Foreign Policy," 51–53. In agreeing to support the decision of President Clinton to send armed forces to the Balkans, Senator Bob Dole conditioned his support on the requirement that American military units *not* take part in multinational peacekeeping operations in the region—or in other words, the USA must be prepared to act unilaterally. See Dole's views in the *New York Times,* December 1, 1995, dispatch by Elaine Sciolino. In his analysis of the conflict in the Balkans, another commentator was persuaded that only forceful action by the USA could resolve the crisis—only forceful and unilateral action by the USA would motivate the European allies to play a decisive part in efforts to stabilize the Balkans. See Michael J. Brenner, "EC: Confidence Lost," *Foreign Policy,* no. 91 (summer 1993): 40–41.

56. In pledging to support President Clinton's decision to send American troops to the Balkans late in 1995, Senator Bob Dole stated that the step would not have been necessary if the White House had intervened earlier in an effort to keep the conflict in the region from escalating to crisis proportions, threatening regional war. See Dole's views in the *New York Times,* December 1, 1995, dispatch by Elaine Sciolino.

57. Late in 1997, President Clinton's moves to augment American military power in and around the Persian Gulf were designed to strengthen Washington's hand in dealing with Iraq's

effort to curtail UN inspections of its territory—and especially to limit America's participation in that process. The dispatch of two aircraft carriers to the area was an obvious exercise in the old tactic of "showing the flag."

58. See Lawrence Freedman, "Why the West Failed," *Foreign Policy,* no. 97 (winter 1994–95): 68–69; and Kagan, *On the Origins of War and the Preservation of Peace.* Another study underscores the admonition that the model of allied cooperation witnessed during the Persian Gulf War after aggression has occurred is not likely to be duplicated in future conflicts. Military planning based on the model of that conflict will almost certainly be "wrong-headed"—a classic example of fighting the next war on the basis of the last one! See Evans, "El Salvador's Lessons," 43–44.

59. Specifically, a strategy of low-intensity conflict would involve such activities as coercive diplomacy, police actions abroad, psychological operations, support for foreign insurgencies and guerrilla movements, counterterrorist activities, and military and paramilitary deployments when they are needed. Another term for this category of activities is "unconventional warfare." See McClintock, *Instruments of Statecraft,* 336.

60. Rodman, "Points of Order," 36; and see the analysis of Bob Dole's views on foreign affairs by Adam Nagourney in the *New York Times,* June 26, 1996.

61. Nixon, *1999,* 21–22.

62. See Maull, "Germany and Japan," 101.

63. An enlightening analysis of the problems besetting the United Nations after some fifty years of its existence is available in Yves Beigbeder, *The Internal Management of United Nations Organizations: The Long Quest for Reform* (New York: St. Martin's Press, 1997).

64. For a more detailed formulation of these core goals by a leading conservative, see the analysis of what is called "the Dole Doctrine," in the *New York Times,* April 1, 1996, dispatch by William Safire. As Senator Dole envisioned it, the following were specific objectives constituting America's vital diplomatic interests after the Cold War: preventing the domination of the European continent by a single power; maintaining a balance of power in East Asia; safeguarding the peace and security of the Western Hemisphere; preserving the nation's access to vital raw materials, especially Persian Gulf oil supplies; expanding global trade and American access to foreign markets; and protecting America's citizens abroad. It must be acknowledged, of course, that no two conservative interventionists would compile identical lists of America's "core interests" in global affairs.

65. See the views of Fareed Zakaria in the *New York Times,* August 21, 1996; and of Rodman in "Points of Order," 36.

66. See the views of Fareed Zakaria in the *New York Times,* August 21, 1996.

67. See Senator Dole's criticisms of the diplomatic behavior of the Clinton administration, in "Shaping America's Future," 33.

68. See the detailed study by Thomas G. Weiss and Cindy Collins, *Humanitarian Challenges and Intervention: World Politics and the Dilemmas of Help* (Boulder, Colo.: Westview Press, 1996).

69. As one example, a former U.S. ambassador to China, Winston Lord, has called attention to the limits of American power in accomplishing a long list of goals in relations with the People's Republic of China. In his view, outsiders have always entertained an exaggerated conception of their ability to influence political and other developments within the Chinese society. See his views, as quoted in *Newsweek,* April 1, 1996, 29–30.

70. Italics are in the original. This analysis continues: "The U.S. Government doesn't have a clue how to resolve most of the world's ethnic conflicts, and never will. The expertise, leverage, and political will simply don't exist" for achieving the objective. Rodman, "Points of Order," 36.

71. See Rodman, "Points of Order," 36; and Dole, "Shaping America's Future," 41.

72. For a timely and informative analysis by a retired American diplomat of European-American relations in the new era, see John W. Holmes, *The United States and Europe after the Cold War* (Columbia, S.C.: University of South Carolina Press, 1997). In contrast to most conservative observers, this author believes that NATO has become moribund; he is convinced that a total withdrawal of American armed forces from the European continent is inevitable. Yet in time the USA and a unified Europe will become increasingly linked, economically and financially.

73. For background, see Edwin F. Fedder, *The Dynamics of Alliance in the Postwar World* (New York: Dodd, Mead, 1973); A. W. DePorte, *Europe between the Superpowers* (New Haven: Yale University Press, 1979); and Gerhard Mally, *Interdependence* (Lexington, Mass.: Lexington Books, 1976). As Richard M. Nixon assessed it, after the Cold War no less than before, Europe remains "the single most strategic piece of territory in the world." For example, Europe has a population of some 345 million people and a combined gross national product of around $7 trillion annually—larger than America's annual GNP. In light of such facts, the preservation of close U.S.-European relations remains an "indispensable" objective of Washington's diplomacy. Nixon, *Beyond Peace,* 83–84, 196–97.

74. See, for example, F. C. S. Northrop, *European Union and United States Foreign Policy* (New York: Macmillan, 1954); and Ernst H. van der Beugel, *From Marshall Aid to Atlantic Partnership: European Integration and American Foreign Policy* (New York: Elsevier, 1966). In the more recent period, right-wing observers continue to emphasize the importance of American initiatives in making progress toward European unification, especially by the European Community. See Mark M. Nelson, "Transatlantic Travails," *Foreign Policy,* no. 92 (fall 1993): 75–92; and Peter Duignan and C. H. Gann, *The United States and the New Europe, 1945–1993* (Cambridge, Mass.: Blackwell, 1994). In another study of European-American relations after the Cold War, Jonathan Dean calls attention to the danger of a possible German resurgence—a development that Washington must make a concerted diplomatic effort to avoid. See his *Ending Europe's Wars: The Continuing Search for Peace and Security* (New York: Twentieth Century Fund, 1994).

75. See Brenner, "EC: Confidence Lost," 24–44. According to one recent study, an increasingly prosperous, democratic, and unified German nation is capable of assuming a leading role in solving regional and global problems. This analysis is confident that the Germans can now be trusted to conduct a peaceful and constructive foreign policy; Germans no longer have "dreams of grandeur" or visions of creating a new empire. See David Schoenbaum and Elizabeth Pond, *The German Question and Other German Questions* (New York: St. Martin's Press, 1996).

76. In Henry Kissinger's judgment, NATO must "deepen its political dimension," enabling the alliance to deal effectively with such phenomena as Islamic fundamentalism, the increasingly critical global energy problem, and a number of other threats jeopardizing regional and global peace and stability. See his views in *Newsweek,* June 17, 1996, p. 43.

77. See Peter W. Rodman, "NATO Looks East," *National Review,* July 15, 1996, pp. 37–38.

78. See Duignan and Gann, *The United States and the New Europe;* see also Nelson, "Transatlantic Travails," 75–92. In the latter commentator's view European-American relations are a matter of reciprocal dependency. The USA still needs NATO and the support of its European allies; for their part, the European nations remain heavily dependent upon U.S. military power. Washington, another commentator asserts, must continue to encourage the emergence of strong regional institutions (which, militarily at least, remain weak) on the Continent. This will enable the allies to shoulder a greater portion of the burden for solving global problems, such as responsibilities involved in international peacekeeping. See Brenner, "EC: Confidence Lost," 33–42. Even while he endorsed the goal of an expanded NATO, Richard Nixon also called for a *reduction*

in the level of American troops within the NATO area. Expanded military contributions by the allies would, in his view, be expected to fill this gap. Nixon, *Beyond Peace,* 90–91.

79. See the analysis of Bob Dole's views on foreign affairs by Adam Nagourney in the *New York Times,* June 26, 1996, and the discussion by William Safire of Dole's approach to external policy in ibid., April 1, 1996.

80. One observer quotes Chancellor Bismarck to the effect that Russia is never as strong, or as weak, as it appears! To the minds of many conservatives, Moscow's defeat in the Cold War in no sense meant that Russia had abandoned its expansionist and hegemonial impulses. To the contrary, Moscow is inclined to reassert "its regional dominance," and it continues to use coercion against neighboring states. See Rodman, "Points of Order," 39. Another conservative observer has cautioned that the end of the Cold War is apt to be a dangerous era in terms of relations with the new Russian state. The possibility cannot be excluded that under increasing domestic pressures, Russia's leaders "will try a military adventure" at the expense of its neighbors. Russia's rulers would not be the first to rely on a "victorious war" to "rejuvenate" their society internally! Drucker, *The New Realities,* 35–36.

81. This is a major theme, for example, of Dean, *Ending Europe's Wars.* See also the views of former secretary of state Henry Kissinger on Washington's relations with Moscow in the post–Cold War era. As Kissinger assesses it, throughout modern history "Russia has subordinated the well-being of its own population to [a] relentless outward thrust and threatened all its neighbors with it." Kissinger is far from sanguine that the Kremlin has abandoned its age-old expansionist impulses. See the summary of his views on U.S. foreign policy in *Newsweek,* June 17, 1996, pp. 41–46. Another analysis of Moscow's behavior after the Cold War referred to "Russia's return to aggressive hegemonism," conduct that "has given Eastern and Central Europe plenty to worry about." This observer believes that, to a greater or lesser degree, *all* of the most influential political leaders in contemporary Russia entertain expansionist and interventionist ambitions in the realm of external policy. See Adrian Karatnycky, "Russia on the Brink," *National Review,* March 25, 1996, pp. 50–51. Another conservative spokesman, who was also concerned about the Kremlin's behavior abroad, urged Washington to inform Moscow in no uncertain terms that any effort to suppress or thwart independence movements within the former Soviet empire would evoke a strong American response and would call into serious question the future of Western aid programs to Russia. Leach, "A Republican Looks at Foreign Policy," 23.

82. Richard Nixon has pointed out that during the czarist era (as during the period of Peter the Great), new domestic policies and reforms were coupled with a strong and expansionist foreign policy. A more recent example of the same phenomenon was provided by the administration of Nikita Khrushchev, who precipitated the Cuban Missile Crisis of 1962 and constructed the Berlin Wall. Nixon, *1999,* 45–46. See also the analysis by Karatnycky, "Russia on the Brink," 51–52: this observer has no doubt that with the passage of time, the Russian government "will attempt to restore the former Soviet Union" and will pose a continuing security threat to its weaker neighbors.

83. See the conclusions of Dimitri Simes in "Gorbachev's Times of Troubles," *Foreign Policy,* no. 82 (spring 1991): 117.

84. See Barbara Amiel, "The Need for NATO," *National Review,* May 1, 1995, 38–39; Muravchik, "Carrying a Small Stick," 59–61; Peter W. Rodman, "Prague Spring," *National Review,* May 6, 1996, 39–42; and Nixon, *Beyond Peace,* 40–42.

85. Muravchik, "Carrying a Small Stick," 60–61.

86. Leach, "A Republican Looks at Foreign Policy," 23.

87. See Benjamin S. Lambeth, "Russia's Wounded Military," *Foreign Affairs* 74 (March-April 1995): 86–99.

88. Muravchik, "Carrying a Small Stick," 58–61; Nixon, *Beyond Peace,* 153–54; and the editorial in *The Chicago Tribune,* November 11, 1996.

89. Nixon, *Beyond Peace,* 265–67.

90. For background on U.S. involvement in the Middle East, see William R. Polk, *The United States and the Arab World* (Cambridge, Mass.: Harvard University Press, 1965); Haim Shaked and Itamar Rabinovic, eds., *The Middle East and the United States* (New Brunswick, N.J.: Transaction Books, 1980); and Emile A. Nakhleh, *The Persian Gulf and American Policy* (New York: Praeger Publishers, 1982).

91. A useful discussion of America's security and diplomatic interests in the Persian Gulf area is contained in the Congressional Quarterly's publication *The Middle East,* 7th ed. (Washington, D.C.: Congressional Quarterly, 1991), 39–123, and later editions of this useful work. See also several of the contributions to the symposium by Micah L. Sifry and Christopher Cerf, eds., *The Gulf War: History, Documents, Opinions* (New York: Random House, 1991), 1–99. As Richard Nixon evaluated the matter, "the question of who controls what in the Persian Gulf and the Middle East is the key to who controls what in the world." Nixon, *The Real War,* 74.

92. As one example, the government of Iran continues to entertain hegemonial ambitions within the Persian Gulf region; and in recent years, Tehran has been engaged in building up its military strength (including the acquisition of a nuclear arsenal) that can be used in pursuit of its external goals. A detailed and provocative scenario portraying the ominous consequences of these and other developments is available in Caspar Weinberger and Peter Schweizer, *The Next War* (Washington, D.C.: Regnery, 1996), 101–63.

93. At the same time, conservative interventionists caution that the preservation of Persian Gulf security is not a commitment that can be successfully assumed by the USA alone. Victory in the Persian Gulf War, it has been repeatedly emphasized, resulted from a collaborative effort by America and its principal allies; and that same strategy will be needed to ensure Persian Gulf security in the years ahead. Nixon, *Beyond Peace,* pp. 94.

94. See Robert D. Kaplan, "War after Peace," *New Republic,* April 29, 1996, pp. 22–23.

95. This is the basic theme of Anthony H. Cordesman in *Iran and Iraq: The Threat from the Northern Gulf* (Boulder, Colo.: Westview Press, 1994). See also Nixon, *Beyond Peace,* 144–47.

96. See the editorial entitled "Mandela's Arms," in the *Wall Street Journal,* January 20, 1997; and the editorial entitled "South Africa, Syria, and Arms," in the *Chicago Tribune,* January 22, 1997.

97. For background, see David E. Long, *The United States and Saudi Arabia: Ambivalent Allies* (Boulder, Colo.: Westview Press, 1985).

98. See the editorial entitled "Taking Off the Gloves with Riyadh," in the *Chicago Tribune,* January 25, 1997. President Ronald Reagan stated that the USA would never stand by and permit Saudi Arabia to become "another Iran." See Reagan's views, as quoted in Charles W. Maynes, "Relearning Intervention," *Foreign Policy,* no. 98 (spring 1995): 105. Recent political developments in this key Middle Eastern nation are discussed at greater length in Congressional Quarterly, *The Middle East,* 215–33.

99. America's role since the 1940s in efforts to resolve the Arab-Israeli conflict are highlighted in William B. Quandt, *Decade of Decision: American Policy toward the Arab-Israeli Conflict* (Berkeley: University of California Press, 1977); in Fred J. Khouri, *The Arab-Israeli Dilemma* (Syracuse: Syracuse University Press, 1968); in Jimmy Carter, *Keeping Faith: Memoirs of a President* (New York: Bantam Books, 1982), 267–431; the same author's *The Blood of Abraham: Insights into the Middle East* (Boston: Houghton Mifflin, 1985); and George Lenczowski, *American Presidents and the Middle East* (Durham: Duke University Press, 1989).

100. For a forceful expression of the idea that after the Cold War, the United States must still be extensively involved in Asian affairs, see James A. Baker III, "America in Asia: Emerging Architecture for a Pacific Community," *Foreign Affairs* 70 (winter 1991-92): 1–18.

101. Douglas MacArthur's views are quoted in Nixon, *Beyond Peace,* 104.

102. The prospect of continuing conflicts and controversies among Asian states is a basic theme of Young Jeh Kim, ed., *The New Pacific Community in the 1990s* (Armonk, N.Y.: M. E. Sharpe, 1996). Most of the contributors believe that the USA must remain actively involved in Asian affairs. For example, Gerald Segal is convinced that in the years ahead, certain aspects of Chinese foreign policy will pose a genuine threat to American interests. Therefore, as the world's only superpower, the USA must be prepared to take the lead in deterring Beijing's expansionist or hegemonial conduct abroad. See Segal's letter to the editor in *Foreign Affairs* 74 (September-October 1995): 187.

103. See the views of Jonathan Clarke in the *Los Angeles Times,* November 1, 1996.

104. See the views of William F. Buckley, Jr., as quoted in J. David Hoeveler, Jr., *Watch on the Right: Conservative Intellectuals in Post-Modern America* (Madison, Wis.: University of Wisconsin Press, 1991), 48.

105. See the editorial in the *Chicago Tribune,* November 11, 1996.

106. According to William E. Odom, for an indefinite period in the future, the peace and security of Asia will depend upon the maintenance of a powerful American military presence within the region. Military power must be available for officials in Washington to deal with potential and actual threats likely to arise within Asia. See his analysis of tendencies and anticipated developments in *Trial after Triumph: East Asia after the Cold War* (Indianapolis: Hudson Institute, 1992).

107. Nixon, *The Real War,* 192.

108. For useful background, see Edwin O. Reischauer, *The United States and Japan,* rev. ed. (New York: Viking Press, 1957); Herbert Passin, ed., *The United States and Japan* (Englewood Cliffs, N.J.: Prentice-Hall, 1966); and Shibusawa Masahide, *Japan and the Asian Pacific Region: Profile of Change* (New York: St. Martin's Press, 1984).

109. Former secretary of state James Baker has called for a "new partnership" between the USA and Japan to preserve peace and stability in Asia. See his "America in Asia," 18.

110. See the editorial entitled "Japan's Diplomatic Offensive," in the *Wall Street Journal,* January 24, 1997; and Nixon, *The Real War,* 111, 191–92.

111. For background on American foreign policy toward Asia historically, see Marvin Kalb and Elie Abel, *Roots of Involvement: The U.S. in Asia, 1784–1971* (New York: W. W. Norton, 1971); Tang Tsou, ed., *China's Policies in Asia and America's Alternatives* (Chicago: University of Chicago Press, 1970); and Foster Rhea Dulles, *China and America: The Story of Their Relations since 1784* (Princeton: Princeton University Press, 1946).

112. This is the contention, for example, of Andrew J. Nathan and Robert S. Ross in *The Great Wall and the Empty Fortress: China's Search for Security* (New York: W. W. Norton, 1997). In the authors' view, these economic constraints will induce the leaders of China to maintain regional stability and cooperative relations with stronger nations like the USA and Japan. Another recent study underscores China's economic weakness, especially its growing inability to feed its burgeoning population. (That same disability, it might be noted, had much to do with Soviet Russia's economic decline and its loss of the Cold War). See Lester R. Brown, *Who Will Feed China? Wake-up Call for a Small Planet* (New York: W. W. Norton, 1995).

113. Nixon, *Beyond Peace,* 122; and the same author's *1999,* 242–43.

114. For more detailed discussion of China's growing military power and its implications for regional security, see Weinberger and Schweizer, *The Next War,* 3–101.

115. See, for example, the views of Asian officials, as quoted in Robert A. Manning and James Przystup, "In Dire Straits," *National Review,* April 8, 1996, pp. 29–30.

116. See the views of Mortimer B. Zuckerman on U.S. relations with the People's Republic of China in "Realism About China," *U.S. News and World Report,* June 9, 1997, p. 104.

117. See, for example, Segal, letter, 187–88. In this commentator's view, at times there will be no alternative to dynamic American leadership designed to block an increasingly assertive China's regional and global ambitions.

118. One of the most powerful interest groups within the American society since the late 1940s has been the pro-Taiwanese lobby. As in the past, this lobby has been extremely active in urging officials in Washington to resist mainland China's latest designs on Taiwan. From the available evidence, this interest group continues to have a potent influence in shaping the course of American diplomacy. See, for example, the *New York Times,* April 9, 1996, dispatch by Elaine Sciolino. Yet one student of Chinese affairs is doubtful that the PRC is militarily strong enough to mount a successful campaign to reclaim Taiwan, even in the absence of American military power in the region. See the letter of Eric Arnett to *Foreign Affairs* 76 (January-February 1997): 173–74.

119. See George F. Will, "Marx in a J. Press Suit," *Newsweek,* June 9, 1997, p. 88. Among conservative groups in the United States, a number of fundamentalist religious organizations have become increasingly outspoken in condemning the PRC's suppression of religious freedoms and in calling on officials in Washington to take a firm position on the issue. According to one analysis, the influence of this group is especially important in explaining vocal congressional opposition to the Clinton administration's policy of "dialogue" with mainland China. See "Pray for China," *Newsweek,* June 9, 1997, pp. 44–45.

120. One conservative source quoted Chinese premier Li Peng to the effect that his government subscribed to "a new doctrine" in its foreign relations, holding that China and Japan together were "ready to assume global leadership." According to this interpretation, the Chinese government was seeking to revert to an earlier era of diplomacy, when the nation was the dominant power in Asia. See "Japan's Diplomatic Offensive." And see also the analysis of the PRC's foreign policy objectives in Manning and Przystup, "In Dire Straits," 29–30.

121. This is also basically the position taken by a report on Sino-American relations in the years ahead in Ezra F. Vogel, ed., *Living with China: U.S.-China Relations in the Twenty-first Century* (New York: W. W. Norton, 1997). This view is based on the fact that Chinese society has made progress in protecting human rights; that Beijing now participates in several international organizations and has signed a number of international conventions; and that it is now a party to the Nuclear Nonproliferation Treaty. Consequently, a policy of "dialogue" and cooperation with the Chinese government is in America's diplomatic interests.

122. Will, "Marx in a J. Press Suit," 88.

123. This is the view of former secretary of state James Baker, for example, in "America in Asia," 16–18. This belief also went far toward explaining why President Clinton's policy of granting China most-favored-nation status, and encouraging its membership in the World Trade Organization (WTO), elicited widespread support among conservatives on Capitol Hill.

124. One commentator believes the best means of fostering democratic tendencies and greater respect for human rights within the society is for America to encourage Chinese economic growth and progress. In this view, improving the lot of the Chinese people is the single most influential step the USA and other outside nations can take in promoting human rights within China. Conversely, a confrontational approach to Beijing is likely to have a number of adverse consequences for the cause of freedom and human rights within the society. See James Lilley,

"Freedom through Trade," *Foreign Policy,* no. 94 (spring 1994): 37–43. Another observer points out that a confrontational approach to China by policymakers in the USA would almost certainly result in an expansion in Chinese military expenditures, would increase tensions between the two nations on a variety of issues, and would strengthen the position of anti-Western "hard-liners" within the Chinese political system. See Zuckerman, "Realism about China," 104. And see similar views by Richard M. Nixon in *Beyond Peace,* 125–26.

125. See the analysis of Sino-American relations by Kenneth Auchincloss in *Newsweek,* April 1, 1996, pp. 28–33. Another observer identifies the following specific Asian problems as requiring China's positive contribution in the search for effective solutions: creating firm regional institutions; preventing new outbreaks of violence and warfare in Southeast Asia; and resolving regional disputes and conflicts involving Russia, India, Burma, Vietnam, and Thailand. See Zuckerman, "Realism about China," 104. Certain other problems—such as preventing further nuclear proliferation in Asia and dealing with environmental problems within the region—will unquestionably require Chinese participation if they are to be solved.

126. See the prediction by Kenneth Auchincloss in *Newsweek,* April 1, 1996, p. 30.

127. One recent study contends that the most immediate danger to the peace and security of East Asia is posed by the expansionist policy of the government of North Korea, even though economically and financially it is a basket case. See Tae-Hwan Kwak and Edward A. Olsen, eds., *The Major Powers of Northeast Asia: Seeking Peace and Security* (Boulder, Colo.: Lynne Rienner, 1996). See also Manwoo Lee, "North Korea: The Cold War Continues," *Current History* 95 (December 1996): 438–43.

128. Early in 1996, authorities in South Korea called for assistance by other nations (the USA, Japan, China, and Russia) in restraining North Korea from engaging in continuing border incursions against it. See the *New York Times,* April 9, 1996, dispatch by Andrew Pollack. According to one observer, North Korea's determination to join the ranks of the nuclear powers—exemplifying the global problem of nuclear proliferation—was America's most urgent diplomatic challenge after the Cold War. See Maynes, "Relearning Intervention," 103. See also the views of John R. Bolton in the *New York Times,* July 28, 1996. Another study of North Korea's manifold problems concluded that it was in the interests of the United States, along with South Korea, China, and other nations, to prevent economic collapse and social chaos in the country—if for no other reason that failure to do so would inevitably mean a growing tide of refugees streaming across the 38th Parallel into South Korea. See Marcus Noland, "Why North Korea Will Muddle Through," *Foreign Affairs* 76 (July–August 1997): 105–19.

129. See the editorial in the *Chicago Tribune,* November 11, 1996; and Nixon, *Beyond Peace,* 137.

130. For a strong case in favor of a new and more constructive relationship between the USA and Vietnam, see Allan E. Goodman, "Dateline Hanoi: Recognition at Last," *Foreign Policy,* no. 100 (fall 1995): 144–55. According to this observer, more co-operative relations between Washington and Hanoi will contribute to a peaceful resolution of regional problems, will strengthen democratic tendencies throughout Southeast Asia, will facilitate arms control agreements, and will be a useful step in undertaking anti-terrorist measures. See Goodman, "Dateline Hanoi," 150–53; and see also Nixon, *Beyond Peace,* 137.

131. The contribution of the Monroe Doctrine to the nation's diplomacy is discussed in detail in Cecil V. Crabb, Jr., *The Doctrines of American Foreign Policy: Their Meaning, Role, and Future* (Baton Rouge: Louisiana State University Press, 1982), 9–56.

132. See the discussion of the Johnson administration's intervention in the Dominican Republic in 1964 in Lyndon B. Johnson, *The Vantage Point: Perspectives of the Presidency, 1963–1969*

(New York: Holt, Rinehart, and Winston, 1971), 180–206; and G. Connell-Smith, "OAS and the Dominican Crisis," *World Today* 21 (June 1965): 229–36.

133. Leach, "A Republican Looks at Foreign Policy," 18.

134. A detailed analysis of the effort to implant stable democratic institutions and processes in a key Latin American state is Wayne S. Cornelius, *Mexican Politics in Transition: The Breakdown of a One-Party-Dominant Regime* (San Diego: Center for U.S.-Mexican Studies, 1996). Other obstacles to democracy throughout Latin America are identified and analyzed in Nora Lustig, ed., *Coping with Austerity: Poverty and Inequality in Latin America* (Washington, D.C.: Brookings Institution, 1995).

135. A highly useful study of the problem—focusing upon one of the most promising contexts in Latin America—is Walton L. Brown, *Democracy and Race in Brazil, Britain, and the United States: Reaching for Higher Ground* (Lewiston, Pa.: Edwin Mellen Press, 1997). In this author's view, lack of progress in achieving racial equality poses a serious barrier to democratization in Brazil and, by implication, several other Latin American states as well. America's own record in that regard has not been a positive influence in promoting democracy south of the border. Another formidable barrier to democracy throughout Latin America is the political role of military elites within these societies. For a recent analysis of the problem, see Richard L. Millett and Michael Gold-Bliss, eds., *Beyond Praetorianism: The Latin American Military in Transition* (Miami: University of Miami Press, 1996). For other examples providing evidence that Washington's efforts to ensure the future of democracy south of the border have for the most part miscarried, see Abraham F. Lowenthal, ed., *Exporting Democracy: The United States and Latin America* (Baltimore: Johns Hopkins University Press, 1991).

136. An analysis of the effort to promote democracy in El Salvador raises real questions about the effectiveness of military intervention in efforts to promote democracy within the hemisphere. The presence of foreign military contingents leads indigenous governments to conclude that other nations "will save them no matter what happens"; and it encourages existing regimes to defer long-needed domestic reforms. See Evans, "El Salvador's Lessons," 45.

137. For example, one study focusing on U.S. policy toward Central America concludes that in most instances, interventionist behavior paid few dividends for the USA, while having numerous negative consequences. See several of the contributions to Kenneth M. Coleman and George C. Herring, eds., *Understanding the Central American Crisis: Sources of Conflict, U.S. Policy, and Options for Peace* (Washington, D.C.: Scholarly Resources, 1991). In a different setting—U. S. policy toward Africa—one commentator is highly critical of Washington's intervention in Zaire, concluding that in the final analysis, it actually created a serious obstacle to the emergence of democracy in this key African state. See the dispatch by Lucy Komisar in the *Los Angeles Times,* January 16, 1997. In more general terms, in time George F. Kennan became extremely skeptical of what he believed was the view of many Americans, that democracy was the "natural state" of mankind. He found little or no evidence to support the widely prevalent idea that democratic political systems could be successfully implanted and operated outside the "narrow parameters" of northwestern Europe and North America. See his views as quoted in Tony Smith, *America's Mission: The United States and the Worldwide Struggle for Democracy in the Twentieth Century* (Princeton: Princeton University Press, 1994), 179.

138. Nixon, *Beyond Peace,* 137–38. For developments that have led to fundamental changes in Cuban-American relations, see Wayne S. Cole, "Shackled to the Past: The United States and Cuba," *Current History* 95 (February 1996): 49–55.

139. See Edmond J. Keller and Donald Rothchild, eds., *Africa in the New International Order: Rethinking State Sovereignty and Regional Security* (Boulder, Colo.: Lynne Rienner, 1996).

140. See the detailed discussion of growing health, social, and economic problems in sub-Saharan Africa—particularly the region's increasingly critical food shortages—in Robert L. Paarlberg, "Rice Bowls and Dust Bowls," *Foreign Affairs* 75 (May–June 1996): 130–32. See also Nixon, *1999,* 280–82.

141. Daniel Deudney and G. John Ikenberry, "After the Long War," *Foreign Policy,* no. 94 (spring 1994): 32–33. The challenges in foreign economic policy confronting American policymakers after the Cold War are identified and examined in Sylvia Ostry, *The Post–Cold War Trading System: Who's on First?* (New York: Twentieth Century Fund, 1997).

142. See the views of Henry R. Nau in "Trading Troubles," *National Review,* December 31, 1996, pp. 39–40.

143. See Smith, *America's Mission,* 292–93.

144. Dionne, *Why Americans Hate Politics,* 351–52.

145. Nixon, *Beyond Peace,* 117, 162–70.

146. President Reagan's views are quoted in Smith, *America's Mission,* 266–71.

147. Secretary Shultz's views are quoted in Smith, *America's Mission,* 270.

148. Secretary Baker's views are quoted in Smith, *America's Mission,* 315.

149. James F. Hoge, Jr., "Media Pervasiveness," *Foreign Affairs* 73 (July–August 1994): 138.

150. See the poll data presented in Rosner, "The Know-Nothings Must Know Something," 124.

151. See the views of C. Michael Armstrong, in "Up to the Challenge?" *Foreign Affairs* 74 (July–August 1995): 21.

152. Nixon, *Beyond Peace,* 173–74.

153. Alfred E. Eckes, "Trading American Interests," *Foreign Affairs* 71 (fall 1992): 153–54. A leading student of public opinion found that an overwhelming majority of the people wants policymakers in Washington to concentrate on the solution of domestic problems. See Daniel Yankelovich, "Foreign Policy after the Election," *Foreign Affairs* 71 (fall 1992): 5–6.

154. Norman J. Ornstein, "Foreign Policy and the 1992 Election," *Foreign Affairs* 71 (summer 1992): 7.

155. See Robert A. Scalapino, "The United States and Asia: Future Prospects," *Foreign Affairs* 70 (winter 1991): 28–29.

156. See Richard Rosecrance, "A New Concert of Powers," *Foreign Affairs* 71 (spring 1992): 75.

157. Nixon, *Beyond Peace,* 6.

CHAPTER 5

1. See the *Baton Rouge Morning Advocate,* May 30, 2000, dispatch by AP commentator Robert H. Reid.

2. See Clinton's views as quoted in Elizabeth Drew, *On the Edge: The Clinton Presidency* (New York: Simon and Schuster, 1994), 146.

3. See the analysis of Secretary Christopher's view in Charles Lane, "A Man of Good Intentions," *New Republic,* July 29, 1996, pp. 15–19.

4. President Clinton's views are quoted by William Neikirk in the *Chicago Tribune,* January 22, 1997.

5. President Clinton's views are cited in Drew, *On the Edge,* 51.

6. See the views of Zbigniew Brzezinski, as summarized in Mark Gerson, ed., *The Essential Neo-Conservative Reader* (Reading, Mass.: Addison-Wesley, 1996), 174–79.

7. See the views of Jacob Heilbrunn, "True Believers," *New Republic,* June 3, 1996, p. 11.

The subject is dealt with in greater detail in Michael McClintock, *Instruments of Statecraft: U.S. Guerrilla Warfare, Counterinsurgency, and Counter-Terrorism, 1940–1990* (New York: Pantheon Books, 1992).

8. See, for example, the symposium on "Global Security" in *Current History* 94 (May 1995). One contributor emphasizes that the evidence leaves little doubt that America's "understandings of world politics have lagged behind the deep transformations that are altering the global landscape." Americans must be prepared to cope with "profound change" in the international system, which will in turn present them with a multitude of novel and difficult foreign policy problems. See James N. Rosenau, "Security in a Turbulent World," *Current History* 94 (May 1995): 193–200.

9. See extended discussion in Joshua Muravchik, *The Imperative of American Leadership: A Challenge to Neo-Isolationism* (Washington, D.C.: American Enterprise Institute, 1996).

10. See Donald S. Zagoria, "Clinton's Asia Policy," *Current History* 92 (December 1993): 402–406.

11. The compelling need of U.S. foreign policy after the Cold War, according to Charles W. Bray, is to replace the containment strategy with the concept of "community-building" in international affairs. This demands that Washington make every effort to create genuine and stable democracies throughout the world. See his letter to the editor of *Foreign Affairs* 72 (spring 1993): 194–95.

12. See Michael S. Lund, *Preventing Violent Conflicts: A Strategy for Preventive Diplomacy* (Washington, D.C.: U.S. Institute for Peace Press, 1996); and Gareth Evans, "Cooperative Security and Intrastate Conflict," *Foreign Policy,* no. 96 (fall 1994): 5.

13. The transition in American attitudes from the isolationist era to the postwar period of interventionism is traced out in H. Schuyler Foster, *Activism Replaces Isolationism: U.S. Public Attitudes, 1940–1975* (Washington, D.C.: Foxhall Press, 1983); and in Ralph B. Levering, *The Public and American Foreign Policy: 1918–1978* (New York: William Morrow, 1978).

14. A poignant example of the phenomenon was provided during President Clinton's first term by newly liberated states in Eastern Europe, whose officials vocally urged the White House to take the lead in extending NATO eastward. See Drew, *On the Edge,* 403–404.

15. Numerous examples of fundamental differences in liberal viewpoints regarding international issues may be found in Charles W. Kegley, Jr., ed., *Controversies in International Relations Theory: Realism and the Neoliberal Challenge* (New York: St. Martin's, 1995).

16. With regard to the actions of the Clinton White House toward Iraq, for example, one liberal critic denounced it as entirely too restrained and indecisive, with the result that the president "has seriously damaged the credibility of American defense in the [Persian] gulf." This observer called for "firmer military action" against Saddam Hussein's regime; he also urged the White House to engage in military action against Iranian troops in northern Iraq in order to demonstrate that "we won't tolerate any attacks, military or terrorist, against American interests in the Middle East." See the analysis by Kenneth R. Timmerman in the *New York Times,* September 4, 1996. Another liberal commentator castigated the Clinton administration's "feeble response" in dealing with Iraq. In this view, Washington needed to take decisive military and diplomatic action to bring about the "elimination " of Saddam Hussein's regime and to destroy Baghdad's increasingly powerful military establishment. See the dispatch by A. M. Rosenthal in the *New York Times,* September 6, 1996. This same observer called upon the White House to adopt effective measures directed against international terrorism, not excluding "standing ready to retaliate militarily against the sponsors of terrorism." See the views of A. M. Rosenthal in the *New York Times,* July 30, 1996. As a general principle, another study concluded, in the post–Cold War era

as in earlier periods, the USA must be prepared when necessary to engage in unilateral military intervention to achieve its diplomatic goals. See the detailed analysis by Jonathan Clarke and James Glad, *After the Crusade: American Foreign Policy for the Post-Superpower Age* (New York: Madison Books, 1995).

17. See the edition of Thomas Paine's *Common Sense,* edited by Nelson F. Adkins (Indianapolis: Bobbs-Merrill, 1953), 3.

18. President Wilson's views are quoted in William Taubman, ed., *Globalism and Its Critics: The American Foreign Policy Debate of the 1960s* (Lexington, Mass.: D. C. Heath, 1973), 97.

19. Winston Churchill's views on U.S. foreign policy are quoted in Walter Johnson, *The Battle against Isolation* (Chicago: University of Chicago Press, 1944), 5.

20. For numerous illustrations of the Roosevelt administration's wartime and postwar goals, see Cordell Hull, *The Memoirs of Cordell Hull,* 2 vols. (New York: Macmillan, 1948); Robert E. Sherwood, *Roosevelt and Hopkins: An Intimate History,* 2 vols. (New York: Bantam Books, 1950); and Warren F. Kimball, ed., *Franklin D. Roosevelt and the World Crisis, 1937–1945* (Lexington, Mass.: D. C. Heath, 1973).

21. For a contemporary exposition of this idea, see the study by Joseph S. Nye, *Bound to Lead: The Changing Nature of American Power* (New York: Basic Books, 1989).

22. See Theodore Saloutos, *The Greeks in the United States* (Cambridge, Mass.: Harvard University Press, 1964), 162, 170–76, 256–57. See also the discussion of America's reaction to the Greek independence movement in Thomas A. Bailey, *The Diplomatic History of the American People,* 8th ed. (New York: Appleton-Century-Crofts, 1969), 181–82.

23. The place of the Monroe Doctrine in U.S. foreign policy is discussed in Cecil V. Crabb, Jr., *The Doctrines of American Foreign Policy: Their Meaning, Role, and Future* (Baton Rouge: Louisiana State University Press, 1982). More detailed expositions are Dexter Perkins, *A History of the Monroe Doctrine, 1823–1826* (Boston: Little, Brown, 1955); Donald M. Dozer, ed., *The Monroe Doctrine: Its Modern Significance* (New York: Alfred A. Knopf, 1965); Arthur P. Whitaker, *The United States and the Independence of Latin America, 1800–1830* (Baltimore: Johns Hopkins University Press, 1941); and Edwin Lieuwen, *U.S. Policy in Latin America: A Short History* (New York: Praeger, 1965).

24. The Kossuth visit to the USA is dealt with in Emil Lengyel, *Americans from Hungary* (Philadelphia: Lippincott, 1948), 37–43. Other instances involving the American reaction to revolutionary movements in Europe during the nineteenth century are treated in Jan Lerski, *A Polish Chapter in Jacksonian America: The United States and the Polish Exiles of 1831* (Madison: University of Wisconsin Press, 1958); and Carl Witke, *The German Forty-eighters in America* (Philadelphia: University of Pennsylvania Press, 1952). For a more general analysis of the impact of ethnic minorities on the nation's foreign relations, see Charles M. Mathis, Jr., "Ethnic Groups and Foreign Policy," *Foreign Affairs* 59 (summer 1981): 975–99.

25. See Cecil V. Crabb, Jr., *Policy-Makers and Critics: Conflicting Theories of American Foreign Policy* (New York: Frederick A. Praeger, 1976), 40–41. The influence of Italian Americans on U.S. foreign policy in the period before World War II is discussed in the chapter by Max Ascoli in R. M. MacIver, ed., *Group Relations and Group Antagonisms* (New York: Harper/Collins, 1944).

26. The George Kennan being referred to here was a distant relative of the influential diplomatic official and post–World War II commentator on American foreign policy, George F. Kennan. The earlier George Kennan was a tireless speaker and author in efforts to rally American public opinion against the czarist regime. One of his most widely circulated books, for example, was *Siberia and the Exile System* (1882). Informed students of Russian-American relations believe

that the American opposition to czarism served as one factor in events leading to the overthrow of the czarist system in 1917. See Thomas A. Bailey, *America Faces Russia: Russian-American Relations from Early Times to Our Day* (Ithaca, N.Y.: Cornell University Press, 1950), 133.

27. Mark Twain's remarks are quoted in Max M. Laserson, *The American Impact on Russia—Diplomatic and Ideological: 1784–1917* (New York: Macmillan, 1950), 311.

28. See William W. Orbach, *The American Movement to Aid Soviet Jews* (Amherst, Mass.: University of Massachusetts Press, 1979); and Bailey, *America Faces Russia,* 125–26.

29. For a forceful expression of President Wilson's views toward the Russian Revolution of 1917, see "Address of the President of the United States," April 2, 1917, Sixty-fifth Congress, lst Session, House of Representatives, Document #1.

30. More extended treatments of the Veracruz affair are available in John S. D. Eisenhower, *Intervention! The United States and the Mexican Revolution, 1913–1917* (New York: W. W. Norton, 1993); R. E. Quirk, *An Affair of Honor: Woodrow Wilson and the Occupation of Vera Cruz* (Lexington, Ky.: University of Kentucky Press, 1962); and Howard Cline, *The United States and Mexico,* rev. ed. (Cambridge, Mass.: Harvard University Press, 1963), 139–62. Recent studies examining the continuing challenge of creating a democratic political system in Mexico are Stephen D. Morris, *Political Reformism in Mexico: An Overview of Contemporary Mexican Politics* (Boulder, Colo.: Lynne Rienner, 1995); and Wayne A. Cornelius, *Mexican Politics in Transition: The Breakdown of a One-Party-Dominant Regime* (San Diego: Center for U.S.-Mexican Studies, 1996).

31. General treatments of Sino-American relations down to the recent period are Foster Rhea Dulles, *China and America: The Story of Their Relations since 1784* (Princeton: Princeton University Press, 1946); John K. Fairbank, *The People's Middle Kingdom and the U.S.A.* (Cambridge, Mass.: Harvard University Press, 1967); and the same author's *The United States and China,* rev. ed. (Cambridge, Mass.: Harvard University Press, 1958).

32. See, for example, Dorothy Borg, *American Policy and the Chinese Revolution, 1925–1928* (New York: American Institute of Pacific Relations, 1947); and Robert McClellan, *The Heathen Chinese: A Study of American Attitudes toward China, 1890–1905* (Columbus: Ohio State University Press, 1971).

33. A British observer of American diplomacy toward China in the nineteenth century declared that "The foreign policy of the United States is foreign missions." See Tyler Dennett, *Americans in Eastern Asia: A Critical Study of the Policy of the United States with Reference to China, Japan, and Korea in the Nineteenth Century* (New York: Barnes and Noble, 1941), 555–76. Another informative treatment of this aspect of American diplomacy toward China is Paul A. Varg, *Missionaries, Chinese, and Diplomats: The American Protestant Missionary Movement in China, 1890–1952* (Princeton: Princeton University Press, 1958).

34. America's "Open Door Policy" toward Asia for a half-century or so after 1898 is examined in Crabb, *The Doctrines of American Foreign Policy,* 56–106. More extended discussions of the meaning and application of the Open Door principle are available in Fairbank, *The United States and China;* in Warren I. Cohen, *America's Response to China: An Interpretive History of Sino-American Relations* (John Wiley and Sons, 1971); in Stephen C. Y. Pan, *American Diplomacy Concerning Manchuria* (Boston: Bruce Humphries, 1938); and in John P. Davies, *Dragon by the Tail: American, British, Japanese, and Russian Encounters with China and One Another* (New York: W. W. Norton, 1972).

35. The episode of Japan's "Twenty-one Demands" on China is discussed more fully in Cohen, *America's Response to China,* 91–94; and in Dulles, *China and America,* 141–43.

36. The Manchurian Crisis of 1931–32 is treated in greater detail in Armin Rappaport, *Henry L. Stimson and Japan, 1931–1932* (Chicago: University of Chicago Press, 1963); and Richard

Current, "The Stimson Doctrine and the Hoover Doctrine," *American Historical Review* 59 (April 1954): 513–42. A briefer discussion is available in Crabb, *The Doctrines of American Foreign Policy,* 78–94.

37. The change in the attitudes of the American people and their leaders from isolationism to interventionism is traced out in the detailed study by Herbert Feis, *The Road to Pearl Harbor* (New York: Atheneum, 1962); in William L. Langer and S. Everett Gleason, *The Challenge to Isolation* (New York: Macmillan, 1952); in Sherwood, *Roosevelt and Hopkins;* and in Kimball, ed., *Franklin D. Roosevelt and the World Crisis.*

38. See Cecil V. Crabb, Jr., and Kevin V. Mulcahy, *Presidents and Foreign Policy Making: From FDR to Reagan* (Baton Rouge: Louisiana State University Press, 1986), 82–83.

39. See, for example, William R. Louis, *Imperialism at Bay: The United States and the Decolonization of the British Empire, 1941–1945* (New York: Oxford University Press, 1978); and John D. Sbrega, "The Anticolonial Views of Franklin D. Roosevelt," in Herbert D. Rosenbaum and Elizabeth Bartelme, *Franklin D. Roosevelt: The Man, the Myth, the Era, 1882–1945* (Boston: Greenwood Press, 1987).

40. American diplomatic leadership in seeking to establish viable international institutions is highlighted in Murray Gilbert, *From the League to the U.N.* (New York: Harper/Collins, 1951); in Richard W. VanAlystyne, *American Crisis Diplomacy: The Quest for Collective Security* (Stanford: Stanford University Press, 1952); and Richard N. Gardner, *In Pursuit of World Order* (New York: F. A. Praeger, 1964).

41. Numerous examples of FDR's diplomatic moves during the war are treated in Gaddis Smith, *American Diplomacy during the Second World War: 1941–1945* (New York: John Wiley and Sons, 1966); Tony Smith, *America's Mission: The United States and the Worldwide Struggle for Democracy in the Twentieth Century* (Princeton: Princeton University Press, 1994), 113–46; Sidney Warren, *The President as World Leader* (New York: McGraw Hill, 1964); and Willard Range, *Franklin D. Roosevelt's World View* (Athens: University of Georgia Press, 1959).

42. America's support of Chiang Kai-shek's Nationalist Party during the Chinese civil war is discussed at length in Fairbank, *The United States and China,* 246–78; and in Cohen, *America's Response to China,* 100–211. Following the civil war, for a generation or so thereafter, Sino-American relations were characterized by mutual suspicions, tensions, and (during the Korean War) overt conflict. See Foster R. Dulles, *American Foreign Policy toward Communist China* (New York: Thomas Y. Crowell, 1972); and A. Doak Barnett, *China Policy* (Washington, D.C.: Brookings Institution, 1977).

43. See, for example, the account of the Truman administration's increasingly firm attitude toward Moscow over the latter's policies in Eastern Europe, as recounted in Harry S Truman, *Year of Decisions,* vol. 1 of *Memoirs* (Garden City, N.Y.: Doubleday, 1955–56), 71–82.

44. Secretary Acheson's views are quoted in Harry S Truman, *Years of Trial and Hope,* vol. 2 of *Memoirs* (Garden City, N.Y.: Doubleday, 1955–56), 254–55.

45. See, for example, Lloyd C. Gardner, *Architects of Illusion: Men and Ideas in American Foreign Policy, 1941–1949* (Chicago: Quadrangle Books, 1970), pp. 3–25.

46. The Greek-Turkish Aid Program of 1947, inaugurating the containment policy, is discussed more fully in Truman, *Years of Trial and Hope,* 93–109; and in Bruce R. Kuniholm, *The Origins of the Cold War in the Near East: Great Power Conflict and Diplomacy in Iran, Turkey, and Greece* (Princeton: Princeton University Press, 1980). In what was thereafter referred to as the "Truman Doctrine," the president declared: "I believe that it must be the policy of the United States to support free peoples who are resisting attempted subjugation by armed minorities or by outside pressures." By "subjugation," the president meant that other nations were attempting to

preserve their independence from foreign threats; by "armed minorities," he was obviously referring to postwar efforts by Communist and pro-Communist groups to seize political power; and by "outside pressures," he meant Soviet-led (and later, Chinese-led) efforts to foment revolution and subversion within other societies. A more detailed discussion of the Truman Doctrine and its implications may be found in Crabb, *The Doctrines of American Foreign Policy*, 107–52. See also the series of essays in Robert E. Osgood, ed., *From the Truman Doctrine to Vietnam* (Baltimore: Johns Hopkins University Press, 1970). The increasingly "tough" position of the U.S. government in dealing with Moscow is traced out in Martin F. Herz, *Beginnings of the Cold War* (New York: McGraw-Hill, 1966), and in Herbert Druks, *Harry S. Truman and the Russians, 1945–1953* (New York: Robert Speller, 1966).

47. The experienced student of Russian affairs and diplomatic official George F. Kennan is widely regarded as the architect of the containment policy, as set forth in his highly influential and widely circulated article under the pseudonym of "X," in *Foreign Affairs* 25 (July 1947): 556–83. Over the years, Kennan denied that he advocated the containment strategy as it came to be understood and applied by successive administrations in Washington. Although his "X" article by no means made the point clear, Kennan contended in time that he was calling for *political*, as distinct from *military*, containment of Communist expansionism and intrigue abroad. He also disclaimed the idea of a general and indiscriminate anti-Communist campaign to be undertaken by the USA throughout the world. For example, Kennan *opposed* America's involvement in the Vietnam War; nor did he favor large-scale programs of American military aid to other countries. For changes in Kennan's ideas in later years, see his *Memoirs, 1925–1950* (New York: Pantheon Press, 1967) and *Sketches from a Life* (New York: Pantheon Press, 1989). An informative commentary on his views is David Mayers, *George Kennan and the Dilemmas of U.S. Foreign Policy* (New York: Oxford University Press, 1988).

48. The formulation, implementation, and implications of the Marshall Plan are examined in Michael J. Hogan, *The Marshall Plan: America, Britain, and the Reconstruction of Western Europe, 1947–1952* (New York: Cambridge University Press, 1987).

49. See Truman, *Years of Trial and Hope*, 227–43, 240–61.

50. The Truman administration's "Point Four" program of aid to developing nations is discussed in Truman, *Years of Trial and Hope*, 236–50. Although the program underwent a number of reorganizations and name changes, in effect it has been continued down to the present day. See, for example, Agency for International Development, *Development and the National Interest* (Washington, D.C.: 1988); Max F. Millikan and Robert Packenham, *Liberal America and the Third World: Political Development Ideas in Foreign Aid and Social Science* (Princeton: Princeton University Press, 1973); Peter J. Schraeder, ed., *Intervention in the 1980s: U.S. Foreign Policy in the Third World* (Boulder, Colo.: Lynne Rienner, 1989); Nicholas Eberstadt, *Foreign Aid and American Purpose* (Lanham, Md.: University Press of America, 1989); Robert J. Berg and David F. Gordon, eds., *Cooperation for International Development: The United States and the Third World in the 1990s* (Boulder, Colo.: Lynne Rienner, 1989); and David L. Cingranelli, *Ethics, American Foreign Policy, and the Third World* (New York: St. Martin's Press, 1993).

51. An informative discussion of the tenets of liberal thought is Louis Hartz, *The Liberal Tradition in America: An Interpretation of American Political Thought since the Revolution* (New York: Harcourt Brace, 1955). See also Frederick M. Watkins, *The Political Tradition of the West: A Study in the Development of Modern Liberalism* (Cambridge, Mass.: Harvard University Press, 1948); and Michael W. Doyle, "Liberalism and World Politics," *American Political Science Review* 80 (December 1986): 1151–69.

52. Richard E. Rubinstein and Jarle Croker, "Challenging Huntington," *Foreign Policy*, no. 96 (fall 1994): 128.

53. See Howard H. Baker and Ellen L. Frost, "Rescuing the U.S.-Japanese Alliance," *Foreign Affairs* 71 (spring 1992): 107. Or as another study concluded, after the Cold War the USA must engage in "tutelary leadership" in its approach to global problems. See Michael J. Brenner, "EC: Confidence Lost," *Foreign Policy*, no. 91 (summer 1993): 41.

54. The term "preventive diplomacy," for example is used by a student of American diplomacy on the African continent. See Shawn H. McCormick, "The Lessons of Intervention in Africa," *Current History* 94 (April 1995): 164. Another study of conflict and violence in that region concludes that (with particular reference to the genocidal conflict in Rwanda), the United States and the West generally were guilty of a grievous sin of omission because of their failure to intervene at an early stage to avert wholesale violence in Central Africa. See Alain Destexhe, *Rwanda and Genocide in the Twentieth Century* (New York: New York University Press, 1995). The concept of "preventive diplomacy" is also employed by a student of American diplomatic activities in the Balkans. See Charles Gati, "From Sarajevo to Sarajevo," *Foreign Affairs* 71 (fall 1992): 77–78.

55. An outstanding example of such thinking is provided by the attitude of many liberal observers about the "reform" of the United Nations, converting it into a viable peacekeeping agency. See, for example, Thomas G. Weiss and Meryl A. Kessler, "Moscow's U.N. Policy," *Foreign Policy*, no. 79 (summer 1990): 94–113. In this view, the successful revitalization of the UN will require a successful "partnership" between the USA and Russia to achieve the objective.

56. A recent study highlighting the liberal emphasis upon rationality in the decision-making process is Albert Breton et al., *Nationalism and Rationality* (New York: Cambridge University Press, 1995).

57. An analysis of the American foreign policy process, emphasizing the importance of nonrational factors in decisionmaking, is Irving L. Janis, *Groupthink: Psychological Studies of Policy Decisions and Fiascoes* (Boston: Little, Brown, 1982). See also Adam B. Ulam, *The Big Two: Soviet-American Perceptions of Foreign Policy* (Indianapolis: Bobbs-Merrill, 1971); and Robert L. McNamara, *Blundering into Disaster* (New York: Pantheon Books, 1987). This is McNamara's account of how the USA was drawn into the Vietnam War—a process of course in which he played a key role. Another study calling attention to the impact of non-rational factors in shaping American policy toward Southeast Asia is Paul Kattenburg, *The Vietnam Trauma in American Foreign Policy, 1945–1975* (New Brunswick, N.J.: Transaction Books, 1980). According to a recent study of Sino-American relations, the approach of each nation toward the other has too often been subjected to the process of "demonization," or the impact of long-lasting stereotypes and misperceptions on both sides. See James Shinn, ed., *Weaving the Net: Conditional Engagement with China* (New York: Council on Foreign Relations, 1996). From another perspective, the crucial impact of forceful personalities, with all their subjective ideas and behavior traits, upon the postwar American foreign policy process is highlighted in Robert D. Schulzinger, *The Wise Men of Foreign Affairs* (New York: Columbia University Press, 1985).

58. According to one recent study, in the twenty-first century a new species of democracy—called "cosmopolitan democracy"—must be created that is capable of controlling the activities of multinational corporations and other forces operating across national boundaries. See David Held, *Democracy and the Global Order: From the Modern State to Cosmopolitan Governance* (Stanford: Stanford University Press, 1995). See also the view of Anthony Lake, President Clinton's national security adviser, that "free markets create middle classes," and that this development in turn will be a positive step in the maintenance of global peace and security. Lake's views are quoted in Drew, *On the Edge*, 324.

59. For a forceful statement of this case for American diplomatic leadership in behalf of global democracy, see Thomas Franck, "The Emerging Right to Democracy," *American Journal of International Law* 86 (January 1992): 46–91.

60. Norman J. Ornstein and Mark Schmitt, "Dateline Campaign '92: Post–Cold War Politics," *Foreign Policy*, no. 79 (summer 1990): 183–84. After entering the White House, Bill Clinton pledged that his administration would "support the advance of democracy everywhere." His views are quoted in Drew, *On the Edge*, 417. Specific actions taken by the U.S. government to promote democracy abroad are recounted in Smith, *America's Mission*. See also Thomas Carothers, *In the Name of Democracy: U.S. Policy toward Latin America in the Reagan Years* (Berkeley: University of California Press, 1991); Larry Diamond and Marc F. Plattner, eds., *The Global Resurgence of Democracy* (Baltimore: Johns Hopkins University Press, 1993); Joan M. Nelson, *Encouraging Democracy: What Role for Conditional Aid?* (New York: Overseas Development Council, 1992); and Brad Roberts, ed., *The New Democracies: Global Change and U.S. Foreign Policy* (Cambridge, Mass.: MIT Press, 1990).

61. In his "war message" to Congress on April 2, 1917, President Woodrow Wilson declared that, by entering World War I, America intended to "vindicate the principles of peace and justice in the life of the world as against selfish and autocratic power"; its goal was "to set up amongst the really free and self-governed peoples of the world such a concert of purpose and actions as will henceforth insure the observance of those principles." In Wilson's view, the war had been brought about by the actions of "autocratic governments" and "not by the will of their people." Wilson went on to say that "We have no quarrel with the German people"—who were, in his view, drawn into war by their authoritarian rulers. See the text of President Wilson's message to Congress, as reproduced in John A. Vasquez, ed., *The Classics of International Relations* (Englewood Cliffs, N.J.: Prentice-Hall, 1996), 35–40. See also William J. Dixon, "Democracy and the Peaceful Settlement of International Conflict," *American Political Science Review* 88 (March 1994): 14–32; and James L. Ray, *Democracy and International Conflict* (Columbia, S.C.: University of South Carolina Press, 1995).

62. According to one commentator, America's dedication to the goal of promoting human rights abroad was a crucial factor determining the outcome of the Cold War. See William Korey, *The Promises We Keep: Human Rights, the Helsinki Process, and American Foreign Policy* (New York: St. Martin's Press, 1993). See also Michael Posner, "Rally Round Human Rights," *Foreign Policy*, no. 97 (winter 1994–95): 133–40.

63. The idea that the post–Cold War international system is favorable for the extension and enforcement of international law is forcefully argued in Thomas M. Franck, *Fairness in International Law and Institutions* (New York: Oxford University Press, 1996).

64. The efforts by the Truman White House to compel Moscow to honor wartime agreements respecting Eastern Europe are described in Truman, *Year of Decisions*, 15–16, 70–71.

65. The importance of national perceptions (and misperceptions) as an element determining foreign policy is highlighted in Everett C. Ladd and Karlyn H. Bowman, *Public Opinion in America and Japan: How We See Each Other and Ourselves* (Washington, D.C.: American Enterprise Institute Press, 1996).

66. See Paul Kennedy, *The Rise and Fall of the Great Powers: Economic Change and Military Conflict from 1500 to 2000* (New York: Random House, 1987).

67. See Carl Kaysen, Robert S. McNamara, and George W. Rathjens, "Nuclear Weapons after the Cold War," *Foreign Affairs* 70 (fall 1991): 110.

68. See James P. Grant, "Jumpstarting Development," *Foreign Policy*, no. 91 (summer 1993): 124–38.

69. See the excerpt from Immanuel Kant's plan for achieving "perpetual peace," in Vasquez, ed., *The Classics of International Relations*, 368–76.

70. The consequences for the USA of uninterrupted conflict and political instability in other

societies are clearly and disturbingly identified in the study by the American Assembly by Michael S. Teitelbaum and Myron Weiner, eds., *Threatened Peoples, Threatened Borders: World Migration and U.S. Policy* (New York: W. W. Norton, 1995).

71. See C. S. Gochman and A. N. Sabrosky, eds., *Prisoners of War: Nation-States in the Modern Era* (Lexington, Mass.: Lexington Books, 1990); and J. Mueller, *Retreat from Doomsday* (New York: Basic Books, 1989).

72. Clinton's observation is quoted in Drew, *On the Edge,* 410.

73. See Ronald Steel's prescriptions for American foreign policy in the new era in *Temptations of a Superpower* (Cambridge, Mass.: Harvard University Press, 1995).

74. See the view of William Schneider in the *National Journal,* January 22, 1994.

75. See, for example the introduction to Arnold Kanter and Linton F. Brooks, eds., *U.S. Intervention Policy for the Post–Cold War World: New Challenges and New Responses* (New York: W. W. Norton, 1995); and Laura Reed and Carl Kaysen, eds., *Emerging Norms of Justified Intervention* (Cambridge, Mass.: American Academy of Arts and Sciences, 1994).

76. See, for example, John L. Hirsh and Robert B. Oakley, *Somalia and Operation Restore Hope* (Washington, D.C.: United States Institute for Peace, 1995). These authors advocate a policy of what might be called "cautious interventionism" by the USA in responding to crises abroad. According to another study, America's policy of interventionism (which the author accepts) must be "redefined" in order to avoid mistakes of the past and to make foreign policy compatible with domestic policy. See David C. Hendrickson, "The Recovery of Internationalism," *Foreign Affairs* 73 (September–October 1994): 26–43.

77. See the views of UN Ambassador Madeleine Albright, as quoted in Drew, *On the Edge,* 145. Speaking of his administration's response to the crisis in the Balkans, President Clinton said that it was imperative that the USA act, "but I don't think we should act alone." Quoted in Drew, *On the Edge,* 153.

78. See, for example, the views of Secretary of State Warren Christopher, that at times the United States must project its military power abroad. When military power is used to achieve diplomatic goals, the president and his advisers must do so, however, "with a clear mission and the means to prevail." See Warren Christopher, "America's Leadership, America's Opportunity," *Foreign Policy,* no. 98 (spring 1995): 8. According to another observer, after the Cold War Washington will need to rely upon a "nuanced combination" of armed force and diplomacy to achieve its purposes abroad. Hopefully, the nation's policymakers will be able to use peaceful diplomatic instruments to accomplish their goals; but at times, there will be no alternative to reliance upon military force. See Richard J. Payne, *The Clash with Distant Cultures: Values, Interests, and Force in American Foreign Policy* (Albany: State University of New York Press, 1994).

79. Jonathan Clarke, "Leaders and Followers," *Foreign Policy,* no. 101 (winter 1995–96): 45–48. One study of American public opinion found that a majority of the people favored an active role by the USA abroad. But they also believed that "economic interests" ought to take priority over military goals and the promotion of human rights in the pursuit of external goals. See poll data presented in John Stemlau, "Clinton's Dollar Diplomacy," *Foreign Policy,* no. 97 (winter 1994–95): 22.

80. See Clarke, "Leaders and Followers," 50–51. In their proposed new foreign policy agenda for the United States, Shuman and Harvey give high priority to Washington's encouragement of multilateralism and collective security. See Michael H. Shuman and Hal Harvey, *Society without War: A Post–Cold War Foreign Policy* (Boulder, Colo.: Westview Press, 1993). See also Steven R. Ratner, *The New UN Peacekeeping: Building Peace in Lands of Conflict after the Cold War* (New York: St. Martin's, 1995). Another commentator has called upon officials in Washington

to establish a "new concert" of democratic nations to promote collective actions to solve global problems—in effect, a contemporary version of the nineteenth-century Concert of Europe. See G. John Ikenberry, "Salvaging the G-7," *Foreign Affairs* 72 (spring 1993): 132–39. In the opinion of another observer, effective international peacekeeping today is beyond the capacity of a single nation—even a superpower like the United States. See Ingvar Carlsson, "The U.N. at 50: A Time to Reform," *Foreign Policy*, no. 100 (fall 1995): 5.

81. For several different proposals involving military intervention by the United States, acting in concert with other nations, see Doug Bandow, "Avoiding War," *Foreign Policy*, no. 89 (winter 1992–93): 156–75; and Clarke, "Leaders and Followers," 50–51. The same basic point about the need for collaboration with other nations is made by a student of international human rights. America is likely to achieve its goal only to the extent that it co-operates with other nations in doing so. See Posner, "Rally Round Human Rights," 139.

82. See W. R. Smyser, "USSR–Germany: A Link Restored," *Foreign Policy*, no. 84 (fall 1991): 125–42. As this observer assesses it, the United States must continue to maintain a military presence on the European continent, although the level of U.S. forces perhaps can be reduced. In his view, Germany remains dependent upon a U.S. military guarantee of its security.

83. See Jerry F. Hough, "America's Russia Policy: The Triumph of Neglect," *Current History* 93 (October 1994): 309; and Richard Holbrooke, "America as a European Power," *Foreign Affairs* 74 (March–April 1995): 38–52.

84. Late in July 1997, largely at the instigation of the Clinton administration, invitations were extended to Poland, Czechoslovakia, and Hungary, to join NATO. This meant, as one commentary expressed it, that "an attack on Lomza [Poland] would demand the same retaliation as an attack on New York." Many Poles remained extremely skeptical that Russia had completely abandoned its historic ambitions at their expense. See the discussion of NATO's expansion in *Newsweek* (July 21, 1997), p. 40. Another national commentator has emphasized the idea that NATO's expansion will inevitably mean a significant increase in the alliance's expenses for the USA and the other members. See the views of David Broder, in the *Baton Rouge Sunday Advocate*, July 20, 1997. The case for NATO's expansion—with emphasis upon the impact of this step upon Russia's behavior—is made in Richard L. Kugler, *Enlarging NATO: The Russia Factor* (Santa Monica: Rand Corporation, 1996). See also Richard Ullman, "Enlarging the Zone of Peace," *Foreign Policy*, no. 80 (fall 1990): 102–21.

85. President Clinton's view are quoted in *U.S. News and World Report*, July 14, 1997, p. 34.

86. See the analysis of political activity by ethnic groups favoring NATO expansion in *U.S. News and World Report*, July 21, 1997, pp. 31–35. According to one calculation, there are some 21 million Americans of East and Central European descent. See *U.S. News and World Report*, July 14, 1997, p. 37.

87. A recent study focusing on the key role of the USA in promoting European unity is Francis H. Heller and John R. Gillingham, eds., *The United States and the Integration of Europe: Legacies of the Postwar Era* (New York: St. Martin's Press, 1996). See also A. W. De Porte, *Europe between the Superpowers* (New Haven: Yale University Press, 1979); Walter Goldsmith, ed., *Reagan's Leadership and the Atlantic Alliance* (New York: Pergamon-Brassey's, 1987); and Glennon J. Harrison, *Europe and the United States* (Armonk, N.Y.: M. E. Sharpe, 1994).

88. Gianni De Michelis, "Reaching Out to the East," *Foreign Policy*, no. 79 (summer 1990): 44–56.

89. See Lawrence S. Eagleburger, "The Twenty-first Century: American Foreign Policy Challenges," in *America's Global Interests: A New Agenda*, ed. Edward K. Hamilton (New York: W. W. Norton, 1989), 249. According to this observer, a pervasive feeling among Americans that

other nations (specifically, Western Europe and Japan) have not been "doing their part" in meeting their global responsibilities has been a major factor in fostering frustration and doubt among the American people and Congress about the global role of the USA after the Cold War.

90. One observer has called for a Marshall Plan–type program of aid and reconstruction for Eastern Europe and Russia after the Cold War. See Richard Parker, "Clintonomics for the East," *Foreign Policy,* no. 94 (spring 1994): 53–69. See also Gregory Flynn and David J. Scheffer, "Limited Collective Security," *Foreign Policy,* no. 80 (fall 1990): 77–102; and William H. Kincade and Natalie Melnyczuk, "Eurasia Letter: Unneighborly Neighbors," *Foreign Policy,* no. 94 (spring 1994): 84–105.

91. For a typical expression of this view, see the editorial in the *New Republic,* November 11, 1996, p. 12.

92. For example, a number of liberal observers urged the Clinton White House to use every resource at its command to gain the withdrawal of Russian troops from Chechnya, where a destructive conflict between Russian authorities and their former Chechnyan province had erupted. As one account saw it, Moscow's military intervention in Chechnya had obviously failed—and it was incumbent on Washington to compel authorities in the Kremlin to come to terms with that reality. See "Free Chechnya," *New Republic,* September 9, 1996; and "Russia's Bloody Mess," *The Nation,* September 23, 1966, pp. 4–5.

93. For an informative analysis of the challenge facing American policymakers in their efforts to bring about a politically stable, democratic, and reform-oriented Russian political system, see Jeremy Lester, *Modern Tsars and Princes: The Struggle for Hegemony in Russia* (New York: Verso, 1995). According to this author, the prospects for the emergence of a politically moderate order within Russian society were not overly promising.

94. See Sherman Garnett, "Russia's Illusory Ambitions," *Foreign Affairs* 76 (March–April 1997): 61–77.

95. See Hough, "America's Russia Policy," 309.

96. See, for example, the forceful plea for an interventionist policy by the USA toward Russia by Georgi Arbatov, "Eurasia Letter: A New Cold War?" *Foreign Policy,* no. 95 (summer 1994): 90–103. This observer calls on Washington to take decisive steps in an effort to solve a number of serious problems existing within Russian society, including the urgent need for sweeping economic reforms, promoting human rights, and achieving the integration of Russia into European regional institutions. At the same time, a high-ranking policymaker in the Carter administration has identified many problems in the path of successfully pursuing such a policy. See Zbigniew Brzezinski, "The Premature Partnership," *Foreign Affairs* 73 (March–April 1994): 67–82. Certain political groups within Russia have also denounced America's interference in the society's political affairs. See Drew, *On the Edge,* 406–407.

97. See Shafiqul Islam, "Russia's Rough Road to Capitalism," *Foreign Affairs* 72 (spring 1993): 66.

98. See the view of Christopher Hitchens, "The Death of Bosnia," *The Nation,* September 23, 1996, p. 8.

99. For an enlightening analysis of problems and conditions in the Balkans that keep the region in a condition of upheaval and turmoil, see Christopher Civic, *Remaking the Balkans,* 2nd ed. (New York: Chatham House, 1995). See also the editorial "The Discovery of Gravity," in the *New Republic,* December 2, 1996.

100. See the views of former American ambassador to Saudi Arabia Richard Murphy in the *New York Times,* June 17, 1996.

101. See Graham E. Fuller, "Moscow and the Gulf War," *Foreign Affairs* 70 (summer 1991):

76. America's involvement in the affairs of the Middle East since World War II is examined in Burton I. Kaufman, *The Arab Middle East and the United States: Inter-Arab Rivalry and Superpower Diplomacy* (New York: Twayne Publishers, 1996).

102. The author of a recent study credits intervention by the United States for success to date in removing obstacles to peace in the Arab-Israeli conflict. See Mark Perry, *A Fire in Zion: The Israeli-Palestinian Search for Peace* (New York: William Morrow, 1994). In the future, America has a key role to play in removing the remaining barriers to peace—especially in the realm of Israeli-Syrian relations. See Aryeh Shalev, *Israel and Syria: Peace and Security on the Golan* (Boulder, Colo.: Westview Press, 1994). Another commentator believes that once a peace agreement has finally been achieved between Israel and the Arab states, the USA and the "new Russia" will have an indispensable contribution to make in guaranteeing its terms. See Marshall Brement, "U.S.-U.S.S.R.: Possibilities in Partnership," *Foreign Policy*, no. 84 (fall 1991): 107–25.

103. See the editorial in the *Los Angeles Times,* January 16, 1997.

104. See, for example, the views of Barry Rubin in "Holy Terror," *New Republic,* April 22, 1996, p. 12; and "Who's Terrorizing Lebanon?" *New Republic,* May 6, 1996, p. 7.

105. See the views of Jim Hoagland, in the *Washington Post,* November 8, 1996.

106. See the editorial in the *New Republic,* May 6, 1996, p. 8. The editors of this distinguished liberal journal stated that "We wouldn't shed any tears" if the Clinton White House decided to launch a military strike against suspected chemical weapons plants in Libya!

107. See the views of McGeorge Bundy, as quoted in William G. Hyland, "Foreign Affairs at 70," *Foreign Affairs* 71 (fall 1992): 182.

108. Anthony Lake, "Confronting Backlash States," *Foreign Affairs* 73 (March–April 1994): 45–46. According to one observer, for an indefinite period in the future the peace and security of the Middle East will depend upon the willingness and ability of outside powers—especially the USA—to act when necessary to achieve the goal. This development will in turn be contingent upon Washington's ability to deploy military power rapidly and decisively within the region. See Michael Sterner, "Navigating the Gulf," *Foreign Policy,* no. 81 (winter 1990–91): 52.

109. See Steve A. Yetiv, *America and the Persian Gulf: The Third Party Dimension in World Politics* (Westport, Conn.: Praeger Publishers, 1995).

110. For example, see William B. Quandt, "The Urge to Democracy," *Foreign Affairs* 73 (July–August 1994): 2–11. A more detailed study of the subject is John L. Esposito and John O. Voll, *Islam and Democracy* (New York: Oxford University Press, 1996). A well-informed student of Middle Eastern affairs cautions, however, that the principal result of Washington's efforts to promote democracy within the region may be to give new impetus to Islamic fundamentalism, a force that is viewed as clearly inimical to American interests. See Judith Miller, "The Challenge of Radical Islam," *Foreign Affairs* 72 (spring 1993): 53.

111. The meaning and implications of the "Open Door Policy" are examined in greater detail in Crabb, *The Doctrines of American Foreign Policy,* 56–107. See also Henry L. Stimson, *The Far Eastern Crisis: Recollections and Observations* (New York: Harper/Collins, 1936); John P. Davies, Jr., *Dragon by the Tail: American, British, Japanese, and Russian Encounters with China and with One Another* (New York: W. W. Norton, 1972); Jerry Israel, *Progressivism and the Open Door: America and China, 1905–1921* (Pittsburgh: University of Pittsburgh Press, 1971); and Dorothy Borg, *The United States and the Far Eastern Crisis of 1933–1938* (Cambridge, Mass.: Harvard University Press, 1964).

112. One study identifies a number of what are called "megatrends" that are fundamentally changing Asia's role in international affairs. According to this interpretation, in time Asia will rival—and perhaps overtake—the United States in power and global influence. See John Naisbitt,

Megatrends Asia: Eight Megatrends That Are Reshaping Our World (New York: Simon and Schuster, 1996). See also Warren I. Cohen, ed., *Pacific Passage: The Study of American–East Asian Relations on the Eve of the Twenty-first Century* (New York: Columbia University Press, 1995).

113. According to a longtime student of Asian affairs, after the Cold War the USA must make a "permanent commitment to an emerging Pacific commonwealth of nations." Washington is called on to exhibit leadership in preserving the peace of Asia and in creating a new "security mechanism" for the region. See the letter from Frank Gibney to *Foreign Affairs* 72 (spring 1993): 191–92. See also the views of Donald S. Zagoria, that a major objective of the Clinton White House was to lead the way in creating a "new Pacific community." Zagoria, "Clinton's Asia Policy," 401. According to another study, Asia is witnessing the emergence of a new "civilization in progress." See Masakazu Yamazaki, "Asia, a Civilization in the Making," *Foreign Affairs* 75 (July–August 1996): 106–20. See also several of the essays in Andrew Mack and John Ravenhill, eds., *Pacific Cooperation: Building Economic and Security Regimes in the Asia-Pacific Region* (Boulder, Colo.: Westview Press, 1995).

114. See Michael J. Mazarr, *North Korea and the Bomb: A Case Study of Nonproliferation* (New York: St. Martin's, 1995).

115. See the editorial in the *Washington Post,* November 13, 1966. It must be kept in mind, as many Americans appear to be unaware, that there has never been a peace treaty between North and South Korea formally ending the Korean War.

116. An objective and well-informed analysis of U.S.-Japanese relations after the Cold War is Michael H. Armacost, *Friends or Rivals? The Insider's Account of U.S.-Japanese Relations* (New York: Columbia University Press, 1996). The author served as American ambassador to Japan during the period 1989–93.

117. America's crucial role in the postwar reconstruction of Japan is underscored in Edwin O. Reischauer, *The United States and Japan,* 2nd ed. (Cambridge, Mass.: Harvard University Press, 1957); a more recent study is Howard B. Schonberger, *Aftermath of War: America and the Remaking of Japan, 1945–1952* (Kent, Ohio: Kent State University Press, 1989).

118. See Bela Balassa and Marcus Noland, *Japan and the World Economy* (Washington, D.C.: Institute for International Economics, 1988).

119. By the end of the twentieth century, Japan had become the second-largest industrial power on the globe (ranking behind the USA). According to one estimate, by the early part of the new century, Japan is destined to become America's economic and financial equal. See the data presented in Zagoria, "Clinton's Asia Policy," 402.

120. Zagoria, "Clinton's Asia Policy," 401.

121. See Joseph S. Nye, Jr., "The Case for Deep Engagement," *Foreign Affairs* 74 (July–August 1995): 95–102. Nye and other commentators are convinced that, in order to achieve its goals in Asia, the USA must continue to maintain a large military presence in the region. See also Robert C. Suter, *East Asia and the Pacific: Challenges for U.S. Policy* (Boulder, Colo.: Westview Press, 1992); and Richard P. Cronin, *Japan, the U.S., and Prospects for the Asia-Pacific Century: Three Scenarios* (New York: St. Martin's, 1992).

122. See Sebastian Mallaby, "Off Base," *New Republic,* December 23, 1996, pp. 17–20. According to this observer, under the Clinton administration, U.S. policy toward Japan has been "a mess," primarily because the Clinton White House has allowed economic questions to eclipse more fundamental political and security issues in relations between the two nations.

123. See Charles W. Maynes, "The New Pessimism," *Foreign Policy,* no. 100 (fall 1995): 45–46. And see also Harry Harding, "Asia Policy to the Brink," *Foreign Policy,* no. 96 (fall 1994): 73–74.

124. For details in the process of achieving "normalization" in Sino-American relations, see Robert S. Ross, *Negotiating Cooperation: The United States and China, 1969–1989* (Stanford: Stanford University Press, 1995).

125. See Sherle R. Schwenninger, "The Debate That Wasn't," *The Nation,* November 18, 1996, pp. 22–24; and see the analysis of China's post–Cold War behavior in foreign affairs by Thomas J. Christensen, "Chinese Realpolitik," *Foreign Affairs* 75 (September–October 1996): 37–53.

126. Jacob Heilbrunn, "Flirting with Disaster," *New Republic,* December 2, 1996, pp. 29–30. See also Richard Bernstein and Ross H. Munro, "China I: The Coming Conflict with America," *Foreign Affairs* 76 (March–April 1997): 18–33. According to these observers, China's leaders will in the not-too-distant future view the USA as the chief obstacle blocking the achievement of their foreign policy goals. Accordingly, Washington's principal diplomatic objective must be to contain China's hegemonial ambitions abroad.

127. The government of contemporary China, one study is convinced, is determined "to drive the USA out of Asia." The PRC's recent efforts to gain control of Taiwan provide dramatic evidence of this intention. For its part, the United States must take any necessary step—not excluding the use of military power—to block Beijing's diplomatic ambitions. This strategy must also include firm American support for Japan in the latter's dispute with China over the possession of certain islands in the South China Sea. See the editorial entitled "Hard Copy" in the *New Republic,* June 10, 1996, p. 7.

128. See the analysis of the viewpoints and activities of labor unions on the question of U.S. trade with China, in the *New Orleans Times-Picayune,* May 15, 2000, dispatch by Thomas L. Friedman; and in the *New York Times,* May 14, 2000, dispatch by Steven Greenhouse.

129. For a forceful statement of this viewpoint, see Robert S. Ross, "China II: Beijing as a Conservative Power," *Foreign Affairs* 76 (March–April 1997): 33–45. In this commentator's view, if Washington treats the PRC as "an enemy," then China will almost certainly become and act like one. Instead, American policymakers must engage in a "dialogue" with Chinese leaders, focusing on issues of national security, trade and economic development, and human rights, in an effort to persuade Beijing to "use its power in a manner conducive to U.S. interests." Ross, "China II," 33.

130. This is the viewpoint advanced, for example, by Andrew J. Nathan and Robert S. Ross, *The Great Wall and the Empty Fortress: China's Search for Security* (New York: W. W. Norton, 1997).

131. One study emphasizes that in recent years, the ability of China's rulers to impose their authority on the nation's burgeoning population has *declined* significantly and is likely to continue to decline. The "iron discipline" of the Chinese Communist Party has been severely eroded. Yet this analysis also cautions that progress in the direction of democracy in China will be slow and uneven. See Liu Binyan, "The Long March from Mao: China's De-Communization," *Current History* 92 (September 1993): 241–44.

132. These and other problems confronting Chinese society in the years ahead are examined in detail in Lester R. Brown, *Who Will Feed China? Wake-up Call for a Small Planet* (New York: W. W. Norton, 1995).

133. According to one liberal source, Washington must maintain effective channels of communication with Beijing, despite incidents from time to time of repressive policies and actions by the Chinese government. In this view, the dominant issues in contemporary Sino-American relations—trade questions, the expanding opportunities for foreign investment in China, the PRC's exportation of weapons of mass destruction and nuclear technology, and the overall prob-

lems of preserving Asian security—can only be successfully resolved *by negotiations* among Chinese, American, and other governments' officials. In turn, the prerequisite for successful negotiations is that the parties to such disputes maintain communications with each other. See the editorial in the *Los Angeles Times,* November 1, 1996. See also the more detailed analysis calling for this approach in Ezra F. Vogel, ed., *Living with China: U.S.-China Relations in the Twenty-first Century* (New York: W. W. Norton, 1997).

134. Robert L. Bernstein and Richard Dicker, "Human Rights First," *Foreign Policy,* no. 94 (spring 1994): 43–44. Similarly, after new outbreaks of political turmoil erupted in Indonesia, one liberal source called on Washington to "use its considerable influence to discourage reflexive repression and encourage timely change" in the direction of democracy in that key Asian country. See the editorial in the *New York Times,* August 1, 1996.

135. See the editorial in the *Washington Post,* November 7, 1996.

136. See the editorial in the *Washington Post,* November 12, 1996; and the editorial in the *New York Times,* July 30, 1996.

137. See Bruce Cummings, "Korea's Labor War," *The Nation,* January 27, 1997, p. 7.

138. See the analysis of the internal conflict gripping Sierra Leone in the *New York Times,* May 14, 2000, dispatch by Norimitsu Onishi.

139. See George W. Shepherd, Jr., ed., *Racial Influences on American Foreign Policy* (New York: Basic Books, 1970); the symposium on "African Policy and Black Americans," *Foreign Policy,* no. 15 (summer 1974): 109–52; and R. Stephen Brent, "Aiding Africa," *Foreign Policy,* no. 80 (fall 1990): 121–45. After noting that to date the provision of several billion dollars in external aid to Africa has failed to solve its increasingly grave problems, one commentator proposed that an American-led "international trusteeship" be imposed upon the continent! See the views of William Pfaff in the *New York Times,* June 23, 1996. An informative analysis of problems existing within contemporary African societies in Edmond J. Keller and Donald Rothchild, eds., *Africa in the New International Order: Rethinking State Sovereignty and Regional Security* (Boulder, Colo.: Lynne Rienner, 1996).

140. The pervasiveness of violent conflicts on the African scene is graphically depicted in Oliver Furley, *Conflict in Africa* (New York: I. B. Tauris, 1995); and Harvey Glickman, ed., *Ethnic Conflict and Democratization in Africa* (Atlanta: African Studies Association Press, 1995). Referring to the genocidal conflict gripping Zaire and affecting other nations in Central Africa, one commentator called for the United States and other advanced nations to "develop a coherent region-wide response" to the phenomenon. In Africa and elsewhere, comparable crises will almost certainly erupt unless and until this occurs. See the views of Ian Guest in the *Washington Post,* November 11, 1996. See also McCormick, "The Lessons of Intervention in Africa," 162–67. As this observer assesses it, the results of U.S. intervention in Somalia were clearly mixed; despite America's efforts, the country's political future remains "uncertain." This analyst is more sanguine about the results of U.S. intervention in Rwanda. A dominant lesson from foreign intervention in Mozambique, on the other hand, is that peace agreements are unlikely to endure without continuing foreign supervision of their terms. Another general lesson derived from recent American intervention in African affairs is that it is not possible to differentiate sharply between "humanitarian" and "political" intervention. In nearly all instances, political considerations will in time almost certainly prove to be unavoidable and all-important in determining the success of humanitarian intervention.

141. The challenges confronting American foreign policy in Africa are identified and analyzed in Michael Clough, *Free at Last? U.S. Policy toward Africa and the End of the Cold War* (New York: Council on Foreign Relations, 1991); in Shain, "Multicultural Foreign Policy," 69–87; and in

Jeffrey Herbst, "Creating a New South Africa," *Foreign Policy*, no. 94 (spring 1994): 120–37. One influential liberal publication contended that Washington had a clear obligation to achieve a peace settlement in Central Africa, involving Rwanda, Burundi, and Zaire. Without active American intervention, the entire African continent was likely to be engulfed in war. See the editorial in the *Los Angeles Times*, November 4, 1996. Similarly, another liberal commentary was convinced that it was Washington's responsibility to lead the way in an attempt to save "central Africa from imminent catastrophe"; this was a mission that must be adopted and pursued "at the highest levels of the United States and its allies." See the editorial in the *Washington Post*, November 9, 1996. According to another commentator, America's failure to act decisively in Central Africa would guarantee the existence of massive and extremely difficult refugee problems on the African continent. See the view of David Rieff in the *Washington Post*, November 10, 1996.

142. See, for example, the views of David Rieff, in "Camped Out," *New Republic*, November 25, 1996, pp. 26–28.

143. One commentary cautions, for example, that while intervention by the USA in Central Africa may be necessary, no one should imagine that such action will automatically lead to durable peace and stability in the region. A number of fundamental problems—such as existing boundary disputes and the lack of an equitable "sharing" of political power by rival ethnic groups—must be solved before conditions of peace and stability are likely to exist. See the editorial in the *Washington Post*, November 15, 1996. See also the views of Rieff, "Camped Out," 26–28.

144. See, for example, the analysis of the continent's problems by a Nigerian observer, in Claude Ake, *Democracy and Development in Africa* (Washington, D.C.: Brookings Institution, 1996).

145. One highly qualified observer is convinced that Africa will most likely experience the most critical internal problems among the major regions of the world. By the late 1990s, for example, African food production was not keeping pace with its population growth, leaving some 40 percent of the region's population malnourished. See Robert L. Parlberg, "Rice Bowls and Dust Bowls," *Foreign Affairs* 75 (May–June 1996): 130–31.

146. President Kennedy's views are quoted in Smith, *America's Mission*, 214.

147. See the analysis of developments in Zimbabwe in the *New Orleans Times-Picayune*, May 15, 2000, by Georgie A. Geyer.

148. See Alain Destexhe, "The Third Genocide," *Foreign Policy*, no. 97 (winter 1994–95): 3–18; the report by Human Rights Watch, *Landmines in Mozambique and Easy Prey: Child Soldiers in Liberia* (New York: Human Rights Watch, 1994); and Adonis Hoffman, "Nigeria: The Policy Conundrum," *Foreign Policy*, no. 101 (winter 1995–96): 146–58. In this analysis of U.S. policy toward the key African state of Nigeria, the author believes that intervention by the United States and other foreign powers offers the best hope of implanting democracy in the society; but he is no less convinced that diplomatic, rather than military, efforts will be the most effective means for achieving the goal.

149. This is a major theme of the symposium by Abraham F. Lowenthal and Gregory F. Treverton, eds., *Latin America in a New World* (Boulder, Colo.: Westview Press, 1994). For an analysis of a number of forces and tendencies likely to shape U.S. relations with Latin America in the future, see Peter H. Smith, *Talons of the Eagle: Dynamics of U.S.–Latin American Relations* (New York: Oxford University Press, 1996).

150. See Peter Hakim and Michael Shifter, "United States–Latin American Relations: To the Summit and Beyond," *Current History* 94 (February 1995): 49–53.

151. Hakim and Shifter, "United States–Latin American Relations," 50–51.

152. See Bradford DeLong, Christopher DeLong, and Sherman Robinson, "The Case for

Mexico's Rescue," *Foreign Affairs* 75 (May–June 1996): 8–14. In this view, Mexico's economic collapse "would likely have caused severe depressions in Latin America and perhaps in Asia," as well. Yet as another student of Mexican affairs concludes, the prospects for democracy and economic progress within the country remain uncertain. See Jorge G. Castaneda, "Mexico's Circle of Misery," *Foreign Affairs* 75 (July–August 1996): 92–106. Another well-informed student of Mexican-American relations is convinced that Washington's *repeated* rescue of the Mexican economy in the long run has not been a constructive approach. Instead, Washington ought to send "strong signals" that it will "no longer bail out Mexico—or any emerging economy—whose problems are a result of political [and] economic mismanagement." See the letter by Robert Krol in *Foreign Affairs* 75 (September–October 1996): 171.

153. Richard L. Millett, "An End to Militarism? Democracy and the Armed Forces in Central America," *Current History* 94 (February 1995): 72.

154. The "profound poverty" and growing inequality of income existing within contemporary Latin America are realities underscored in Nora Lustig, ed., *Coping with Austerity: Poverty and Inequality in Latin America* (Washington, D.C.: Brookings Institution, 1995).

155. These and other examples are examined in Gabriel Marcella, ed., *Warriors in Peacetime: The Military and Democracy in Latin America* (Portland, Ore.: Frank Cass, 1994); and Sidney W. Mintz, "Can Haiti Change?" *Foreign Affairs* 74 (January–February 1995): 73–87. Referring to increasingly critical problems in Mexico (but the point could well be made about other Latin American societies), one author says that it is not "in the U.S. interest to have a well of Third World misery on its southern frontier." See M. Delal Baer, "North American Free Trade," *Foreign Affairs* 70 (fall 1991): 138.

156. See the discussion of the Clinton administration's efforts to gain congressional and public support for the North American Free Trade Agreement (NAFTA) in Drew, *On the Edge,* 285–300, 338–55.

157. These and other problems confronting the United States within the hemisphere are examined in greater detail in several of the essays in "Latin America," *Current History* 95 (February 1996); and in Tom Farer, ed., *Beyond Sovereignty: Collectively Defending Democracy in the Americas* (Baltimore: Johns Hopkins University Press, 1995)

158. President Wilson's views are quoted in Smith, *America's Mission,* 60.

159. U.S. intervention in Haiti is discussed more fully as a case study in Chapter 6.

160. See Joshua Muravchik, *Exporting Democracy: Fulfilling America's Destiny* (Washington, D.C.: AEI Press, 1991). In effect, this observer called on policymakers in Washington to establish a new kind of *Pax Americana* abroad—a regime of "harmony, not of conquest." Similarly, a former U.S. diplomatic official has said, concerning Turkish-American relations, that a high-ranking American goal must be maintenance of "a stable, secular democracy in a Muslim country" within a region marked by "turbulence, poverty, and religious radicalism." See Morton I. Abramowitz, "Dateline Ankara: Turkey after Ozal," *Foreign Policy,* no. 91 (summer 1993): 181.

161. See Ornstein and Schmitt, "Dateline Campaign '92, 181–82.

162. See, for example, the views of Gareth Evans in "Cooperative Security and Intrastate Conflict," 8–12; and Morton H. Halperin, "Guaranteeing Democracy," *Foreign Policy,* no. 91 (summer 1993): 105–24. Halperin is convinced that a dominant diplomatic objective of the USA in Latin America and other regions must be "to help fledgling democracies prevail against internal and external enemies." See 117–18.

163. According to one recent study, thirty-one (out of a total of thirty-five) governments within the hemisphere could be classified as "democratic." See the findings in a study by Freedom House, as reported in the *New York Times,* August 4, 1996. Yet the criteria for classifying a

society as "democratic" of course remain highly debatable. Historically, a wide gap has existed between professions of faith in the democratic ideal, on the one hand, and the practices engaged in by Latin American governments, on the other hand; and that disparity continues to characterize the political process in most Latin American states today.

164. Major obstacles confronting efforts to create and maintain stable democratic institutions and processes in Latin America are examined in Jorge I. Dominguez and Abraham F. Lowenthal, eds., *Constructing Democratic Governance: Latin America and the Caribbean in the 1990s—Themes and Issues* (Baltimore: Johns Hopkins University Press, 1996); and the same editors' *Constructing Democratic Governance: South America in the 1990s* (Baltimore: Johns Hopkins University Press, 1996). See the detailed report on human rights throughout the world in *Human Rights Watch World Report: 1995* (New York: Human Rights Watch, 1995). Another study is persuaded that America's commitment to the cause of human rights was a key factor explaining the outcome of the Cold War. See Korey, *The Promises We Keep.* One liberal source believes that after the Cold War, the president and Congress must make a concerted effort to deny modern arms to Latin American states, in an effort to reduce the likelihood of coups against democratic governments. See the editorial entitled "Lick Those Chops," *The Progressive,* January 1997, p. 9.

165. See the data on public opinion included in Stemlau, "Clinton's Dollar Diplomacy," 22.

166. See the analysis by Stanley Reed in "Clinton's Split Personality on Foreign Policy," *Business Week,* November 1, 1993, p. 58.

167. One study of President Clinton's first term concluded that in appointing Warren Christopher as secretary of state, and Anthony Lake as national security adviser, Clinton's dominant aim was "to keep foreign policy from distracting the President from his domestic agenda." During his first presidential campaign, Clinton endeavored to keep debate focused on domestic policy and to keep foreign policy issues "submerged." As he entered the Oval Office, Clinton was viewed as having "few strong instincts on foreign policy questions." Unlike most postwar chief executives, Clinton did not have regularly scheduled meetings with his foreign policy advisers. See Drew, *On the Edge,* 28, 138, 144, 146. Another analysis of the approach of President Clinton to diplomatic issues observed that during his first (if not necessarily his second) term, Clinton viewed foreign affairs as a major "distraction" from his efforts to solve domestic problems. See the analysis by Michael Elliott in *Newsweek,* August 18, 1997, p. 46. Similarly, the crucial influence of domestic issues in shaping the foreign policy of the Carter administration is highlighted in David Skidmore, *Reversing Course: Carter's Foreign Policy, Domestic Politics, and the Failure of Reform* (Nashville: Vanderbilt University Press, 1995). A preoccupation with domestic issues also significantly influenced the worldview of President Lyndon B. Johnson, whose attitudes reflected the Populist political tradition. LBJ's mind-set on foreign affairs is examined at greater length in Crabb and Mulcahy, *Presidents and Foreign Policy Making,* 198–236. A recent study of American foreign policy emphasizes how the neglect and derogation of diplomatic challenges by the American people and their leaders have seriously impeded the nation's ability to achieve its goals abroad. See Monteagle Stearns, *Talking to Strangers: Improving American Diplomacy at Home and Abroad* (Princeton: Princeton University Press, 1996).

168. According to one study, democratic political systems are especially prone to having major foreign policy decisions influenced by domestic factors and forces. See Susan Peterson, *Crisis Bargaining and the State: The Domestic Politics of International Conflict* (Ann Arbor: University of Michigan Press, 1996). For an analysis highlighting the crucial influence of domestic factors on one aspect of American foreign policy during the past half-century, see Vernon W. Ruttan, *United States Development Assistance Policy: The Domestic Politics of Foreign Economic Aid* (Baltimore: Johns Hopkins University Press, 1995). The impact of internal economic tendencies and forces upon

the nation's external policies is also underscored in Michael E. Brown, ed., *The International Dimensions of Internal Conflict* (Cambridge, Mass.: MIT Press, 1996).

169. The point is developed further in Robert C. Johnson, *The National Interest and the Human Interest: An Analysis of U.S. Foreign Policy* (Princeton: Princeton Press, 1980). For a forceful case underscoring the relationship between internal budgetary and financial concerns, on the one hand, and diplomatic success on the other hand, see Lawrence S. Eagleburger and Robert L. Barry, "Dollars and Sense Diplomacy: A Better Foreign Policy for Less Money," *Foreign Affairs* 75 (July–August 1996): 2–8.

170. At this point it is worth calling attention to a fundamental dichotomy in the public mind about the relationship between domestic and foreign policy. On the one hand, except perhaps when the USA faces a threat or serious crisis abroad, the people unquestionably accord highest priority to domestic issues and expect their leaders to do likewise. On the other hand, they also expect that officials in Washington will manage foreign affairs *successfully,* avoiding embarrassing diplomatic failures that damage the nation's credibility abroad. At times, the Clinton administration was quite clearly entrapped in this dilemma. See Drew, *On the Edge,* 427–37. A helpful analysis of the concept of America's "national interest" in a world of rapid and often radical change in Donald E. Nuechterlein, *America Recommitted: United States National Interest in a Restructured World* (Lexington: University of Kentucky Press, 1991).

CHAPTER 6

1. See the report on President Clinton's trip to South Africa in the *New York Times,* March 27, 1998, dispatch by James Bennet.

2. This is the conclusion of Thomas L. Friedman in the *New York Times,* October 1, 1993.

3. See Elaine Sciolino, "Madeleine Albright's Audition," *New Times Magazine,* September 22, 1996, pp. 66–70.

4. See the view of this official, as quoted in Ivo H. Daalder and Michael E. O'Hanlon, "Unlearning the Lessons of Kosovo," *Foreign Policy,* no. 116 (fall 1999): 128–29.

5. See the views of Senator Mitch McConnell (R–Ky.), as quoted in Robert S. Greenberger, "Dateline Capitol Hill: The New Majority's Foreign Policy," *Foreign Policy,* no. 101 (winter 1995–96): 169.

6. Our emphasis in this chapter upon the pragmatic orientation of the Clinton White House in foreign affairs should not be interpreted to mean that there is anything necessarily unique in the nation's diplomatic experience about this approach. A long list of instances could be cited from the American diplomatic record to show that pragmatic calculations and factors have frequently influenced Washington's actions abroad. Changing American attitudes during the late 1930s—from firm support for the classical isolationist position to growing public approval of the Roosevelt administration's policy of interventionism in behalf of the Allies—serves as a significant case in point. The American people abandoned isolationism because it did not work; it failed to protect the nation's interests as ominous challenges arose abroad. Over some two centuries of diplomatic experience, public attitudes have been subject to wide "swings" or alterations of mood and opinion concerning the role the nation ought to play abroad. For an able exposition of this view, see F. L. Klingberg, "The Historical Alteration of Mood in American Foreign Policy," *World Politics* 4 (January 1952): 239–73. It was said of President Thomas Jefferson (who is often cited as a symbol of an "idealistic" approach to public policy questions) that he could be "as hard, as practical and as cynical . . . when the occasion arose, as any veteran diplomat of the Old World." See Nathan Schachner, *Thomas Jefferson: A Biography,* 2 vols. (New York: Appleton-Century-Crofts, 1951), 407.

7. Thus, one analysis of voter attitudes during the presidential race in 2000 found that what

was described as "a lopsided majority" of citizens wanted the next president to take "small, steady steps" toward solving national problems. Only one in five respondents favored a candidate who has "big, new ideas" on national issues. See the analysis of the New Hampshire primary election in the *New Orleans Times-Picayune,* January 18, 2000, dispatch by Richard Morin and Dan Batz. See also the earlier analysis of public attitudes on foreign policy issues by John E. Reilly, "The Public Mood at Mid-Decade," *Foreign Policy,* no. 98 (spring 1995): 76–93. And see the views of Ben J. Wattenberg, *The Real America: A Surprising Examination of the State of the Union* (Garden City, N.Y.: Doubleday, 1974), 203–13.

8. See the views of Peter Rodman in "Points of Order," *National Review,* May 1, 1995, p. 88.

9. See the views of Mortimer B. Zuckerman in *U.S. News and World Report,* January 26, 1998, p. 74.

10. See the analysis by Charles W. Maynes, "A Workable Clinton Doctrine," *Foreign Policy,* no. 93 (winter 1993–94): 4–6.

11. See Elizabeth Drew, *On the Edge: The Clinton Presidency* (New York: Simon and Schuster, 1994), 283. This observer expressed basically the same conclusion with regard to the nation's international trade policy. See pp. 292–99.

12. See the views of John M. Broder, in the *New York Times,* March 28, 1999. Another commentator characterized President Clinton's foreign policy of "engagement" by saying that his diplomatic behavior has been "ad hoc and patchwork." His actions abroad have been "inconsistent," and the rationale for engaging in interventionist behavior "has never jelled into a coherent foreign policy." See the views of Marshall Whitmann, a foreign policy analyst at the Heritage Foundation, in the *New Orleans Times-Picayune,* October 23, 1999.

13. This was the judgment of Senator Robert Dole, as quoted in the *New York Times,* June 8, 1995, dispatch by Elaine Sciolino.

14. These are the views of Representative Lee H. Hamilton (D–Ind.), a longtime member of the House Foreign Affairs Committee, in "A Democrat Looks at His Party," *Foreign Policy,* no. 71 (spring 1992): 30–33.

15. This is the conclusion of Colonel James H. Aarestad (retired), in *Newsweek,* March 23, 1998, p. 15.

16. See the views of Gregory D. Foster, a professor at National Defense University, in the *Baton Rouge Sunday Advocate,* February 22, 1998. Another commentator on the Clinton presidency believes that fundamental differences among his advisers not infrequently produced an ad hoc, erratic, and unpredictable approach to foreign policy issues. See Drew, *On the Edge,* 145–46.

17. See the views of the last British governor of Hong Kong, Christopher Patten, *East and West: China, Power, and the Future of Asia* (New York: Random House–New York Times Books, 1999), p. 269.

18. For example, see the views of Senator Mitch McConnell (R–Ky.), in Greenberger, "Dateline Capitol Hill," 169. As this observer assesses the matter, in the post–Cold War international system, it is simply not possible to formulate and adhere to "a totally coherent foreign policy." Secretary of State Warren Christopher agreed with this conclusion. In his view, prevailing external conditions required the United States to pursue a policy of "pragmatic engagement" abroad. See his views as cited in Bill Bradley, "Eurasia Letter: A Misguided Policy," *Foreign Policy,* no. 101 (winter 1995–96): 84. Referring to America's involvement in the conflict in the Balkans, another observer concluded that the nation's policy must be flexible and adaptive, avoiding both the extremes of non-involvement in the crisis and of overinvolvement in it. See the views of William Safire in the *New York Times,* June 18, 1998. In more formal terms, one of the nation's

most experienced diplomatic officials totally rejected what he called "diplomatic monism," or the attempt to make conditions in a highly variegated political universe "fit" into some kind of preconceived diplomatic framework. In his view, such efforts always distort reality and may well, in the end, damage the nation's interests abroad. See the views of Louis J. Halle as set forth in detail in *Civilization and Foreign Policy: An Inquiry for Americans* (New York: Harper, 1955).

19. Some commentators attributed President Clinton's preference for an ad hoc approach to policymaking to the fact that "he had trouble defining policy even in a given case, and seemed uncomfortable talking about it." Clinton frequently gave the impression of being basically uninterested in international problems and of being poorly informed about them. According to one observer, when he appointed Warren Christopher as his first secretary of state, Clinton did so in the hope that the president would then be able to concentrate his efforts mainly on domestic questions. See Drew, *On the Edge,* 28, 144–45.

20. According to one commentator, the Clinton administration was devoted to a "balanced" or "cautious" policy abroad; it was committed to "doing nothing rash" in the foreign policy field. See Barry Schweid, "Dateline Washington: Warren's World," *Foreign Policy,* no. 94 (September 1994): 119–41. To his critics, President Clinton justified his approach to the People's Republic of China as being at the same time "principled and pragmatic." To his mind, it was a "moderate" and "balanced" policy that avoided the extremes of either confrontation with the PRC or of accepting the Chinese government's behavior at home and abroad. In the end, Clinton was convinced, this approach would yield "concrete results." See Clinton's views, and the commentary on his planned trip to mainland China, in the *New York Times,* June 12, 1998, dispatch by John M. Broder.

21. Early in his presidency, Bill Clinton declared that at the dawn of a new century, the most essential requirement for a successful foreign policy was to "find ways to make people triumphant in the face of change"; Americans must make their "major institutions friendly to change and change friendly to them." Clinton's views are cited in Drew, *On the Edge,* 51. Answering the criticism that the administration's foreign policy was subject to frequent change, Secretary of State Warren Christopher replied: "I don't suppose you'd want anybody to keep a campaign promise if it was a very unsound policy." His views are quoted in Drew, *On the Edge,* 139. One informed student of the Clinton presidency observed, following his State of the Union Address early in 2000, that "what we've seen is an incredibly adaptable politician conforming to the political necessities of the time." See the views of Professor Ross K. Baker in the *New York Times,* January 27, 2000, dispatch by John M. Broder. Referring to the Clinton administration's policy toward Africa, an earlier analysis described the "new model" that officials said would guide their diplomatic activities toward that continent. Instead of a foreign policy derived from rigid ideological principles, the Clinton White House proposed to work constructively with those African leaders who will "manage their governments well, taking care of basic services." This meant in effect that Washington would employ "varying standards," or judge each case on its merits, on the African continent. Once again, the well-known pragmatic test of *results* would determine the Clinton's approach to sub-Saharan Africa. See the analysis of U.S. policy in the *New York Times,* March 25, 1998, dispatch by James C. McKinley. On a different diplomatic front, similar pragmatic calculations governed the Clinton administration's policy toward Russia in efforts to solve its critical economic and financial problems. Along with most Americans, President Clinton and his aides firmly opposed Moscow's effort to suppress separatist movements in Chechnya and elsewhere. Yet aid from the USA would *not* be denied to the Russian government on that account. A spokesman for the administration said that the question of financial assistance from the United States and other external sources would be considered "on a case-by-case basis"; there would be

no "umbrella political standard" for determining Washington's position on the issue. See the *New York Times*, December 29, 1999, dispatch by Joseph Kahn.

22. This state of mind was exhibited by President Clinton's secretary of defense Les Aspin, when he lamented regarding proposed intervention in the Balkans: "Nobody likes this deal, it's really one of those thankless tasks—but I don't know what else to do." His views are quoted in Drew, *On the Edge*, 282.

23. Policymaking during the Cuban Missile Crisis of 1962 is discussed more fully in Theodore Sorensen, *Kennedy* (New York: Harper/Collins, 1965); Elie Abel, *The Missile Crisis* (Philadelphia: J. P. Lippincott, 1966); Robert F. Kennedy, *Thirteen Days: A Memoir of the Cuban Missile Crisis* (New York: W. W. Norton, 1970); and Henry M. Patcher, *Collision Course: The Cuban Missile Crisis and Coexistence* (New York: Praeger, 1964).

24. For the key role played by experience in pragmatic thought, see the more detailed discussion in Cecil V. Crabb, Jr., *American Diplomacy and the Pragmatic Tradition* (Baton Rouge: Louisiana State University Press, 1989), 64–66, 80–83.

25. See the reprint of William James's work *The Meaning of Truth* (Cambridge, Mass.: Harvard University Press, 1975); and his *Essays in Radical Empiricism* (New York: Longmans, Green, 1922).

26. In the pragmatic conception, "meliorism" implies that progress in human affairs is *possible*, although it is by no means automatic or inevitable. Pragmatists reject the view of many right-wing groups that all change is inimical and that schemes for improving human society are doomed to failure. At the same time, they are equally skeptical about proposals by utopian and liberal groups that often envision a radical and rapid remaking of human society (as, for example, in many schemes to "outlaw war" or to eliminate global armaments). Perhaps the best terms for describing the pragmatic state of mind on the question are *adaptation* and *development*. Gradually, over time, society's existing (and presumably deleterious) "habits" must be replaced by a new set that are an outgrowth of experience.

27. See William James, *A Pluralistic Universe: Hibbert Lectures to Manchester College on the Present Situation in Philosophy* (New York: Longmans, Green, 1909). A briefer account is available in Marcus P. Ford, *William James's Philosophy: A New Perspective* (Amherst, Mass.: University of Massachusetts Press, 1982).

28. Thus, one student of the post–Cold War international system has referred to the "fundamental transformation" that has occurred within it. In contrast to the era of bipolarity, when "all moves appeared to be connected," today "foreign policy is about discrete problem-solving" in "an increasingly complex world in which U.S. interests are not so clearly defined." "There is . . . no magic or universal formula to [international] problem-solving, nor is there any guarantee of success." Clinton's pragmatic approach to external problems recognizes these realities. See the views of Jurek Martin, "Clinton Abroad," *Washington Monthly*, March 1999, pp. 22–26.

29. According to one analysis, like FDR before him, President Clinton drew on "a dozen different rationales for using power in the pursuit of peace." See the view of John W. Broder, in the *New York Times*, March 21, 1999.

33. A long list of studies of the New Deal is available. An informative one is James M. Burns, *Roosevelt: The Lion and the Fox* (New York: Harcourt, Brace, 1956). For examples of FDR's pragmatic approach to foreign policy issues during the New Deal period, see Cordell Hull, *The Memoirs of Cordell Hull*, 2 vols. (New York: Macmillan, 1948); Robert E. Sherwood, *Roosevelt and Hopkins: An Intimate History* (New York: Harper, 1950); and Warren F. Kimball, ed., *Franklin D. Roosevelt and the World Crisis: 1937–1945* (Lexington, Mass.: Lexington Books, 1973).

31. President Clinton's National Security Adviser, Anthony Lake, characterized the adminis-

tration's approach to foreign policy by the term "the new Wilsonianism." See his views as cited in the *New York Times,* October 31, 1993, dispatch by Thomas L. Friedman.

32. In President Bill Clinton's last budget for the fiscal year 2001, a total of $278 billion was proposed for national defense spending—or some 15 percent of the total federal budget. This sum was approximately equal to the outlay for Medicare and Medicaid combined. See the budgetary data in the *Baton Rouge Morning Advocate,* February 8, 2000.

33. Early in the new millennium, for example, the People's Republic of China renewed its campaign of harassment against the Republic of China (Taiwan) in an ostensible effort to influence the outcome of the latter's forthcoming national elections. As earlier administrations had done, the Clinton White House reiterated America's long-standing commitment to the security of Taiwan, in the face of ominous threats from the mainland; and Washington carried out naval exercises in the region to reinforce its policy.

34. See Lester Brune, *America and the Iraq Crisis, 1990–1992: Origins and Aftermath* (Claremont, Ca.: Regina Books, 1993), 21. An authoritative and detailed account of events leading up to the Persian Gulf War and America's response to them may be found in George Bush and Brent Scowcroft, *A World Transformed* (New York: Alfred A. Knopf, 1998), 302–450.

35. See Arthur H. Blair, *At War in the Gulf: A Chronology* (College Station, Tex.: Texas A and M University Press, 1992), 13.

36. See Bush and Scowcroft, *A World Transformed,* 302–33; and *Keesing's Record of World Events,* August 1990, p. 37638.

37. Bush and Scowcroft, *A World Transformed,* 334–56; and *Keesing's Record of World Events,* 37936.

38. A detailed account of Baghdad's domestic and foreign policies after the Persian Gulf War, and of Washington's response to them, may be found in Andrew Cockburn and Patrick Cockburn, *Out of the Ashes: The Resurrection of Saddam Hussein* (New York: Harper/Collins, 1999). Efforts by the Bush White House to bring about the ouster of Saddam Hussein's regime are recounted on pp. 30–58. For a prolonged period, American officials operated on the erroneous assumption that Saddam Hussein would be overthrown by a military-led coup—one instance in which Washington did not object to a military-dominated government! See pp. 36–37.

39. For example, early in his administration, President Bill Clinton directed the Central Intelligence Agency to undertake efforts to unseat Saddam Hussein. Among other approaches relied upon, American officials supported Kurdish dissidents and other Iraqi opposition groups in their efforts to oust Saddam Hussein's regime. These efforts also proved unsuccessful. In time, a number of well-informed American officials became highly dubious about the probability of success. See Cockburn and Cockburn, *Out of the Ashes,* 164–90.

40. See Cockburn and Cockburn, *Out of the Ashes,* 148–50.

41. See the transcript of the address by President Clinton in the *New York Times,* June 27, 1993.

42. See the transcript of President Clinton's address in the *New York Times,* June 27, 1993; and on the same date, the dispatch by Tim Weiner. According to one commentator on the incident, the president and his advisers believed that they had used the opportunity to "show our toughness" in foreign affairs. See Drew, *On the Edge,* 229–30.

43. *Keesing's Record of World Events,* October 1994, p. 40255.

44. Other examples of Baghdad's repeated, and often successful, efforts to defy UN directives, inspection procedures, and constraints on its actions are recounted in detail in Bill Gertz, *Betrayal: How the Clinton Administration Undermined American Security* (Washington, D.C.: Regnery, 1999), 194–210.

45. *Keesing's Record of World Events,* May 1997, p. 41661.

46. *Keesing's Record of World Events,* February 1998, p. 42098.

47. See *Keesing's Record of World Events,* September 1998, p. 42526, and December 1998, p. 42697.

48. See Cockburn and Cockburn, *Out of the Ashes,* 294; and *Keesing's Record of World Events,* December 1998, pp. 42697–42699, and January 1999, p. 42755.

49. An example of this constraint on U.S. policy toward Iraq was the effort made by American officials to take into consideration the Turkish government's viewpoints and policies with regard to its politically dissident Kurdish population. Washington's encouragement of a separate Kurdish state, for instance, would prove destabilizing for Turkey and would have a highly negative effect upon Turkish-American relations. See Drew, *On the Edge,* 288–90.

50. Informative background treatments of the crisis in the Balkans are Susan L. Woodward, *Balkan Tragedy: Chaos and Dissolution after the Cold War* (Washington, D.C.: Brookings Institution, 1995); and Christopher Bennett, *Yugoslavia's Bloody Collapse: Causes, Courses, and Consequences* (New York: New York University Press, 1995).

51. For a summary of the principal elements of the Dayton peace agreement on Bosnia and Herzegovina, see Leonard J. Cohen, "Bosnia and Herzegovina: Fragile Peace in a Segmented State," *Current History* 95 (March 1996): 107–109.

52. Kosovo is a region in southern Serbia of just over 4,000 square miles (slightly smaller than Connecticut), with some two million people, a majority of whom are ethnic Albanians, who practice the Muslim region.

53. This was the judgment of Maynard Glitman, as quoted in Joyce P. Kaufman, "A Challenge to European Security and Alliance Unity," *World Affairs* 198 (summer 1998): 26. According to another commentator, even some of President Clinton's own advisers complained that "his attention to foreign policy was sporadic" and devoid of any sustained or long-range understanding of America's global role. See the *New York Times,* January 3, 2000, dispatch by David E. Sanger. Another observer is convinced that toward Kosovo, the USA had pursued "a piecemeal foreign policy . . . which assures long-term instability" in the region. Only the adoption of a "far-reaching plan" that endeavors to solve the problems of the region as a whole has any chance of producing peace and stability. See the views of Michael P. Butler, in the *New York Times,* February 17, 2000.

54. See Cohen, "Bosnia and Herzegovina," 104. One study has summarized public attitudes toward U.S. military intervention abroad by saying that it must satisfy several criteria: the costs of such intervention must be "contained" or limited; victory should be assured; and the burden of intervention must be shared with other nations, if possible. See Daalder and O'Hanlon, "Unlearning the Lessons of Kosovo," 134–35.

55. See, for example, the views of Thomas L. Friedman in the *New York Times,* March 17, 2000.

56. Ibid.

57. See the *New York Times,* March 12, 2000, dispatch by Jane Perlez; and the views of UN administrators in Kosovo, in *New York Times,* March 13, 2000, dispatch by Steven Erlanger.

58. The views of one American senator unquestionably expressed the dissatisfaction of many members of the House and Senate over U.S. policy in Kosovo. He complained about the fact that American forces were still "at constant risk" in the Balkans and about the lack of real progress that had been made in bringing lasting peace to the region. Under these circumstances, he called for "a safe, orderly and phased withdrawal" of American armed forces from the troubled region. See the views of Senator John W. Warner (R–Va.), as reported in the *New York Times,* March 12,

2000, dispatch by Jane Perlez. In the same period, another influential legislator, Senator Robert Byrd (D–W.V.), concluded that the situation in Kosovo was on the verge of "unraveling." He called on the White House to turn the task of peacekeeping in the Balkans over to the European allies. The USA would continue to provide financial, logistical, diplomatic, and other forms of support for the peacekeeping operation. See his views in the *New York Times,* March 20, 2000.

59. See the views of NATO's commander, Gen. Wesley Clark, as cited in the editorial in the *New York Times,* March 17, 2000.

60. As merely one example of this recurrent criticism, see the views of Marshall Whitmann, a foreign policy analyst of the Heritage Foundation, that President Clinton's approach to the Bosnian problem and other global issues has been "ad hoc and patchwork. . . . There is no Clinton doctrine. Or if it exists, it is a deep, dark secret." His views are quoted in the *New Orleans Times-Picayune,* October 25, 1999, dispatch by Christopher Marquis. It ought to be noted, however, that basically this same criticism was leveled against the Truman administration in the early post–World War II period. The alleged deficiency had much to do with the establishment of the Policy Planning Council (designed as a kind of diplomatic "general staff") in the State Department. Yet the basic criticism of U.S. policy remains undiminished to this day!

61. See Madeleine Albright, "North Atlantic Treaty Organization: Collective Defense against Threat of Aggression," *Vital Speeches of the Day,* June 15, 1998, pp. 518–21.

62. See Robert Cooper, "Europe: The Post-Modern State and World Order," *New Perspectives Quarterly* 14 (summer 1997): 46–58.

63. Because America's national interest in the Balkan conflicts was never clearly defined or understood, either by officials or the people, the degree of public support for the commitment of NATO forces in response to the crises "was severely limited." This reality dictated that, when it did intervene, NATO would resort to a "risk-free" military campaign of air strikes. But this strategy made little positive contribution toward laying the basis for lasting peace in the Balkans. See Michael Mandelbaum, "A Perfect Failure: NATO's War against Yugoslavia," *Foreign Affairs* 78 (September–October, 1999): 5–6. The question of U.S. military involvement in the Balkans conflicts, according to another commentator, was but part of a larger question that had long troubled Americans, especially members of the House and Senate: How much longer would a large contingent of U.S. forces have to be stationed on the European continent? See Peter W. Rodman, "The Fallout from Kosovo," *Foreign Affairs* 78 (July–August 1999): 49.

64. The "wag the dog" strategy takes its name from a popular movie, in which an incumbent president resorts to a foreign crisis to draw public and media attention away from his domestic troubles and problems.

65. See George Perkovick, "Nuclear Proliferation," *Foreign Policy,* no. 112 (fall 1998): 12.

66. Almost every time American officials explained the rationale of America's policy in the Balkans, the reasons cited were different. For example, to the minds of many Americans the ethnic Albanian Kosovars were asserting the cherished Wilsonian concept of "self-determination" (although in fact officials in Washington *opposed* the existence of Kosovo as an independent nation). President Clinton and his advisers also repeatedly stated that "ethnic cleansing" and other atrocities constituted war crimes, whose perpetrators ought to be tried and convicted. Moreover, continuing violence in the Balkans threatened to "spillover" into neighboring countries, jeopardizing the peace and security of the European continent. In addition, the crises in the Balkans created a number of ancillary problems—such as a rising tide of refugees—with which the international community was required to deal. The Clinton White House also sought to provide convincing evidence that its emphasis upon "multilateralism" was a feasible approach to global problem-solving. Two other objectives unquestionably motivated Washington's diplomacy in the

Balkans. One was a desire to demonstrate America's capacity for global leadership, at a time when questions were being raised on that score at home and abroad. Failure by the USA to take a decisive leadership role in solving the Balkans problem, one official said, would inevitably mean that "more people would be killed, more refugees, more ethnic hatred in the Balkans" and "the war would likely spread." See the views of Secretary of Defense Les Aspin, in Drew, *On the Edge*, p. 282. Then there was also the parallel goal of providing proof that NATO had not lost its usefulness during a period when widespread doubts were being raised about the alliance's utility and future. A successful demonstration of an enlarged NATO's ability to resolve the crisis in the Balkans, in the words of one commentator, would serve as "an affirmation of shared values and common defense" within the Western community. See Kaufman, "A Challenge to European Security and Alliance Unity," 225. For some Americans, achieving the last goal was viewed as an important step in permitting the USA in time to *reduce* its global commitments. These and other reasons are adduced in Cooper, "Europe," 46–58; Albright, "North Atlantic Treaty Organization," 518–21; Kaufman, "A Challenge to European Security and Alliance Unity," 25–31; and Drew, *On the Edge*, 280–83.

67. According to the Rambouillet peace formula, Kosovo remained under nominal Serbian authority in a new Yugoslav Federation, although its ethnic Albanian majority was granted substantial political autonomy. Serbians have never accepted the principle of complete independence for Kosovo.

68. In the view of one commentator, external intervention in Bosnia served as a forceful communication of the idea that the international community would intervene to avert a "humanitarian catastrophe" in other settings, as well. See Rodman, "The Fallout from Kosovo," 46. Yet another observer has pointed out, U.S. intervention in Bosnia in fact serves as a dubious precedent. In recent years, many more people have died in civil strife in such countries as Sierra Leone, the Sudan, and Rwanda *without* evoking "humanitarian interventionism" by the United States and its allies. Mandelbaum, "A Perfect Failure," 6.

69. See the assessment of U.S. policy toward Kosovo by Michael Mandelbaum, "A Perfect Failure," 2–5.

70. One observer's judgment is that, all things considered, the most lasting lesson of humanitarian intervention in the Balkans is that "ethnic conflicts are a swamp, and NATO may not want to wager its future on its ability to 'solve' them." Rodman, "The Fallout from Kosovo," 51.

71. Haiti occupies the western portion of the island of Hispaniola. Covering 10.5 thousand square miles, it is about the size of the state of Maryland. With over 7 million people, Haiti has one of the fastest-growing populations in the world. Formerly part of French Empire in the New World, Haiti became independent of France in 1804.

72. The transition in American diplomacy toward Latin America during the New Deal is discussed more fully in Cecil V. Crabb, Jr., *The Doctrines of American Foreign Policy: Their Meaning, Role, and Future* (Baton Rouge: Louisiana State University Press, 1982), 40–45.

73. See Mike Blakley, "Haiti," in *The Costs of Conflict: Prevention and Cure in the Global Arena*, ed. Michael E. Brown and Richard N. Rosecrance (Lanham, Md.: Rowman and Littlefield, 1999), 95. As a measure of the depths of poverty to which Haiti had sunk, it is worth noting that before the coup in 1991, foreign aid accounted for some 25 percent of the country's gross national product.

74. See Steven W. Hook, "The White House, Congress, and the Paralysis of the U.S. State Department after the Cold War," in *After the End: Making U.S. Foreign Policy in the Post–Cold War World*, ed. James M. Scott (Durham: Duke University Press, 1998), 324–26.

75. Blakley, "Haiti," 94.

76. See Chetan Kumar, *Building Peace in Haiti* (Boulder, Colo.: Lynne Rienner, 1998), 20–21.

77. The Economist Intelligence Unit, *Country Profile: Dominican Republic, Haiti, and Puerto Rico* (London: Economist Intelligence Unit, 1998), 32.

78. Blakley, "Haiti," 96.

79. Sentiment in Congress in favor of action by the United States to deal with the Haitian refugee problem rose steadily, although polls indicated that public opinion was not enthusiastic about such intervention. See the discussion in James M. Scott, ed., *After the End: Making U.S. Foreign Policy in the Post-Cold War World* (Durham: Duke University Press, 1998), 36–38, 116–18.

80. According to one analysis, the Clinton White House was concerned about the impact of a vast influx of "boat people" upon economic, social, and political conditions in Florida. See Drew, *On the Edge,* 139.

81. See Drew, *On the Edge,* 417.

82. See the discussion in Ralph G. Carter, "Congress and Post–Cold War U.S. Foreign Policy," in *After the End: Making U.S. Foreign Policy in the Post–Cold War World,* ed. James M. Scott (Durham: Duke University Press, 1998), 114–16. According to this analysis of Washington's activities toward Haiti, President Clinton's policy "can largely be attributed to pressure brought by TransAfrica and the Congressional Black Caucus." Ibid., 118. Or, as another study found, the actions of these two interest groups were largely responsible for keeping the Haitian issue on the foreign policy agenda during 1993 and 1994 and in pushing for "stronger action" by the USA against the Haitian junta. See James M. McCormick, "Interest Groups and the Media in Post–Cold War U.S. Foreign Policy," in *After the End: Making U.S. Foreign Policy in the Post–Cold War World,* ed. James M. Scott (Durham: Duke University Press, 1998), 181–82.

83. Economist Intelligence Unit, *Country Profile,* 32.

84. Blakley, "Haiti," 97–98.

85. Kumar, *Building Peace in Haiti,* 23.

86. See Drew, *On the Edge,* 331–34. According to this observer, *both sides* in the Haitian conflict violated the terms of the Governor's Island Accord.

87. See William Hyland, *Clinton's World: Remaking American Foreign Policy* (Westport, Conn.: Praeger, 1999), 98. The *Harlan County* episode, one commentator contended, presented the unseemly "picture of the mighty United States sailing away from a clutch of rioters." According to Secretary of State Warren Christopher, the earlier abortive attempt by the USA to bring peace and security to Somalia—resulting in the death of eighteen American soldiers in October 1993—unquestionably "cast a shadow" over later interventionist moves abroad. Christopher's views are quoted in Jennifer Sterling-Folker, "Between a Rock and a Hard Place: Assertive Multilateralism and Post–Cold War U.S. Foreign Policy Making," in *After the End: Making U.S. Foreign Policy in the Post–Cold War World,* ed. James M. Scott (Durham: Duke University Press, 1998), 288; and in Drew, *On the Edge,* pp. 334–35.

88. Economist Intelligence Unit, *Country Profile,* 32.

89. Kumar, *Building Peace in Haiti,* 26.

90. Blakley, "Haiti," 99.

91. For more extended discussion of American intervention in Somalia and its impact on U.S. policy, see Sterling-Folker, "Between a Rock and a Hard Place," 287–291; and Hyland, *Clinton's World,* 63–64.

92. Economist Intelligence Unit, *Country Profile,* 32.

93. Hyland, *Clinton's World,* 64.

94. One student attributes this result largely to the fact that the Haitian operation was per-

ceived (correctly or not) as successful—or at least, it was not viewed as a failure—by the American people. See Jerel Rosati and Stephen Twing, "The Presidency and U.S. Foreign Policy after the Cold War," in *After the End: Making U.S. Foreign Policy in the Post–Cold War World,* ed. James M. Scott (Durham: Duke University Press, 1998), 44.

95. One leading student of the nation's foreign affairs, for example, cites the intervention in Haiti as an example of an undertaking that was ultimately "doomed to failure," just as most attempts to promote democracy abroad by relying on military means are usually unsuccessful. See the view of Richard Falk, as cited in H. W. Brands, *What America Owes the World: The Struggle for the Soul of Foreign Policy* (Cambridge: Cambridge University Press, 1998), 310–11.

96. For an assessment of the Haitian society's economic, social, and political prospects, see the *New Orleans Times-Picayune,* March 20, 2000, dispatch by Monique Guillory. This commentator uses such terms as "rampant corruption," governmental "incompetence," "chaos," and general "pandemonium" in characterizing overall conditions in contemporary Haitian society.

97. Economist Intelligence Unit, *Country Profile,* 33.

98. This is the contention of Blakley, in "Haiti," 101–108.

99. Hyland, *Clinton's World,* 65. One commentator concluded that Washington's policy toward Haiti represented a mixture of idealism and realism. See Brands, *What America Owes the World,* 315–16. Further insight into the historic role of the Monroe Doctrine in U.S. policy toward Latin America is provided in Crabb, *The Doctrines of American Foreign Policy,* 1–56.

100. For more detailed discussion of the rationale guiding President Clinton's foreign policy, see the *New York Times,* March 28, 1999, dispatch by John M. Broder; and Jurek Martin, "Clinton Abroad," *Washington Monthly,* March 1999, pp. 22–26.

101. One study of public attitudes toward foreign affairs found relatively little enthusiasm among citizens for interventionist moves designed to promote American values and democracy in foreign societies. See Oli Holsti, "Public Opinion and U.S. Foreign Policy after the Cold War," in *After the End: Making U.S. Foreign Policy in the Post–Cold War World,* ed. James M. Scott (Durham: Duke University Press, 1998), 146–48. Among seven reasons listed why the public would support stationing American troops abroad, promoting the cause of democracy overseas was not listed among them. See ibid., 152.

102. The emphasis in this chapter upon the pragmatic quality of President Clinton's foreign policy should not be construed as meaning that pragmatic calculations and influences play no part in the diplomacy of other administrations. One student of recent American foreign relations, for example, has said concerning the foreign policy moves of the Bush administration, that they were characterized by a "mixture of competence and drift, of tactical mastery set in a larger pattern of strategic indirection." Toward many important global issues, the Bush White House was "usually quite tentative and cautious, allowing others to take the foreign policy initiative." Toward other issues, as in the Persian Gulf War, however, it was capable of acting decisively and with a reasonably clear sense of direction. See the views of Rosati and Twing, "The Presidency and U.S. Foreign Policy after the Cold War," 36.

103. See the discussion of fundamental disagreements among President Clinton's foreign policy aides in Drew, *On the Edge,* 427–28.

104. One spokesman for the Clinton administration said regarding America's role in the Haitian crisis that, based on experience, officials in Washington had to be skeptical "about the ability of the United Nations to operate without vigorous involvement" by the USA. In his view, "Ultimately the UN is us." See the views of an unidentified White House adviser, in the *New York Times,* October 10, 1993.

105. See the text of President Clinton's speech dealing with his scheduled trip to mainland

China in the *New York Times,* June 12, 1998; and the commentary on Clinton's China policy by John M. Broder in the same issue. See also Edward N. Luttwak, "Our Prudent, Incoherent China Policy," *Harper's Magazine,* June 1998, pp. 19–22. According to this observer, a policy of "muddled but prudent moderation" toward the PRC was preferable to any conceivable alternative approach.

106. Relations between China and America before World War II are discussed in detail in Foster R. Dulles, *China and America: The Story of Their Relations since 1784* (Princeton: Princeton University Press, 1946); and in John K. Fairbank, *The United States and China* (Cambridge, Mass.: Harvard University Press, 1958).

107. See the discussion of the contemporary lure of the China market in the *New Orleans Times-Picayune,* April 21, 2000, dispatch by Eric Schmitt. One member of the House, for example, expressed a prevailing view when he said that, if a pending trade deal between the United States and China could be concluded, opening up this new market for American-made goods "will keep leverage over China's behavior on human rights, religious tolerance and the environment." See the views of Rep. Sander M. Levin (D–Ill.), as reported in the *New York Times,* April 17, 2000, dispatch by Eric Schmitt.

108. Many students of World War II believe that the war actually began in the early 1930s, when Japan annexed the mineral-rich Chinese province of Manchuria. See the extended discussion of the Open Door Policy and the "Stimson Doctrine" issued during the Manchurian crisis in Crabb, *The Doctrines of American Foreign Policy,* 56–107.

109. See Crabb, *The Doctrines of American Foreign Policy,* 90–95.

110. An illuminating discussion of U.S. policy toward China down to the end of the Chinese civil war, focusing on Washington's ties with Chiang Kai-shek's regime, may be found in Herbert Feis, *The China Tangle* (Princeton: Princeton University Press, 1953). An official compilation of documents and official statements related to this period is United States Department of State, *United States Relations with China,* Publication No. 3573, Far Eastern Series (Washington, D.C.: GPO, 1949).

111. An enlightening analysis of the steps leading to the "normalization" of relations between Washington and Beijing is Patrick Tyler, "The (Ab)normalization of U.S.-Chinese Relations," *Foreign Affairs* 78 (September–October 1999): 93–122.

112. See Henry Wei, *China and Soviet Russia* (Princeton: D. Van Nostand, 1956); and Robert North, *Moscow and Chinese Communists* (Stanford: Stanford University Press, 1953). Chinese revolutionary activities abroad during the Maoist period are discussed in Devere E. Pentony, *China: The Emerging Red Giant* (San Francisco: Chandler, 1962).

113. An informative analysis of American attitudes toward China is available in Harold R. Isaacs, *Scratches on Our Minds: American Images of China and India* (New York: John Day, 1958). Chinese viewpoints toward the United States and other foreign nations (often referred to as the "Barbarians") are examined in John K. Fairbank, *Chinese Thought and Institutions* (Chicago: University of Chicago Press, 1957).

114. For idealists, like President Jimmy Carter, the "normalization" of relations with China was viewed as "a redemption, a moral crusade, and a piece of farsighted diplomacy that . . . transcended politics." See Tyler, "The (Ab)normalization of U.S.-Chinese Relations," 122. See also the analysis of public opinion on major foreign policy issues in John E. Reilly, "The Public Mood at Mid-Decade," 76–93. This study found that relations with China did not rank high on the American people's scale of major issues abroad. For example, citizens accorded the promoting of democracy in mainland China very low priority among America's important diplomatic objectives. See also the analysis of public attitudes toward China in *U.S. News and World Report,* June

8, 1998, pp. 20–23. This study cites evidence of very deep ambivalence in the American mind on the subject of Sino-American relations.

115. From the beginning of the process of "normalization" in Sino-American relations, *Realpolitik* calculations played a part in the negotiations, as, for example, in the desire of both nations to contain Russian ambitions in Asia and globally. See Tyler, "The (Ab)normalization of U.S.-Chinese Relations," 108–10.

116. See Ross Y. Koen, *The China Lobby in American Politics* (New York: Harper/Collins, 1974).

117. See Jordan Singer, "A Watchful Eye: Monitoring the Conventional Arms Trade," *Harvard International Review* 18 (winter 1995–96): 40–45.

118. According to the last British governor of Hong Kong, China and Japan have never engaged in the kind of "reconciliation" that has occurred between Germany and France, permitting the peaceful stabilization of Europe. That reality continues to pose a major threat to the peace and security of Asia. Only American military power can keep that threat under control. See Patten, *East and West,* 285.

119. A well-informed student of Asian affairs has said that Americans have always had what he calls a "Marco Polo–like obsession with the Chinese market." In his view, the market for American-made goods within China has always been—and for the foreseeable future is likely to remain—limited. See Patten, *East and West,* 267.

120. This is the contention of Seymour M. Lipset in "Some Social Requisites of Democracy: Economic Development and Political Legitimacy," *American Political Science Review* 53 (January 1959): 69–105. Yet this view is not without its critics. For example, see the views of one commentator that on the eve of the new millennium, despite a rising standard of living in China, political conditions within the society were *worse* than they had been in earlier years. Patten, *East and West,* 306.

121. The subject is dealt with more fully in the study by the World Bank, *World Development Report, 1999–2000: Entering the Twenty-first Century* (New York: Oxford University Press, 2000).

122. See the analysis of prevailing attitudes in the House and Senate on the policy of the Clinton White House toward China, in the *New Orleans Times-Picayune,* April 21, 2000, dispatch by Eric Schmitt; and the analysis of the same subject in the *New York Times,* April 18, 2000, dispatch by Jane Perlez.

123. A particularly significant development in this regard was the Chinese government's use of overwhelming force to suppress pro-democracy demonstrations by students and workers in Tiananmen Square in June 1989, when several thousand demonstrators were killed or wounded by the military. This episode had a long-lasting impact upon viewpoints on Capitol Hill regarding attempts to maintain "a dialogue" with Beijing. Long-standing concerns on Capitol Hill about mainland China's policies at home and abroad are highlighted in Cecil V. Crabb, Jr., "An Assertive Congress and the TRA: Policy Influences and Implications," in *Congress, the Presidency, and the Taiwan Relations Act* ed. Louis W. Koenig (New York: Praeger, 1985), pp. 85–111. According to one commentator, underlying distrust of the PRC in the minds of legislators has been evident ever since the normalization of Sino-American relations by the Carter administration. See Tyler, "The (Ab)normalization of U.S.-Chinese Relations," 122.

124. An analysis of public attitudes toward foreign policy issues found that over half of the respondents expressed concern about the growing military prowess of the PRC; a majority feared that in the not-too-distant future, an increasingly powerful China would pose a serious threat to American diplomatic and security interests in Asia. See Reilly, "The Public Mood at Mid-Decade," 76–93. A number of commentators have also expressed concern about the rising mili-

tary power Beijing would rely on to support its "strategic ambitions" in Asia and globally. According to one observer, Clinton's policy of "pragmatic engagement" was an overt failure because it invited "Chinese adventurism abroad and repression at home." See the analysis by Robert Kagan and William Kristol in the *New York Times,* June 22, 1998. A former high-ranking official of the Reagan administration has likewise expressed apprehension about what appears to be a revival of Chinese "expansionism," supported by an increasingly potent military arsenal. See the *New York Times,* June 15, 1998, analysis James Webb. Still another observer believes that mainland China will likely become "a strategic threat" to the USA in one or two decades. See the views of Michael Barone, in *U.S. News and World Report,* September 6, 1999, p. 38.

125. After witnessing a significant increase in tensions between the PRC and the Republic of China at the turn of the millennium, one observer called attention to the fact that according to the ancient Chinese military strategist, Sun Tzu, the "acme of skill" was to "subdue the enemy without fighting." This goal was to be achieved by "attacking the mind of the enemy . . . by intimidating him, subverting his will to fight, dividing him internally and from his allies." In other words, in this view, Beijing would most probably pursue its goals toward Taiwan by means of psychological warfare, intimidation, and the old Chinese tactic of "setting off fireworks" over a long period of time. See the views of Albert L. Weeks in the *New York Times,* March 12, 2000.

126. See the views of George F. Kennan, as quoted in Patten, *East and West,* 257. The author, a longtime observer of Chinese affairs, has stated that he is "not scared witless by China." He is more fearful of "things going wrong in China" (e.g., a total breakdown of law and order) than he is of the nation's military power and external ambitions. China is "not an economic superpower today and is a very long way from becoming one." See ibid., 258–60.

127. See the views of Gerald Segal, "Does China Matter?" *Foreign Affairs* 78 (September–October 1999): 24–36. This commentator underscores China's deteriorating position among the world's manufacturing nations. In 1900, for example, China accounted for some 6.2 percent of the world's manufactured goods; by 1997, this figure had fallen to some 3.5 percent. By the latter date, its per capita gross national product ranked eighty-first among the nations (just ahead of Papua New Guinea). Ibid., 25. In the military dimension, he has calculated that China is "a second-rate military power." For example, its annual defense spending is only some 4.5 percent of the world's total (vis-à-vis 33.9 percent for the USA). This observer does not believe that the PRC poses a credible military threat to Taiwan. Ibid., 29–30. Similarly, the PRC "is in no position to matter much as a source of international political power." Ibid., 33.

128. Minxin Pei, "Will China Become Another Indonesia?" *Foreign Policy,* no. 116 (fall 1999): 95–96. This commentator is not optimistic that China's leaders will be able to undertake the required reforms in time to prevent political disaster. See pp. 107–109. Other assessments of the prospects for democracy in China are available in Andrew J. Nathan, ed., *China's Transition* (New York: Columbia University Press, 1997); and in Murray S. Tanner, *The Politics of Lawmaking in Post-Mao China: Institutions, Processes, and Democratic Prospects* (Oxford: Clarendon Press, 1999).

129. One experienced commentator has stated that America's goal was bringing about "the stable, steady transformation of China into a responsible member of the world trading system and into a more free and open society." The "best tool" Washington has for accomplishing the purpose is "globalizing China"—that is, exposing the society to the kinds of external influences that would result from Beijing's membership in the World Trade Organization, expanding trade ties with the USA and other nations, and preserving the kind of "dialogue" with China's leaders envisioned by the Clinton White House. In turn, successfully implementing this strategy demanded that Americans discount "Chinese bluster" regarding Taiwan, even while the USA continues to maintain a strong military presence in East Asia. See the views of Thomas L. Friedman in the *New York Times,* February 29, 2000; and see the editorial in the *New York Times,* March 20, 2000.

INDEX